Yellowstone's LOST LEGEND

"UNCLE" BILLY HOFER, RENAISSANCE MAN OF THE EARLY PARK

BY SCOTT HERRING
UNIVERSITY OF CALIFORNIA, DAVIS

RIVERBEND
PUBLISHING

Yellowstone's Lost Legend:
"Uncle" Billy Hofer, Renaissance Man of the Early Park

Copyright © 2020 Scott Robert Herring

Published by Riverbend Publishing, Helena, Montana

ISBN: 978-1-60639-125-9

Printed in the USA

1 2 3 4 5 6 7 8 VP 26 25 24 23 22 21 20

Cover and text design by Sarah Cauble, sarahcauble.com

Riverbend Publishing
P.O. Box 5833
Helena, MT 59604
1-406-449-0200
riverbendpublishing.com

Contents

Acknowledgements

This book would not have been possible but for historical forces I had nothing to do with, specifically the death of the typewriter and the advent of the personal computer. As this book will note, Thomas Elwood Hofer's life is not poorly documented. People wrote about him regularly; he wrote letters to the kind of VIPs whose letters get saved when they die; he worked as a professional journalist. As an example illustrating, not the problem, but the windfall that made this book writable is a relatively minor issue: the precise number of articles Hofer produced for the journal *Forest and Stream*. Working in the early 1990s, entirely in the paper-and-typewriter era, historian Paul Schullery found "more than 50 articles, notes, and letters."[1] The historian Sarah Broadbent, searching exhaustively through the Yellowstone National Park archives a little later in the 1990s, but still well within the age of paper, found 80 articles by Hofer, and 45 references to him.[2] Working between 2012 and 2016, entirely in the digital era, I scared up 83 articles and 53 references. That was not my doing, but the computer's, and the list is not yet complete. The machine also unlocked distant archives filled with letters and the like concerning Hofer. Online libraries like HathiTrust and Google Books opened up his life in a way that would have been impossible just twenty years ago. So to the electrons and silicon go the major credit.

Humans were involved, of course. In Yellowstone National Park, I benefitted greatly from the help of historians Lee Whittlesey, Ruth and Leslie Quinn, Paul Schullery, ecologist Mike Tercek, and wildlife educator Ashea Mills. At the University of California, Davis, librarians Dan Goldstein and Ruth Gustafson provided crucial assistance. Dozens of others helped, of course. I have only named my most crucial allies.

I must pause here and explain that I have a personal stake in this story. Like Thomas Elwood Hofer, I come from one of the centers of civilization—Los Angeles, in my case. I fled the place to live and work in Yellowstone National Park. I got deeply addicted, and stayed through much of the 1990s. What happened to Hofer was identical to what happened to me and my friends, quite a few of whom are still up there. People who get hooked on the place will often do any crazy thing to stay. Hofer stayed for over forty years, so he had to cook up a startling array of things to do that allowed him to stay.

My point is simply that his experiences are intensely familiar to me, and it does not matter that he first arrived in the park nearly a century and a half ago, during an era when there may have been only five hundred visitors to the park a year, or possibly a thousand. Today, four million people assault the place in a dizzying array of motor vehicles—and yet there is, for those who live there, some core to the Yellowstone experience that cannot be destroyed, but that can still be lived, given time and work. That core was there for Hofer in 1879, and it was there for me. Its existence made it immensely easier to write this book, because I continually found myself reading of Hofer's experiences—no matter how outlandish they were—then nodding, and saying, "Yeah, I remember that."

Introduction

On a cold, cold morning in mid-February, at the edge of the remote Montana village of Gardiner, an ordinary-looking man turned his face south and set out to do the extraordinary.

He must have drawn little notice, except that the locals, all of whom knew him, would have wished him luck, knowing he might need it. Or he might not. Unimpressive to look at, he was clean-shaven—for now—except for a mustache that was modest for the era and the year, 1887. Under his winter clothes, he was, to borrow an item from the twenty-first century's supply of slang, in terrific shape. His face was weathered and scorched; and to borrow an item from the twenty-first century's supply of neuroses, he should have been worried about melanoma. By his own account, and from all that we know about him, he was not worried about much of anything.

He stepped onto the snow and into a pair of deceptively simple objects, relatively familiar in the Old World, but not in the New. In the language of 1887, they were "snowshoes," and were actually what we would call "skis," a Norwegian word that had not yet been incorporated into English.[1] In North America, they were known mainly to Scandinavian immigrants in places like the upper Mid-west, and the immigrants only occasionally used them for fun. Today's winter sports industries were then in the distant future, and unimaginable. So were our bindings and poles; these skis (this book will call them that, to avoid confusion) had only leather straps, two each, for the toes and the heels. The pole—singular—was a shaft of pine, seven feet long. It was called, to add to the general strangeness of the situation, a "lurk."[2] It would double as a measuring stick to plot the depth of the snow, "until," the man later explained, "the snow was too deep for the pole to touch bottom."

The wooden skis were nine feet long, petite for the era, when skis were regularly twice as long as the skier was tall. They had been expertly honed and waxed by their proprietor, who aimed them south and shushed off without fanfare. He would have gone alone, as he normally did in the winter, but this time he brought along a youngster, Jack Tansey, who was included, it seems, for the companionship. He was not there as a porter; the two carried everything they needed in backpacks, and the packs weighed a mere 18 pounds. They could count on at least some resupply on the snowed-over trails ahead, but not much, not in that distant era. Nor was Tansey there for his expertise; astonishingly, he had no experience as a skier, but his leader, who was not in a rush, assumed he would pick it up as they went along. The need for companionship makes sense given the length of the trip, and the aim. The two would be skiing over 200 miles, through the interior of the still relatively new national park called Yellowstone.

Worry would be sensible. Their starting point lay at a gentle 5300 feet above sea level, gentle by local standards. Ahead, to the south, loomed a wall of rock, ice, and snow. Stretching from horizon to horizon, this line of mountains strongly suggested what awaited them. The first stop was park headquarters, at a still-gentle 6200 feet. After that, they entered the park interior, where elevations tended to run between 7000 feet and 8000 feet. Finishing the trip would require them to negotiate passes over 10,000 feet high. It would have taken many ski poles to measure the depth of the snow, in the lee of the wind at 10,000 feet.

It was particularly so that year. The winter of 1887 had already proven itself an epic, and not an uplifting one, unless you hate cows (many had already frozen to death). In the words of historian Paul Schullery, it "was, at least in the short memory of western settlers and ranchers, the mother of all winters, the one that broke the back of many western cattle operations, killing 362,000 cattle in Montana alone. It started in November, and except for a brief thaw in January, the extreme cold and deep snow did not relent until spring." Even at that still-gentle 6200 feet at headquarters, the park superintendent "would report that snow fell on 23 days in January, a total of 77 inches. The coldest temperature at Mammoth that month was 21°."[3]

By chance, two other groups had attempted to traverse the park interior that fatal winter. One had penetrated not much farther than the Norris Geyser Basin, a little more than 25 miles, before sputtering out in exhaustion. A second group, composed of members of the first who refused to give up, had completed the tour, but not before nearly killing themselves trying to cross one of the passes in a blizzard.

Yet the leader was not worried. The genuinely dangerous ice-scape up ahead was as familiar as home, because it was his home. He loved that blinding, wind-blasted nightmare as much as a man can love anyone or anything. He completed the trip with what looked like ease, although only he could make it look that way.

His name was Thomas Elwood Hofer, or "Billy" Hofer to his many friends—and, as he grew older and became nearly as much a fixture of Yellowstone Park as Old Faithful Geyser, he became Uncle Billy. He was to Yellowstone what John Muir was to Yosemite: its first and greatest all-around expert, perhaps the greatest single expert that Yellowstone has ever known.

He should arguably be recognized as Yellowstone's John Muir. Instead, he is widely forgotten. No biography has ever been produced of him, despite repeated calls for one from nearly anybody who has gotten to know Billy and his half-century-long Yellowstone adventure. This book is intended to fill that void.

That he has been forgotten is a matter of bad luck and circumstances unique to both his era and our own. During his lifetime, from at least the occasion of the 1887 ski around the park, he was not obscure. He was nearly famous. He undertook the trip at the behest of his temporary employer, the influential weekly *Forest and Stream*. On the surface an outdoor sportsman's newspaper, *Forest and Stream* was more importantly one of the leading conservation journals of its time. Its editor was George Bird Grinnell, the Yale-trained, scientific jack-of-all-trades with influence throughout the East Coast's upper crust, influence he could use to push a wildlife and wild-land conservation agenda that was often decades ahead of its time.

Billy was one of Grinnell's foremost soldiers, Our Man in Montana, and his influence was amplified by the extraordinary cast of characters who passed through Billy's life. As his expertise grew, so did his reputation, and soon everyone with the means to afford one sought him out as a guide. He guided big-game hunters, statesmen, celebrities, European aristocrats, European royalty, and American presidents. He guided explorers, scientists, and his fellow journalists. The knowledge that he developed brought him, at an early date, to Grinnell's attention.

In the course of his travels, decade after decade, he developed an expertise that makes it all the more important that we elevate him from the state of obscurity into which he has slipped. Yellowstone is a peculiar place in millions of ways—literally millions—but some of its peculiarities are more important and cause more trouble than others. It was the first parcel of land on earth to be given the label "National Park," and the US government bestowed that label at a time when the place had not been much disturbed by humans with knowledge of industry or large-scale agriculture. It today occupies the center of what has come to be called the Greater Yellowstone Ecosystem, a block of land that, by conservative estimates, measures twenty million acres. Others would put the number higher, a few lower. It is the largest mass of land in the temperate zones of the earth that is, ecologically, relatively intact.

Relatively. At 2.1 million acres, Yellowstone National Park itself is only a fraction of the Greater Ecosystem that we have named for it, but it has served as a bastion in which species hunted to death elsewhere, like the grizzly bear and the bison, have in effect hidden out until the general public's attitude toward them got a little less murderous. It has done similar duty for less well-known species, and surely some that remain unknown to us. The federal agency charged today with running it, the National Park Service, operates under a famously schizoid directive. In the act of Congress that had established the NPS in 1916, the new Service was directed "to conserve the scenery and the natural and historic objects and the wild life" in the parks, but at the same time "to provide for the enjoyment of the same in such manner and by such means as will leave them unimpaired for the enjoyment of future generations."[4]

During the early history of the park, near the start of its management by the NPS, and during the long stretch when the park was run by the US Army in the absence of any other body capable of handling the job, the soldiers and rangers tended to overdo the "provide for the enjoyment" part, and they had ideas we today would find bizarre. They "fixed" what they regarded as nature's mistakes, introducing some species of animals, plants, and fish, protecting others, gunning down still others on sight. They ran off or ejected the last of the native tribes. They suppressed every wildfire they could find. They dammed rivers, they felled timber, they blasted and built and destroyed.

Historians have long since come to understand that there never was a "pristine" or "perfect" Yellowstone. For one thing, those native people moved across the landscape in waves soon after the last glaciers receded about 10,000 years ago. Just from the different weapons archaeologists have collected, we know those peoples hunted different animals in different ways at different times. They built small villages, the remains of some of which are visible today. They built fish traps; they built elaborate structures for channeling and controlling the animals they hunted; they set fires; they even dug mines, if small ones, and hauled away the mineral booty to make tools and other useful things. They changed the place, then they changed what they had changed, over and over and over.

Nevertheless, in the first half of the nineteenth century, what would become Yellowstone National Park was a place in which nature was in charge. It still is. "Nature" includes meteors and volcanoes, and if one of those intervenes, we shall see how omnipotent humanity really is. Still, natural systems—the relationships between living creatures and their inanimate surroundings—were the dominant forces.

Trappers, mountain men, and other footloose *voyageurs* had visited repeatedly after the turn of the nineteenth century, and they were armed to the teeth, but they could not impose the kind of violent intervention that happened after the park began its official public life as the National Park in 1872. Everyone involved argues incessantly about the details, but the National Park Service today operates under a broad, general agreement that what we want in Yellowstone National Park is the nearest thing we can get to what the place was like in that first half of the nineteenth century, before the big lead-based interventions began. That means undoing some of the loonier interventions.

But to do so requires a goal or target, and that requires knowledge of what the place was like back then. The native tribes had no alphabet, and surprisingly few early visitors from the East thought to talk to them much, even through interpreters. The other records are sketchy. Those that exist have often gone ignored.

The major examples of problems arising from this ignorance, the ones that have caused the most heat and least light for over a hundred years, are the elk and the wolves. By the 1920s, various government agencies and independent actors, working together, had killed the last wolf in Greater Yellowstone, their bright idea being that the elk would benefit. Ever since, a constant fight has simmered and flared over whether the elk herds grew too large. Nor was there quiet in the early years, when nearly all sides assumed the elk to be headed for extinction.

Early in the years of the Bill Clinton presidency, the Department of the Interior prepared to restore the wolves to Yellowstone (a goal long since attained, with outlandish success where the number of wolves is concerned). Early in the process, the former Yellowstone National Park Historian, Paul Schullery, joined by a later Historian, Lee Whittlesey, assembled every important source they could find giving contemporary accounts of just what kind of animals lived in Yellowstone before the 1880s, and how many. It was an immense effort, one that no one had ever undertaken, probably because it was so immense (and besides, who wants knowledge when it might undermine your arguments in the fight?). The resulting document, 170 pages long, is still only a partial accounting.[5]

Some years later, Schullery commented on his and Whittlesey's ordeal: "We learned that it is impossible to make trustworthy generalizations without having a huge amount of such informal, anecdotal material and that it is apparently very easy to misinterpret whatever evidence you do find."[6] Indeed, much, or most, of the invective about the wolves and the elk had always been thinly-sliced baloney. What is needed today, still, is more and better material. What is really needed is something like both science and a scientist, and a highly experienced one, on the ground in the Yellowstone of the distant past. If only we had one!

Billy Hofer, unsurprisingly, takes his historical place in that monster document about Yellowstone's animals, and it is an important place. His expertise surpasses that of anyone else in it. He had arrived in the area in 1877. He did not leave until the era of the First World War, when events conspired to finally force him indoors for good.

Again, it may be that no single person before or since has known the place as a whole as well as Hofer. There are plenty of specialists then and now who had, or have, him beat. But who has known the entire place to such a degree and as well as he? When he got his first extended tour of it, in 1879, the park as an official entity was just seven years old. He probably met and, given his personality, befriended people who had been there much earlier. Once settled into the area, he set out to walk or ski every bit of it. By 1887, then, he had been at it nonstop for years, and he had been skiing, we know, for over a decade.

Billy Hofer's 1887 journey was not a climax, but rather just another job. Still, when it came time to write up his 1887 tour of the park, among other feats, he created an astonishing artifact: on one full page of *Forest and Stream*, at that time a broadsheet, he produced, with the help of Grinnell's graphic artists, a map of the entire park giving the locations of major concentrations of each species of animal that his readers would be interested in, and quite a few they might not have cared about. His major limitation appears merely to have been space on the page.

"What made it matter, then and now," Schullery stated of the 1887 ski journey, "was that it was, thanks to Grinnell's orders and Hofer's superior skills as an observer, the first serious attempt to survey winter wildlife and conditions in the park." Unlike earlier winter explorers,

> Hofer was on park business, even though not funded by park management. His detailed accounting of wildlife numbers and distribution, and his many observations on what winter was really like, were the first such report produced. A few earlier reports had come in on conditions in some specific location or about some single species population, but nothing like this had even been proposed before, which makes Hofer's achievement all the more impressive.
>
> He reported on all the animals he saw—not just the favorite large mammals, but the small mammals and birds and even the fish he might glimpse while crossing various park

streams (he was an avid fisherman, so his attention to fish isn't surprising). Some of his descriptions of snow depths and vegetation conditions were just as revealing as his wildlife reports. He left us a singular vignette of an earlier Yellowstone—a colder, more isolated, and considerably less disturbed park, in the throes of one of American history's great winters, and he did it all in a calm, matter-of-fact, and often quite charming manner surpassed by few other park visitors before or since.[7]

Grinnell was obviously pleased with what Hofer had sent him. His compositors set the series in dense type, and Grinnell let it sprawl across the pages of much of five issues, allowing it finally to become the length of a short book. No journal carrying such a wide readership would likely do any such thing today. I said earlier that Billy's reputation has risen and fallen based on circumstances unique to his era and our own. He was the star of the April and May 1887 issues of *Forest and Stream* because he was writing near, but before, the end of the era of the celebrity naturalist.

Every age has its favorite science. Today, the geneticist is the star. Around the turn of the twentieth century, during the quantum revolution, it was the physicist. During Hofer's youth, and stretching back into the age of exploration, it was the buccaneering naturalist, sailing the seven seas and braving the elements to return with strange and wondrous beasts. Yet those naturalists were not just entertainers or stuntmen. They were scientists. Charles Darwin was, in his youth, one of them.

And Billy Hofer was one of their number, too. He was, in fact, among the truly accomplished naturalists of his era, and the first to live, full-time and year-round, in greater Yellowstone. His observations were too precise, his knowledge too encyclopedic, and his written records of his counts, measurements, and other studies too careful to be called anything other than "scientific." And that was during the months of summer; the observations he made during winter were unprecedented and unique. Since I am the first person to make this claim for him—that the man was a scientist, and one of the first caliber—it needs a closer look.

Pronounce the word "scientist" today, and whether we first picture Jonas Salk, Peter Higgs, or Bill Nye the Science Guy, we know what one looks like and how that person is supposed to behave. Wearing white coats, surrounded by mysterious equipment, working for a large bureaucracy, and possessing Ph.Ds. as mere tickets of admission, scientists are engaged in a massively-funded and centrally-important enterprise, both creations and creators of the modern world. We do not understand their experiments, but they produce data that other scientists can check and verify. If something goes wrong, we feel, they will figure it out. In all forms, science requires high intelligence, but given scholarships and government support, anyone with the brains can enter its ranks.

That is, of course, the popular conception, one full of misconceptions. Science will never be a perfect meritocracy, nor will it follow its own rules perfectly. Nobel laureates can lose their minds utterly and still retain their force-field of Nobel prestige among the general public, the news media, and even the fellow scientists who ought to know better. Still, most branches of science—both experimental and observational—do today regulate themselves according to rules that are established and accepted by the scientists themselves. Lunacy, junk science, pseudoscience, and outright fraud will always be with us (the amount of money changing hands alone will guarantee that they will always be with us). The mere fact that such terms as "junk science" and "pseudoscience" exist, however, is a testament today to the ability of the professionals to eventually wake up and smell the garbage. Reputation and the well-dressed lie will not normally hold out forever.

In the mid-nineteenth century, as Billy Hofer was growing to adulthood, and well beyond, reputation was nearly all that science had. The terms "science" and "scientist" themselves had scarcely caught on; around the time Hofer was born, "natural philosophy" would have come more readily to the tongue. Only the wealthy had time and money for it, and universities, innately conservative (note how, at graduation, everyone dressed—and still dresses—like medieval nobility), stuck with the Latin and Greek classics as their primary focus for as long as they could. Each science remained the province of aristocrats, who accepted one another as respectable—and believable—natural philosophers in large part out of sheer social prestige.

To understand the situation back then, we can learn much from the relationship between Alfred Wallace and Charles Darwin. Wallace is today known almost entirely for a letter, or letters, he wrote to Darwin that outlined the theory of what we now call evolution, one that Darwin had already been working on for years. They really deserve credit as co-discoverers of the central idea underpinning all the life sciences. It is, instead, Darwin who is today as prominent, historically, as Newton or Einstein or any other scientist who comes to mind.

David Quammen gave a useful summary of the situation in his popular science classic *The Song of the Dodo*, and made it clear how Darwin eclipsed Wallace. The latter was a man of humble origins who made his living—and learned the "life sciences" when they barely existed—collecting specimens in the tropics. In 1855, Wallace published a paper that anticipated some of the key ideas that made *On the Origin of Species* famous when it appeared four years later. The paper, too, remains little-remembered:

> A few other scientists had taken notice of Wallace's paper, and two even said so to Darwin. One of these was Sir Charles Lyell, England's preeminent geologist. The other was Edward Blyth, an Englishman stationed in India with whom Darwin corresponded. But neither Lyell nor Blyth communicated appreciation to the author. To them, this fellow Wallace was an unknown, a commercial collector and trader, a purveyor of stuffed birds and mounted insects

for the curio market. Collection was crucial to the advancement of biology, but if the collector sold specimens (as Wallace did, in order to live), he was liable to be looked on a déclassé.[8]

In truth, Quammen's language here is not strong enough. The mid-nineteenth century gentility lived by an unwritten law that might as well have been set in stone and mounted on high: A gentleman did not engage in trade.

Furthermore, Wallace was still tramping his way from one island to the next all-hell-and-gone out in the Malay Archipelago. He had no social standing and no fixed address. Did anyone know how to reach him? Did anyone care? Having attended some meetings of the Entomological Society during his last sojourn in London, he was not quite a total outsider, but he stood out more than in. And though the discipline of biology had not yet in those years become a profession, regulated by academic credentials and protocols, it was at least a semi-exclusive club. The club's membership consisted largely of gentlemen with inherited wealth, such as Darwin, and of country clergy, who performed their clerical chores mainly on Sunday and were free to watch birds or collect beetles during the week. The club met in London, in Paris, in Edinburgh, in Cambridge, in Berlin, in a few other places, while Alfred Wallace on the far side of the world coped with malaria and rotting feet.[9]

Billy Hofer did his future reputation no favors by behaving rather like his near-contemporary Wallace: tramping to some of the wildest parts of his world, knocking about for a living, and never making any great effort to achieve the status of Gentleman.

In picturing him driving his skis up those two long hills at the start of their 1887 journey, Tansey hustling along in his wake—

the first hill the climb to park headquarters, the second the even harder struggle up through the gunsight pass leading south, onto Swan Lake Flat and toward the interior of the park—one pictures a face so scorched by that brutal February that it resembled worked leather. Yet if he could hear me, he would probably be blushing. He was self-deprecating to a great fault.

Here is just one example. As they headed south, he and Tansey found the damage left by one of the more violent storms of that year, one that had struck a month earlier: "Many trees had been blown down, some were broken off 20ft. up and had brought down in their fall telephone wires and poles. The wide wagon road was piled up with snow fully 12ft. deep, drifted in long ridges, the tops of which we were obliged to follow as if traveling on the comb of a house."[10]

Later, in the same canyon, he found the tracks of three avalanches, as he had been expecting. What was his conclusion about this place? "I really think there is no danger here at all."[11]

It was a typical moment, and one that captures for us today a facet of his defining characteristic: that of a man of the most acute contrasts. He was as tough and physically skilled as a professional athlete, but he had none of the exalted ego that goes with that position. He came from humble origins, but did not strain himself in the slightest in interacting with some of the most wealthy and powerful men of his era. He could pal-around with the likes of Theodore Roosevelt; he could, without flinching, do the same with the roughest Army private or frontier eccentric, in the same minute, if necessary. His formal education was adequate, but unspectacular; his scientific understanding of the Yellowstone region went unrivaled.

His "Aw, shucks, nothin' to it" attitude toward his own feats also helped him disappear down the memory hole. To be famous, as we know today, it is always best to be a self-promoter.

And, to be famous, it is also necessary to be lucky. He should be remembered today as Yellowstone's John Muir, yes, and he is not, but it would have required more than merely a haughtier ego to make him so. Muir was Billy's near-contemporary, one who achieved great fame during his lifetime, fame that has if anything only grown more potent in the century since his death. Yet when one compares the two, they reveal strikingly similar lives. Only Muir could have matched Hofer in his simple delight at natural phenomena that most people today find terrifying. In his book *The Yosemite*, Muir described crossing a snowfield that chose that moment to become an avalanche. That was no problem: "as the whole mass beneath and about me joined in the flight there was no friction, though I was tossed here and there and lurched from side to side. When the avalanche swedged and came to rest I found myself on top of the crumpled pile without a bruise or scar. This was a fine experience."[12] Today, it would probably be a felony, or at least "Driving While Intoxicated."

Both men were born and raised in humble circumstances, learning in their childhood all manner of practical skills. In their young adulthood, they both wandered—purposefully—away from anything that looked like civilization, then found and fell in love with their respective parks. Abandoning anything that looked like regular life, embracing with pure joy huge blocks of raw wilderness, they did whatever was required to stay in those parks permanently. They stayed for years and years, learning every detail about the places and exploring every corner. They wrote about those places for large audiences, and in the end, the rich and well-connected sought them out to take advantage of their expertise.

They shared an attitude toward the wilderness that, surprisingly, was more common in their era than ours. Its abandonment marks a change—for the worse, honestly—in environmental politics over the last century. The old style of environmentalism, which Muir and Hofer arguably shared, made an emotional appeal: love nature, and it will love you back. You need not fear it, because it is not anything like as dangerous as advertised. Since their era, however, people in developed countries have changed. In the 1970s, in another context, the journalist Hunter S. Thompson remarked that "Most natives of Manhattan Island are terrified of all animals except cockroaches and poodles."[13] Today, everyone is terrified of all animals except poodles—cockroaches have slipped over into the "Terror" column. Environmental activists have long since given up trying to get people to love nature; the conscious goal, today, at least in some quarters, is to get them to fear it. Except for the occasional Sierra Club outing and the like, environmentalism is focused almost entirely on global catastrophe.

So why did Muir end up famous, and Billy only a local hero? The crucial difference lay in what amounts to an accident of geography—a matter of luck. Yosemite was, by the later decades of Muir's life, an easy day's travel from San Francisco, Berkeley, and the whole greater Bay Area, then the single major urban area on the West Coast. Yellowstone was and remains in the middle of nowhere. Muir had another stroke of luck. His major scientific contribution was to explain the formation of Yosemite Valley; he was the first to see that it was substantially the work of glaciers, not of Noah's flood or some other hypothetical catastrophe. "Respectable" scientists recognized the force of his ideas, and he became at least an honorary member of the club.

Although he never entirely lost touch with the mountains, Muir married, then spent years accumulating wealth on a ranch in Martinez, California, not too far from either the Sierra or San Francisco. Having amassed enough of a fortune to keep his family comfortable, he returned full-time to his career as a book author, lecturer, and activist that created the fame he enjoys to this day. He could have done none of that living in the middle of nowhere.

While Hofer's output of words was about as large as Muir's, his outlets were journalistic. He had an audience for only so long as he had original news to report from the ground, in Yellowstone. He could easily have written books—he had the discipline for it—but the opportunity never arose. He never married, and his retirement years, spent far from Yellowstone, were financially pinched, but not unhappy, to the extent that he could keep in touch, a little, with his old friends from Yellowstone. He was like Alcyoneus, the giant in Greek mythology who draws his power from his native, nourishing soil, and whom Hercules can only kill when he drags him to an alien place. Having died like the giant, Hofer appears today only fleetingly, and then mainly in the more thoroughgoing histories.

But Hofer, if he had known or thought it mattered, could have taken better care of his future reputation. He was born into a town that provided unique opportunities to at least meet and learn from some of the most accomplished scholars and "natural philosophers" in the United States of his time. It was like being born in Athens when Plato's Academy was at its peak.

And what did Billy do? He fled one of the most respectable places on the North American continent and made a beeline for several of the least.

CHAPTER ONE

Stay East, Young Man, and Die of Boredom

If we could choose our birthplaces, surely Thomas Hofer would not have chosen New Haven, Connecticut. It was wrong in too many ways.

At the time, in 1849, few would have felt the same. After all, New Haven was among the most sophisticated towns of its size in the whole country, sophisticated and prosperous. New Haven was also a place that took its New England values seriously. It was, indeed, early New England on steroids, a menagerie of both high-mindedness and propriety, not at all appropriate for the man Hofer became in his future. From a deeper perspective, though, we can look back and see that his birthplace was in fact crucial in giving him the skills he would need in that rough-and-ready future.

Even though it is located all the way up north in Connecticut, New Haven is today regarded by many as the northern end of metropolitan New York City and thus near the middle of the great Northeast megalopolis, the continuous city that runs from Boston to Washington and beyond. It was never the middle of nowhere. It sits astride the Quinnipiac River—named for the native people who called it home first—which spreads through a series of marshes before debouching into New Haven Harbor and Long Island Sound, with the open Atlantic not far to the east. The Harbor is itself only one of the deeper embayments on the Connecticut shore, which owes its shark-tooth profile to the glaciers that scored the coast during the ice ages, a detail of which young Thomas was unaware, although his older self would probably have smiled at it.

So it was a wet and salty place, and it could offer him an apprenticeship in the art of surviving a routinely cold and threatening environment where help, in an emergency, was the responsibility of the victim. Of course, if that seemed forbidding, the child could simply avoid it…but what boy, born next to the sea, simply avoids it?

Vast swaths of Hofer's early childhood are, as the historian always says, "not well documented." In fact, they are not documented at all, and the documents are not hiding. Some things about him we will never know, and why would we? He was born into an average family, with nothing resembling wealth, not far from two centuries ago. We can, however, reassemble that childhood from some of the extraordinary skills he exhibited as an adult. He was, for instance, so comfortable around boats that they were central to one of his earliest guiding ventures in Yellowstone National Park. Among his first clients was William Pickett, an influential figure in Wyoming politics and a future member of the Boone and Crockett Club, the conservationist society whose most famous founding member was Theodore Roosevelt. Pickett scrambled around the new national park in 1879, when it remained the rawest wilderness, and returned in 1880, with some expert help: Hofer had by then been in the Yellowstone area several years and was supporting himself with whatever work he could invent. With a cousin, Hofer had the idea of taking tourists around the vast, vast Yellowstone Lake during an era when the interior of the park was scarcely served even by roads, much less watercraft. Writing much later, Pickett recalled the events that attended his arrival in 1880:

As early in the spring as the snows would allow, T. Elwood Hofer, (affectionately called "Billy" Hofer by his friends) and his cousin of the same name, fought their way through the snows and located near our present camp, determined to build a sailboat of size adequate for the accommodation of the large influx of visitors, expected to visit the park that summer. They packed in all the tools necessary for such work, including a whip-saw.[1] They had gone into the timber, cut down trees, sawed them into suitable lengths, "roped" them by the horn of the saddle, to their scaffold, "whip-sawed" them into suitable lumber for a sailboat from 30 to 35 feet in length. This job had been done before our arrival, the sailboat being then ready for business.[2]

Pickett called this a "notable achievement," although he thought it paled when compared to Hofer's ski around the park in 1887. It surely deserves stronger language. Pickett had been camped at "the outlet of the Yellowstone Lake into the river of that name"—that is, on the north shore of the lake, in or near the present-day village of Fishing Bridge. Even in the twenty-first century, the trip from the north entrance of the park to Fishing Bridge—the trip that Hofer and his cousin made to reach Pickett—is a tedious journey of over fifty miles, and we have cars and roads. Hofer and his cousin did not, and yet they made the trip at a date when all trails turn into creeks. They punched through snow and mud and multiple mountain passes to reach a spot on the map that was not even a spot. The only hint of civilization was a primitive cabin at Topping Point, a mile south of the river outlet, an earth-roofed affair built by Eugene S. Topping that only lasted until about 1884. Topping had had the same idea as the Hofers, to run a boat service on the lake. He had launched a vessel in 1874 and a second in 1875,[3] but the effort failed—as was inevitable, given how few people visited the lake shore throughout the 1870s. The statistics are comical by today's standards, when four million people visit the park every year, throughout the twelve months. All these numbers are estimates, but the first year of the park's existence, 1872, saw 300 visitors, the next four years 500 visitors, then 1000 each year between 1877 and 1882, all arriving during about an eight-week period in the high summer.[4] Nevertheless, in this isolated and surpassingly primitive place, with no electricity, no workshop, no power tools, and no architect except Hofer, they built what amounted to a small yacht.

We might imagine that Yellowstone at least provided them a decent supply of wood, but we would be wrong: the kind of hardwoods that boat builders prefer, like oak, were nowhere available. The dominant tree-species all over the region is the lodgepole pine, *Pinus contorta*, mainly useful as firewood; the spruce and fir forests that did appear regularly around the lake were not much help either, as they rotted when sawed and exposed to weather. As always, Hofer was able to make do with what Yellowstone provided him, but the materials may have played a role in what followed.

Pickett and his party wanted to reach the farthest shore of West Thumb, the wide circular bay that juts toward Old Faithful. The distance from his camp by water, Pickett guessed, was twenty miles, a figure that accords well with modern maps. As so often on the lake, it was an idyll that turned into a nightmare. The party, eight men and Pickett's dog, was becalmed long enough to break out a set of oars; Hofer would have had to craft the oars by hand with a spoke shave, a detail that Pickett omitted. Then Yellowstone sprang one of its surprises:

> About the time all hands had become tired out, a slight and favorable breeze sprang up, becoming brisker and brisker and we were again sailing along at a comfortable gait, the spirits of the party rising with the wind. The oars were stowed away, and every one was looking forward to a quick run to our destination.
>
> About this time an angry looking, threatening cloud, just peeping over the Continental Divide, was observed in

the northwest. The wind soon became brisker and stronger, and waves began to splash up against the sides of the craft. To reach our destination, it became necessary for the skipper to sail close to the wind. Could he hold that course for twenty minutes longer, we would be so close to shore as to be in smooth water. We were now in the deepest part of the Thumb, measured by Prof. Hayden as about 100 feet; but the wind was increasing in violence, the waves rising and threatening to swamp the boat. Bailing became imperative.

Then the worst of the storm burst upon us, with the fiercest of winds and a downpour of blinding rain. The gaff could not stand the strain and snapped. The sail came tumbling down over our heads, and the boat soon drifted into the trough of the waves, which threatened to engulf the craft. Skipper Hofer kept his head admirably and by vigorous work with the steering oar, he placed the craft out of the trough and across the waves, the crew in the meantime taking care of the flapping sail as best they could. Had our craft been swamped in that storm with waves running high, with temperature of the water 40 to 45 degrees F. and at least two miles from shore, not a soul of that party would have reached land, unless perhaps the dog. It is questionable whether he would have left his master.

Pickett was not being melodramatic; nor is this a nineteenth-century version of *Gilligan's Island*. It is not uncommon today to cast off from any shore of any lake in Greater Yellowstone under the brightest sunny skies, only to face what amounts to a typhoon once the boat is too far from shore to summon help. The weather can go foul so rapidly that even experts are killed, and not just on gigantic Yellowstone Lake. On the much smaller Shoshone Lake in 1994, a highly qualified backcountry ranger was swamped and drowned by just such a storm.[5]

With such a wind, no other sail than our bodies was needed, and the boat soon obtained sufficient headway to answer to the steering oar, and we were running before the wind at a good speed. One great danger had been passed, the next one was lest the waves should flow over the stern. The vigorous bailing could not entirely remove that danger, but as the water of the lake became of less depth, the waves decreased and that imminent danger had seemingly passed.

The making of a safe landing was the next cause of anxiety. With the fierce wind still blowing, it was imperative to sail before the wind. Looking ahead through the driving rain a faint outline of the pine forests on the shore was seen, about four miles ahead. The shore of the lake was known to be sometimes a sand beach, but sometimes shoal and with a beach of boulders. If we should run on the sand beach we felt safe.

Going along at a clipping gait, we came to within a half mile of land, but the shore was very indistinct. When within a quarter of a mile, a sand beach was plainly seen. Just to the left of the landing ahead of us, was a rock beach. It was arranged that the two in front, Herendeen[6] and myself, should leap ashore with the head line and hold the craft steadily until the balance scrambled ashore, for it was anticipated after the prow was beached that the first waves would pile over the stern.

As the bow ran up on the beach, Herendeen and myself leaped ashore with remarkable agility, climbed the bluff at the water's edge, and held fast to the line while the balance scrambled ashore from the boat, now filled with water....[7]

It was all in a day's work—Hofer never had a client die under his care, although he would come close again and again. The boat, they discovered, remained filled with water because the landing had been so violent as to stove in the hull. They spent the night in the open, unfed. They were, of course, hungry during the night and jokingly discussed a media sensation of that time: in June, 1880, Dr. Henry S. Tanner launched, in New York, a widely publicized and successful effort to fast forty days and nights (like so many doctors of his day, Tanner was a nut: he believed starvation cured disease).[8] The party separated. Headed back toward civilization, Pickett stopped at the old Topping cabin to see how Hofer and his cousin were doing, but they had long since departed to find something to eat. Pickett found only a note on the door, typical of the Hofer sense of humor: "I am no relation to Dr. Tanner."[9]

Hofer would eventually repair the craft and sail it back to the cabin at what is now Fishing Bridge, but gave it up shortly afterward and literally moved on to greener pastures. The boat was effectively disposable—he could always build another—and according to one source, it had a Viking funeral: having come unmoored, it drifted down the Yellowstone River until it went over the Upper Falls of the Yellowstone, where it was atomized.[10]

Incidents like this one—and Hofer's time in Yellowstone was jammed with thousands of such incidents—today give the historian some of the details about his early life. Here was a man who could turn the biological debris strewing the north shore of Yellowstone Lake into a serviceable sailing vessel with nothing but his cousin's help and such hand tools as a mule could carry. He was like that: he could do absolutely anything with his hands.

Hofer was, however, thirty-one-years old when he and Pickett set sail and had only been in the park about three years. He had not learned those skills in three years, nor had life in the mountains taught him how to build a yacht and sail it safely through a storm after being dismasted. Maritime New England surely taught him that, and watery New Haven would have served as an ideal schoolhouse. It even provided something like "grades," namely environments that graduated through greater and greater challenges, from creek, marsh, and river to New Haven Harbor, to Long Island Sound, and finally to the open sea.

Expertise of the kind Hofer displayed in Pickett's account could only have been acquired through hands-on training. It is highly unlikely Hofer ever went to sea, in the sense we usually mean by that phrase—as a blue-water sailor, voyaging around the world—but he knew his way around a carpenter's shop and a boat-builder's yard, and that afternoon with Pickett was quite obviously not his first time sailing. As we shall see, he would come back to the lake and its boat traffic later in life, to his regret. On the positive side, he was an accomplished angler with a love for water and aquatic life that ran deep. Coastal New England had a say in all this, as Hofer himself confirmed in a letter he wrote late in life. He had tried sailboats as his first Yellowstone venture, he explained, because he knew them from his early youth, although his description is brief: "Having been interested in sail boats on Long Island Sound, and especially Sharpies in New Haven harbor, I decided to build one at Yellowstone Lake."[11] As we will see, a sharpie was a variety of sailboat invented in New Haven to meet highly specific local needs, which he adapted for use on the lake.

Hofer did not learn his skills as a craftsman through a formal apprenticeship. We have the good fortune to possess documents from Hofer's many friends who recalled what he had said about his past, and there are even a number of such items in which Hofer himself reminisces. A crucial example is *The Yellowstone National Park: Historical and Descriptive*, a book written by Hiram Chittenden, the Army engineer who built much of the park's early infrastructure around the turn of the twentieth century. Later editions of his book include thumbnail biographies of influential early residents, and among them is Hofer. The family history in this elderly book is actually more thorough (so far) than Ancestry.com, although it omits his parents. His mother was born Mary Weeks, and his father was John C. Hofer. He had a sister, Catherine, but no other siblings. Chittenden explained:

In this little group of early Park celebrities it is only fair to include the most distinguished representative of a very important business in the early days of the Park—that of guide or conductor of tourist and hunting parties. "Billy" Hofer was born in New Haven, Conn., February 19, 1849. His father was a native of Switzerland; his mother was an American. His great-great-grandfather on his mother's side fought under John Paul Jones in the Revolutionary War under the name of Thomas Ellingwood, though his real name was Thomas Elwood.[12]

Ellingwood was a Lieutenant of Marines, which, during that era, involved jumping onto the deck of an enemy ship and fighting that enemy with whatever was handy, a saber, a dirk, a club. The family had a rugged streak. The muster list in the Library of Congress for the ship USS *Alliance* for 1780, captained by the famous John Paul Jones, shows Hofer's ancestor as both Thomas "Ellwood" and "Ehlenwood"—the former was the name he went by, the latter was his family name, in each case a near miss to Chittenden's rendering of the moniker.[13] Another list of the crew of *Alliance*—a 36-gun frigate—shows Ellwood serving as Marine Lieutenant from August 24, 1778 to May 1, 1783—that is, through most of the long, exhausting War of Independence.[14] He had also served on land, before the war even started.[15] Chittenden continued about Ellwood:

The fact that he was at the time a British subject may have had something to do with his temporary change of name, which was later abandoned when he took up his residence in America. Being a thoroughly non-religious member of a very religious family, none of his descendants would name their boys after him, until finally one, of the surname Hofer, as worldly as himself, did honor his distinguished ancestor by giving his son the Christian name Thomas Elwood. In later years when the grown-up lad fell in with the rough-and-ready yeomanry of western Montana, they wouldn't accept "Thomas Elwood" at all, it being too "dude-ish" for their pioneer taste. So they substituted the handy prefix "Billy," and it stuck to him ever after. Hofer's childhood was spent in different parts of Connecticut, and he received a fairly good common school education there.[16]

As Chittenden noted, while Hofer spent much of his childhood wielding a spoke shave, he also spent a good deal of it in a schoolroom. A number of other sources testify to his literacy, none so eloquently as Hofer's own writing and accomplishments. He worked, after all, as a journalist for a national weekly, *Forest and Stream*. The newspaperman Emerson Hough, who was friendly with Hofer, found him to be a voracious reader. On their epic journey through the park by ski in 1894, Hough noted how Hofer, on those rare occasions when they got a prolonged rest, could be found "reading a novel describing the trials of the Lady Evalina, or something of the sort."[17] Hofer loved novels, the bigger the better.

Hough thought it amusing that one of the toughest mountain men in the West went in for middlebrow romance novels, but reading is a transferable skill, and Hofer always exhibited that trait that produces learning and that learning produces: curiosity. Hough noted a striking instance during their ski trip when Hofer gave him an expert guided tour of the snowy and abandoned Norris Geyser Basin. From the number of geysers and springs that Hough named in his description, they must have walked several miles through the most active part of the Norris basin. It was not the scenery alone that impressed Hough:

> I can only say that even those to whom the geysers are an old story in summer became enthusiastic over them in this winter aspect, and even Hofer was eager to go over the entire basin again. To Hofer, of course, much of our pleasure was due here, for he knows every geyser thoroughly, and is

a most interesting and thorough and enthusiastic guide. If I had a friend wishing to make the Park trip, I should by all means advise him to get Billy to go along, for he knows the Park inch by inch, and even its scientific features and scientific history are not strange in the least to him, since he has been so much associated there with parties of scientists of all sorts. Billy could talk of rhyolite and algae and silicates in a way to make your head swim.[18]

Thomas Elwood Hofer was a rare man in many ways, and here is another. Then and today, all but a small minority of people who live and work in the park lose interest in the geysers with great speed; indeed, they become the enemy, because they are the very factor that is attracting that army of irritating tourists. When Hough made that tour, Hofer was approaching the end of his second full decade in the park, and he still had a childlike enthusiasm approaching joy for Norris Geyser Basin. Only a highly positive early experience with books and learning could have created such a person.

Here again, he was served well by his native region. New England was settled by religious separatists who wanted everyone in the colony to be able to read the Bible, and so they built what was surely the best school system in the world. New Haven itself was most famous as the home of Yale University, nearly a century and a half old by Hofer's birth. A classic history of New England Puritanism, Edmund S. Morgan's *The Puritan Dilemma*, makes this point repeatedly: "Fortunately, reason could heal differences as well as create them, and the Puritans were extraordinarily reasonable men. The zeal with which they studied the Bible sprang from supreme confidence in the ability of reason to find the truth there. Not knowledge but ignorance, they believed, was the mother of heresy."[19]

At the same time, you can learn a lot about a man by what he flees, and there was another side to those religious separatists that made New England the wrong place for Thomas Elwood Hofer. The separatists were Puritans, a word that is today associated almost exclusively with black capes and sexual repression (rather stupidly, given the double-digit size of Puritan families). The black cape, at least, was correct. "Puritan" is the generic name for the English Protestants who sought to purify the Church of England of any lingering traces of Roman Catholicism. The history of Connecticut is of the successive arrivals of such groups, often as refugees from the larger and more settled Massachusetts Bay Colony to the north. New Haven itself began life as an independent colony, separatists from the separatists.

The government was of course a theocracy, and it took its religion seriously. The standard history of Connecticut for schoolchildren during Hofer's childhood was a book by Benjamin Trumbull, who was, tellingly, both a preacher and a historian, and whose volume was graced by a typically uninviting early nineteenth-century title: *A Complete History of Connecticut, Civil and Ecclesiastical: From the Emigration of Its First Planters, from England, in the Year 1630, to the Year 1764, and to the Close of the Indian Wars.* It had this to say about the founding of Hofer's native town of New Haven, originally named Quinnipiac after the river that flows into New Haven Harbor: "Soon after they arrived at Quinnipiack, in the close of a day of fasting and prayer, they entered into what they termed a plantation covenant. In this they solemnly bound themselves, 'That, as in matters that concern the gathering and ordering of a church, so also in all public offices, which concern civil order, as choice of magistrates and officers, making and repealing laws, dividing allotments of inheritance, and all things of like nature, they would, all of them, be ordered by the rules which the scripture held forth to them.'"[20]

Even as late as Hofer's childhood, it was difficult for New Haven residents to get away from radical Protestantism, which infiltrated every aspect of life. For generations, a common truism among historians was that New England Puritans left their stamp on the character of the whole country.[21] Their relentless work ethic and brutally demanding standards helped drive the nation down a path toward wealth and power. Contemporary historians tend to go easy on this theory; a nation of hundreds of millions can only owe so much any longer to a few tens of thousands of English religious enthusiasts living centuries ago. No one would dispute, however, that they left their stamp on New England, especially before the Civil War.

And what a stamp it was, from young Hofer's point of view. The official motto of Connecticut is the Constitution State, but it was also long called the Land of Steady Habits.[22] Morgan left us a description of what it was like:

> Puritanism was a power not to be denied. It did great things for England and for America, but only by creating in the men and women it affected a tension which was at best painful and at worst unbearable. Puritanism required that a man devote his life to seeking salvation but told him he was helpless to do anything but evil. Puritanism required that he rest his whole hope in Christ but taught him that Christ would utterly reject him unless before he was born God had foreordained his salvation. Puritanism required that a man refrain from sin but told him he would sin anyhow. Puritanism required that he reform the world in the image of God's holy kingdom but taught him that the evil of the world was incurable and inevitable.[23]

Morgan was writing about the seventeenth century, but as he said, it was a power not to be denied, and this kind of aggressive piety still ruled the New England of Thomas Elwood Hofer's childhood.

At some point, Hofer must have thought, to hell with that. He did not find the world evil, certainly not the natural world, and if he ever darkened the door of a church after his early youth, it is difficult to imagine when or where. He was a classic frontier heathen, a kind of spiritual refugee. The nineteenth-century West was full of such men.

Furthermore, that Puritan work ethic had changed Connecticut. By the time Hofer arrived, the state had transitioned from a simple economy based on farming and fishing to the bustling economy of the industrial age. New Haven is an example of the extent and vigor of the boom. When Hofer was born, New Haven had about 20,000 residents and was adding a thousand people every year or so.[24] Especially for that era, it was no longer a town or village; it was a small but booming city, and distinctly industrial. Eli Whitney is known today primarily for his cotton gin, but his greatest invention was the original assembly line—Henry Ford's was a refinement, not an invention. Whitney built a factory (manufacturing firearms) in New Haven. Samuel Colt invented the revolver there, and later Oliver Winchester would build his Winchester Repeating Arms Company there. An intellectual-industrial complex developed between Yale and the increasingly grimy city around it: inventions often issued from the university, and capitalists set up shop outside the ivy walls to mass produce them. Everything from the submarine to the corkscrew was invented in New Haven.[25]

Hofer certainly had some use, later in life, for Winchesters and Colts, but probably did not enjoy living next to their factories. For decades Hofer carried on a correspondence with George Bird Grinnell, running to thousands of pages. Grinnell was the pioneering anthropologist and conservationist who edited Hofer's work at *Forest and Stream*, and the two shared a deep friendship. In 1907, the local authorities where he was living passed a $10 fishing license, and Hofer told Grinnell about it with disgust. He supported "the principle of the thing," but it also smacked of creeping civilization: "If there were any use I'd pray I could sell out here this summer, but you know how the prayers of the wicked turn out! I only hope to sell out and get away from a state that passes such laws. I don't want to live, stay, or camp here. I'm willing to hit the trail any day for Alaska. So far that country 'looks good to me.' I suppose I'm getting old and cranky and it's time I got off out of sight any way. This country is filling up with a lot of bums any way."[26] He left dozens of similar comments in the letters to Grinnell. As we shall see, Hofer in fact did both: he stuck it out, and he went to Alaska. The point is that he was writing from his longtime home in Montana. This was his normal reaction: he would light out for some other territory, literally, at any attempt to civilize him. We might well read the portents in the year of his birth, 1849: in spirit, he was one of the Forty-niners.

Hofer was too young for the Civil War, but after it was over, a longing began to grow in him as it grew in countless other youngsters, a longing to see the wild frontier. During the end of his time in New England—during, say, the second half of the 1860s and the start of the 1870s—the western United States really did at least resemble the Wild West of popular culture. Hofer left Connecticut in 1871. What was the West like at that date? It was not his first destination, but his major destination (to the extent he planned the journey ahead of time, which he appears not to have done) was indeed the Rockies and the northern Great Plains. What were they like?

They were rather like the Western movies, at least the better movies. For one thing, the native tribes were not the hunted, starved, or caged refugees that they became. The various groups we call the Sioux, for instance, governed the Northern Plains as nearly the sole sovereign authority. They produced a number of authentic military geniuses; Crazy Horse of the Oglala was only the most famous. During the 1860s, in what is now called Red Cloud's War, Crazy Horse helped lead an attack on the Bozeman Trail, the route that departed the Oregon Trail and led to the gold fields that had been discovered in southern Montana Territory (one of Hofer's destinations, when he left home). They focused on Fort Phil Kearny, which guarded the trail near what is now the town of Buffalo, Wyoming. The campaign reached its climax when the grossly overconfident Captain William Fetterman led eighty men in a chase after Crazy Horse and a large number of his warriors. The greatest number of Sioux stayed hidden until the last minute, when they surrounded Fetterman and chopped him and every one of his men into pieces, quite literally. In the end, the U.S. government abandoned the Bozeman Trail and retreated, if temporarily. For a time, the Sioux and their allies appeared to be winning.[27]

The Sioux were doing well because their traditional economy was relatively intact: the great continental buffalo herd was still there to feed them, although the numbers were falling fast, down to about five million in 1870.[28] Things were changing rapidly (the completion of the first transcontinental railroad in 1869 was the key event in that change). But for a while, the old West was still there. The U.S. government was a distant and impotent thing represented on the frontier largely by companies and troops of soldiers who spent much of their time huddled in stockaded forts, when they were not deserting. Settlements remained small: Denver—another of Hofer's destinations—contained only about 5000 residents in 1870.[29] In other words, what is today one of the larger cities in North America was then less than a quarter the size of New Haven. Likewise, the infrastructure between settlements in the West was just as tenuous as Denver, and vulnerable to disruption by the real forces on the frontier, people like the Cheyenne and Sioux. It was a land of wild, violent, dangerous adventure. For a while, it genuinely was.

And it was more. Much has been written about the Wild West as a place where youngsters went for the romance of it (as depicted in dime novels), or to slip out of the restraints of civilization and live an anarchic or larcenous life, or to flee the law, or to get rich by any means fair or foul. However, there was more to Thomas Elwood Hofer than that. The western wilderness had a spiritual pull that reached out to him, all the way to New England. This intangible but hallowed quality of the place is hard to reduce to words. One of its greatest disciples, John Muir, said it well: "The tendency nowadays to wander in wildernesses is delightful to see.

Thousands of tired, nerve-shaken, over-civilized people are beginning to find out that going to the mountains is going home; that
wildness is a necessity; and that mountain parks and reservations
are useful not only as fountains of timber and irrigating rivers, but
as fountains of life."[30] Writing much later, Edward Abbey helped
complete Muir's thought:

> We need wilderness because we are wild animals. Every
> man needs a place where he can go to go crazy in peace. Ev-
> ery Boy Scout troop deserves a forest to get lost, miserable,
> and starving in. Even the maddest murderer of the sweetest
> wife should get a chance for a run to a sanctuary of the hills.
> If only for the sport of it. For the terror, freedom, and de-
> lirium [Abbey, we should note, married an astonishing five
> times; Hofer, going the opposite route, never even tried].
> Because we need brutality and raw adventure, because men
> and women first learned to love in, under, and around trees,
> because we need for every pair of feet and legs about ten
> leagues of naked nature, crags to leap from, mountains to
> measure by, [and] deserts to finally die in when the heart
> fails.[31]

Thomas Elwood Hofer would likely have had no problem with a
single word of Abbey's philosophy.

And so he fled New England, leaving his family behind in Canton, Hartford County.[32] We have no evidence of any trouble at
home, and he remained close emotionally to his sister Catherine,
although they were separated for years. For a time, Billy seemed to
sail off the edge of the earth. Hiram Chittenden's thumbnail biography now becomes crucial:

> Upon reaching his majority he struck out for himself and
> went first to Chicago (1871), where he worked for a time
> for the Pullman Palace Car Company. In the spring of 1872

he went to Denver and remained in the State of Colorado during the next five years. In 1877 he went to the Black Hills and thence across the country to Bozeman, Mont., reaching there in mid-summer at the time of the great Nez Perce excitement. Next year, 1878, he found employment with a party going to the Park.[33]

Like so many young bachelors on the frontier, Billy Hofer drifted; he stayed in one place until the gold played out or until he simply got bored, and then he moved on. Such a person will generally not leave much of a record, and following Hofer during this era is a little like following Shakespeare during the famous "missing years" after he first left Stratford. Happily, we do not need conspiracy theories, because we have other writers to corroborate the bare account that Chittenden's book left for us.

One who added to Chittenden was the journalist Emerson Hough, who wrote his own thumbnail biography of Hofer, a sketch that matches Chittenden's in spirit if not in detail. Writing just after the turn of the twentieth century, Hough explained that Hofer had gone "West in time to see the West when it was a land of adventure and hardships. He served as pack master, mail carrier and guide in the wildest parts of the West from Colorado to the Missouri river." Hough also helped us to firm up the date at which Hofer began his western wanderings. Long a resident of Chicago, Hough confirmed that that city was Hofer's first stop. He lived there, said Hough, until the fire of 1871—that is, the Great Fire of Chicago, the one that started in the O'Leary's barn (the cow and the lantern are likely a myth).[34]

Hofer left immediately afterward. The Chittenden biography further tells us that Hofer departed Connecticut "Upon reaching his majority." The age of majority is today 18, but throughout the English speaking world, the age for centuries was twenty-one. The ultimate authority on the matter was *The Institutes of the Lawes of England* by Sir Edward Coke, and it proclaimed quite clearly:

anyone under the age of twenty-one was an "infant."[35] So the crucial year was 1871. Hofer turned twenty-one that year, left home, worked in Chicago until his workplace burned down, then headed west into the unknown. He supported himself doing whatever came to hand and gravitated toward the various mining regions around the West of the 1870s. To the extent that his movements followed a pattern, he drew a triangle across the northern mountains and plains, spending at least five years in Denver and the mountains above, before moving briefly to the Black Hills and then to Montana, where he lived in Bozeman and environs before he reached Yellowstone National Park.

Happily, we have another source for this period: Hofer himself. As noted, he maintained an extensive correspondence with George Bird Grinnell, and, thanks to Grinnell, much of Hofer's half of the correspondence survives today (the vast bulk of Grinnell's personal papers, including the correspondence, is preserved at his alma mater, Yale University). Hofer regularly paused when the subject under discussion jogged a memory from decades earlier, at which point he would give us some key information. A letter from August, 1921—this part was tongue in cheek—purported to express frustration that Grinnell had reached the frontier in 1870, as a recent magazine article had discussed, and so beat Hofer there: "You got the best of me by two years as I did not reach Denver until '72, April. Our train on the K.P. was stuck in the snow for almost four days between Hugo and Deer Trail."[36] So he made the long journey by train—the Kansas Pacific—but it was not a happy trip. Hugo and Deer Trail, Colorado (they still exist) were nearly at the end of the line; Hugo, for instance, was barely a hundred miles from Denver. Imagine, today, spending four days trapped in a railroad car in the snow, so close to your destination, with the car becoming a de facto refrigerator. No wonder Billy took up skiing

As he grew older and less able to get around, Hofer read more and more about the beloved West of his youth, Grinnell occasionally sending him books and articles, and Hofer writing back with what was often an expert opinion. In January 1923, for instance, the two carried on a long discussion about Bent's Fort, the old adobe trading post in what is today southeastern Colorado, occasioned by a monograph Grinnell wrote for the Kansas State Historical Society about the fort in 1923.[37] Hofer could never have visited Bent's Fort, because it was destroyed in the year of his birth, but every old frontiersman knew about it:

> I never was in that country except over the Santa Fe R.R. I went or came west over the old K.P. to Denver then over the Denver Pacific to Ft. Lupton and Ft. St. Vrain[;] the little town just started[.] Platteville was halfway between these two old 'Dobe' Forts. That Fall I went down the Platt[e] with Egbert Johnson to Beaver Creek to within about 70 miles of Julesburg[.] There were quite a number of the old 'Dobe' stations at Beaver Creek South Side[.] After So Platte we camped with Jack Sumner (who had been with Powell down the Grand Cañon of the Colorado). The old station was warm and very comfortable. We saw lots of Buffalo and there was a man there who had just come Skin Hunting. Sumner was making a rifle for him and was to have his pay in skins. The two old Forts Lufton and St. Vrains was used for Ranches.
>
> I noticed you must have worked hard to get together all your story of Bent's Fort.... I used to hear old timers (in '72) talk of Bents Fort and all the other places and see you give the old names as they used them.
>
> I want to thank you for sending the Old Forts.[38]

It was indeed a kind thing for Grinnell to have done, especially because, judging from the dates, Grinnell appears to have sent the monograph while it was still in manuscript form.

It may be that he did so because he could never tell what memories from Hofer such a manuscript might uncover. Hofer wrote in a kind of "telegraphese," because Grinnell was privy to the details, but the story he told was a remarkable little vignette of the Old West. Hofer had left Denver and followed the South Platte River downstream to one of the tributaries of the South Platte, Beaver Creek. "Dobe" of course refers to adobe; Hofer, in traveling to Denver, entered the cultural sphere of the old Southwest, where adobe, for lack of proper wood, was the premier building material. During the fur trading era, in the first decades of the nineteenth century, a number of such outposts existed, Bent's Fort being perhaps the most famous. Ft. Lupton and Ft. St. Vrain started life as just such adobe trading posts. The year, 1872, is today far enough back in time that the Plains were still covered with bison, in large enough quantities that being a market hunter, or, as Hofer put it, a man engaged in "Skin Hunting," was a viable profession. It was just such hunting that would destroy the continental herds by 1885.

In the letter, Hofer also gave us an early taste of a strange and delightful anomaly that characterized his entire life. He could be travelling in the absolute middle of nowhere, and a frontier celebrity—minor or major—would poke his head out of the bush and say hello. John Wesley Powell, in an act of outlandish courage (or outlandish foolhardiness that he happened to survive), had been the first to take boats down the Grand Canyon of the Colorado. Jack Sumner, the gunsmith whom Hofer had fallen in with on Beaver Creek, was not merely a member of Powell's expedition. He helped crew the Major's boat.[39]

What was Hofer doing at Beaver Creek? The date and location suggest that he was prospecting, but there is another possibility. Years later, in Yellowstone National Park, he would be asked by the authorities to try to catch some of the park beavers alive. He wrote about the experience at length in *Forest and Stream* and dropped an offhand comment that was incidental to the subject at hand, but suggests a vast experience behind the language: "I had had some experience trapping them for their pelts, and when doing this I had always tried to set my traps so as to drown them." This seems brutal, perhaps, but that was how pelt hunters dealt with beavers. He also employed language ("I used Nos. 2 and 3 Newhouse traps," etc)[40] that would only come naturally to a trapper. What we normally think of as the "fur trapping era"—the West of the early nineteenth century—was long gone, but pelts were still worth money. So it appears, reliably, that Hofer spent at least part of those years wandering as a trapper. A *Forest and Stream* article published in 1903 included another offhand comment from Hofer with vast experience behind it: "I have been on the plains in the buffalo days when they could be seen by the thousands; I have seen antelope by the thousands and other animals in great number."[41] The destruction of the bison herd is well known to us today, other animals less so. His memory of antelope in such numbers dates from the early 1870s, a time of the truly wild frontier.

Hofer had more to say about Jack Sumner and Beaver Creek in a letter from May 1925. This time, he was commenting on an article Grinnell had written about how plentiful game animals were in the past (and here, I should note that as he grew older, Billy's spelling and syntax became more erratic. Throughout, I will preserve his words as he wrote them):

> I could add a lot to it from my observations from 72 on as in the fall—November—72 I was with a party after their winter supply of Buffalo meat. We went down the South Platt[e] to Beaver Creek. There was a chap there with a small bunch of Texas cattle—no cattle east of there untill you got to Julesburg or further east, I don't know how far. There were no cattle west of there untill you got allmost to Greeley. When I got to Montana in 77 there were very few cattle untill you got to Big Timber and the Crazy Mts. At Beaver Creek there were a few Skin Hunters. Skin Hunting had started in there. A Jack Sumner was running the Beaver Creek ranch his Brother was P.M. [Postmaster] at Denver.

But Montana had the Buffalo and the Elk ranged way down the Yellowstone. I'm thankful I got to Montana way ahead of the railroads.[42]

What Hofer was doing in writing this was using the spread of cattle westward as a marker of the spread of civilization, which (as his various writings confirmed) he spent his life trying to outrun. Cows and railroads went together—the latter hauled the cows from western states to places like Chicago, where they were turned into shoes and tinned beef and the like. The wild animals were still living their traditional lives in Montana, which meant there was yet no railroad—and that was the way Hofer liked it.

In May 1923, in another letter to Grinnell, Hofer produced an extended memory from his discussion of the novel *North of 36* by Emerson Hough. Hofer liked the novel, but had some information to add to it:

> Don't know where he picked up his history of the "Old Texas Trail[.]" When I first came west [in] 72 we used to hear of it and see some of the "Longhorns[.]" They some times got as far north as Wyoming and Montana, young steers to grow and fatten and quite a lot of cows. I think there were some on Grey Bull [River, Wyoming] and there was allways more or less Texas Jacks Bills and other Texas Cowboys working north. Bah! Now as to guns.... All the gun men I ever saw[,] two gun men [,] carried both guns with the grip forward and I could see the advantage for quick shooting. They could draw and kill a man who carried his guns the other way, before he got them started. I've often years ago seen men practicing to see how quickly they could draw and shoot. A Texas Cowboy[43] shot the man that shot him—after he had a bullet in his lungs. As he was sinking to the floor of the saloon he drew and shot as quick as a flash and was dead when he got to the floor. That was [also

true of] Bill Roberts and he shot the man who fired first
[namely] Elias Keeney. If Roberts had to reach back or pull
his gun back before getting it out he could not have fired[.]
I think I showed Hough how they used to carry guns, when
they wanted them quickly.[44]

The only potentially confusing element here is the bit about
how a gunslinger wears his guns. For edification, we can look at the
famous photograph of Wild Bill Hickok wearing fringed buckskins
with a knife in his belt, and note how the handles of his revolvers
stick out like broken thumbs, the butt ends of the handles facing
the camera. That is what Hofer likely had in mind.

The Old Texas Trail—also the Great Western Cattle Trail—
was perhaps the most famous of the routes by which cattle were
driven out of Texas to railheads in the north, to Dodge City, Kansas, in this case. As Hofer noted, the business eventually expanded
into his part of the world, and he found himself dealing with various guys named "Texas" whom he would rather not have had in his
life. The gunfight he describes actually happened, although later,
in Bozeman on Halloween, 1879. It was reported at length in *The
New North-West* of Deer Lodge, Montana,[45] and Hofer actually left
out some of the colorful details: drunkenness, some creative verbal
abuse, a spectacular fistfight, and more, ending in the memorable
gunplay he described.

The time in Colorado was especially crucial for Hofer, because
it was here that he learned to ski. Hofer thereby took part in a
now largely forgotten episode in the history of the U.S. mail: the
delivery of letters to mining camps in the mountains in winter,
delivery which of necessity could only be made by ski. Throughout the Sierra and Rockies, swashbuckling postmen delivered the
mail, giving new meaning to that bit about "Neither snow nor
rain nor heat nor gloom of night," when any single letter could
lead its deliverer into an avalanche. Hough mentioned this side of
Hofer's early experience, above, and one researcher has specifically

identified 1875-76 as the years Hofer carried the winter mail in the Colorado Rockies.[46] In a letter he wrote to Grinnell in 1925, Hofer remembered a typical day on the job: "Soon I'll be 77 and have a right to be comfortable—still I can't say I never enjoyed the dry cold weather in the mountains. I did like it. The winter of 75-76 I put in, in the San Juan Country, carrying mail on my back on skis—I enjoyed—used to start out before daylight so as to be through before the sun warmed the snow and made it stickey. Then too I would not get too warm myself."[47]

Introducing Hofer to its readers in 1900, the *Chicago Tribune* made much of the year he spent at this job, letting fly with a great deal of the journalistic hyperbole typical of that era:

> He carried mail for the United States in the Rocky Mountains in the winter of 1875 and 1876, when the snow was twenty feet deep and one could not stir except upon the long wooden skis or snowshoes of that region. His route was from Tellurium, Colo., over the Grizzly Pass into Animas Forks, and he took up a work which two other carriers had laid down, frightened by the terrors of that wild mountain journey alone amid the snows. He was once caught in a snow slide and barely escaped with his life from an experience out of which but few men have ever come alive.[48]

Hofer's own description, as always, played down the risk to the point of disappearance and focused instead on the delights of the world around him. In a chapter Grinnell wrote for one of the many books that he also edited, Hofer contributed an extended description of the bighorn sheep and of how they become less skittish over time—a small band, for instance, has occupied the Gardner River canyon, near the North Entrance to Yellowstone National Park, for as long as the park has been there, and to many visitors they seem as tame as so many puppies. Hofer knew they were not normally so friendly:

On the other hand, when I carried the mail down In San
Juan county, Colorado, in the winter of 1875-'76, going
across from Animas Forks by way of the Grizzly Pass to
Tellurium Fork, I was the only person in that section of the
country all through the winter, and yet, although the sheep
saw only me, and saw me every day, they always acted wild.
Sometimes a ram would see me and stand and look for a
long time, and then presently all along the mountain side
I would see sheep running as if they were alarmed. On the
other hand, if I met any of them on top of the mountain,
they scarcely ever ran, they just stood and looked at me.[49]

When he skied around Yellowstone in 1887, Hofer was thus merely returning to a well-known discipline that he learned early.

Eventually, he moved on from Colorado. The few researchers who have looked into the matter have identified a simple
reason that Hofer spent such a brief time in the Black Hills:
he had no luck finding gold.[50] What he did find was what for
any other prospector might have been dross but was perhaps
the greatest treasure Hofer ever turned up. He found, as we will
see, Nathaniel Langford's lengthy description of Yellowstone in
Scribner's Magazine.[51] Langford had been part of one of the first
thorough and "official" explorations of what became the park
and described what the expedition saw at length in *Scribner's*.
The publicity indeed ultimately helped make it a national park
in 1872.

Hofer had been drifting, but once his Black Hills prospecting
failed, his career trying to get rich quick by chasing various gold
rushes came to an end. As Hiram Chittenden explained, Hofer
arrived in Bozeman, Montana, in summer 1877 and only avoided
Yellowstone National Park because the Nez Perce were tearing
through the place. His time in Bozeman was episodic and continued into what we can think of as his Yellowstone era (various
sources confirmed his residence there, including a newspaper re-

port from the 1890s that called him "a mountaineer formerly of this city").[52]

He did not know it at the time, but his movements were now assuming a definite direction. He turned west again, and events conspired to draw him toward what he did not yet know was his goal. Happily, we have excellent records from this point forward, because when he put down his pick and shovel, he started—occasionally at first, then regularly—to pick up a pen and earn part of his living with it. From this time on, Thomas Elwood Hofer, rechristened Billy, would write his own story.

In 1887, Forest and Stream *magazine gave Billy Hofer a high-quality plate-glass-negative camera. Teaching himself to use it, he took a series of photographs around Gardiner and the northern part of Yellowstone National Park. This image, along with others rescued from a junk heap, is likely one of those first photographs. Billy, dressed for work the way genuine cowboys did, drives a wagon with Electric Peak in the background. The barrel may be filled with water. Residents of Gardiner laboriously hauled their water from the Yellowstone River or other watercourses.* COURTESY OF BRIGHAM YOUNG UNIVERSITY.

CHAPTER TWO

Seeing More of the Elephant

Decades later, when he was simply too old to drag parties of tourists over some of the worst terrain in North America, Hofer retired to Sunlight Beach on Whidbey Island, across Puget Sound from what is now greater Seattle. Unsurprisingly, he never lost interest in Yellowstone, and happily, although he did live what for him was likely a boring life on that then-isolated island, Yellowstone did not forget him, at least until after he died: he kept up a correspondence with the friends he had made there. From our point of view, one of those connections was crucial.

Yellowstone National Park had been governed by the U.S. Army for much of its history, until, in 1916, a new agency, the National Park Service, took over. Horace Albright, a Department of the Interior attorney who had helped set up the new Service—and who would one day direct it—became superintendent of Yellowstone in 1919 and stayed for ten years. Even though he arrived at about the time Uncle Billy departed, Albright, surprisingly, possessed that rare quality of seeing in the elderly a living repository of history. Billy had known the place when, as a park, it was new—and when it was also a gigantic block of raw wilderness visited by a few hundred adventurers during the short summers and left abandoned the rest of the year. A correspondence between the two followed, with Albright asking Hofer simply what he could remember. Albright apparently wanted to publish a lengthy and polished magazine article of the sort Hofer had produced readily when he was younger, but Hofer at this time had reached an age when he no longer had it in him to sit down at an Underwood typewriter and pound out ten thousand words of elegant prose. Still, Uncle Billy came through. On April 27, 1926, he sent the following letter to Albright, signing it, above his name, "'A Tillicum' of the Park," using the local Chinook word[1] for a member of the tribe, or simply a friend:

> Today I was looking over a lot of old letters and papers when I ran on to the inclosed stuff. This I had sent to Mr. Gr[i]nnell and he had returned some ten years ago. Reading it over I thought it would be the best I could do for you. I had started in on an article for you but there are so many I and Us-es that I was disgusted with it. Fortunately, I ran on this inclosure and if you have no use for it, you can return it—The story of my work in the park and for it and the many people I've met would be a long one.
>
> For instance, a year ago I received a letter from a party I had taken through the park twenty-five years ago. I met them in Seattle. They came here to visit me, later sent me a radio set. Mr. Grinnell came out of his way to see me, Prof. Horey (now over the Great Divide) came out here. Dr. [E.O.] Horey was in charge of a division of the A.M.N. History N. Y. N. Y. I hear from many whom I've traveled with in the mountains but so many have crossed the Great Divide. I miss them and I'm getting to be a "has been" as I'm past 77.[2]

The "Great Divide" was originally the Continental Divide, but in frontier slang, it of course became a synonym for death.

So the letter ends on a sad note, as many of Billy's letters from this period do—but there follows the "inclosed stuff." Billy did have a habit of understating his own accomplishments. The "stuff" is a remarkable treasure-trove for us today, with its thousands and thousands of words that describe Billy's trip to the Black Hills, his journey to Yellowstone amid at least three separate Indian wars and his initial tentative, dangerous steps toward making a living there—a vignette of the Old West at its most exciting.

In trying to produce the article Albright wanted, Billy ran into the same problem that every memoirist writing about the natural world must face: all those personal pronouns made the document sound childishly egotistical. What he sent instead was in effect a rough draft of that article, although it was written a decade earlier for George Bird Grinnell. The result was prose that was even more packed with information than that hoped-for magazine article would likely have been. Furthermore, in an unintended effect, by describing his own introduction to the park, he inadvertently introduced it to us.

In the early spring of 1877 I left Denver for the Black Hills via Cheyenne, Wyoming. Mined a bit in the hills of Iron Creek, very poor digging. Left Black Hills for Big Horn country early in July, traveled via Spearfish Sundance Hills, Pumpkin Butte to Cantonment, Reno. Reached the Cantonment the day after a soldier killed a whiskey peddlar. There was a woman mixed up with the whiskey business called Beaver Tooth. Her man and their teams traveled with our wagons to where the government was building a new post, known then as Big Horn Post #2, at the mouth of the Little Big Horn, afterward named Fort Custer. Visited all the ground of the Big Horn, Custers fight and Reno's stand after his retreat from the bottoms of the Little Big Horn. Then we crossed the Big Horn on the government ferry the day it was completed. There were camped on the Little Big

Horn over 250 men about three miles above the post, men
from all parts of the country.[3]

The notes only gave the facts; Billy would surely have filled in the
background and details, if he had finished the article for Albright.
It did not matter, because the details spoke for themselves. We
know nothing more about the business with the whiskey peddler,
but such incidents were common and stand here as pieces of frontier mayhem—emblematic of the time, place, and people.

Violence was the theme, inevitably, because Billy was crossing a
war zone, and he was furthermore part of the war. The United States
had ceded the Black Hills to the Sioux, but when an expedition led by
George Armstrong Custer found gold there in 1874, the inevitable
rush followed; Billy was merely coming to it late, three years after the
best diggings were taken. The Sioux reacted with rage to this violation of their land, and when the Army attempted to get them under
control and onto the reservations, Custer was again at the forefront,
this time riding to his death at the Battle of the Little Bighorn.[4]

Billy's movements can today be followed with some ease on a
good modern map.[5] He approached the Black Hills from a souther-
ly direction, then mined at Iron Creek in the mountains above
Spearfish, South Dakota. When he gave up, he descended to Spearfish and followed the modern route of Interstate 90 west to Sundance, Wyoming Territory, then continued west until he reached
Cantonment Reno, a temporary base established near the site of
the old Fort Reno on the Powder River, abandoned after the Sioux
had shut down the Bozeman Trail. It was on the Powder River, not
far from the site of the massacre that sealed the earlier Sioux vic-
tory. Here, place-names today become confusing. Fort Reno and
Cantonment Reno were named for a Union hero who died in the
Civil War.[6] The "Reno's stand" Billy referred to was a different action, fought on a hilltop at the Little Bighorn battlefield by Major
Marcus Reno, who was widely blamed for Custer's defeat. No one
was in a hurry to honor him.

Now in north-central Wyoming Territory, Billy fell in with the unfortunate whiskey peddlers. Whiskey was one of the plagues of the frontier, and the native people were not its only victims: the peddlers moved from military camp to military camp also, selling alcohol that was almost always adulterated and regularly poisonous. Billy traveled overland to the junction, in Montana Territory, of the Little Bighorn with the Bighorn River, where the Army had built Fort Custer as one of its responses to the Little Bighorn disaster the previous year. Still traveling overland, Billy headed south to the battle site, then just over a year old, the battle having taken place on June 25, 1876. He found not the tidy, peaceful landscape of the present National Monument but instead saw it in its chaotic wildness. The Seventh Cavalry had left well over 250 dead on the battlefield, along with their dead horses (the Sioux did not like or need Cavalry horses; those horses needed grain and so could not survive the winter). What Billy saw would have looked, from a distance, like a municipal landfill. Only close up would the rubbish have come into focus, as personal effects and human remains.

This occasion was one of many when Billy's life intersected major historical events. To have gotten a look at the Little Bighorn battlefield only a year after the fight was an extraordinary privilege, at least for the strong of stomach. We know, in some detail, exactly what he saw there. The Army had returned during summer 1877 to try to bring some order to the chaos. In his eccentric, if bestselling, biography of George Armstrong Custer, novelist Evan S. Connell collected testimony about what the Army found there: "The first bluecoats to return were cavalrymen of the Seventh.... They arrived in the summer of 1877 from newly built Fort Keogh at the junction of the Tongue and the Yellowstone. Followed by ox-drawn wagons carrying pine boxes they came to pick up what remained of Custer and fifteen officers." Part of the "detail collected the skeletons of enlisted men and dumped them in a pit near the summit of the ridge. A rock cairn was erected to mark the site, topped by a buffalo skull."

Just after the battle, an attempt was made to inter the troopers: "It is probable that each man was covered up, although what was done beyond that remains conjectural. Rain, wind, and snow had worked on these graves. Vultures, ravens, wolves, and other scavengers had come to feed, and some of the identifying stakes that marked the locations of soldiers' bodies might have been knocked over by animals tugging at the bodies. These stakes might have washed downslope or they could have been tumbled by wind from one corpse to another." As for Custer himself, they found little. "Scout George Herendeen said only a few small bones lay in Custer's grave—'a double handful.' He thought the general's corpse had been torn apart by wolves."[7]

Because Billy was at the Little Bighorn battlefield during summer 1877, it is possible he was there at the same time as the Seventh Cavalry. The small, post-battle force they sent could never have "cleaned" the battlefield, and we happen to have a second eyewitness account from that summer, written by William Allen, an old frontiersman who produced his memoirs in 1903. He arrived at the battlefield on August 18. A brief tour, if only a highly simplified one, will help clarify what Allen and Billy Hofer saw there.

On the day of the battle, the Sioux, Cheyenne, and some Arapaho were camped in great numbers in the Little Bighorn valley, west of the river. When the Seventh attacked from the east, pell-mell and in different groups, they fell onto the Indians' encampment, away from the high ground and beyond the river to the west. When their attack was repulsed, they retreated back across the river onto the high ground where Marcus Reno—who by that point in the action was very probably drunk—made his haphazard stand on the cliffs. Meanwhile, most of the dead were scattered through the hills, including Custer, far to the north of Reno's position.

Allen camped in the valley where the Sioux, Cheyenne, and Arapaho had camped a little over a year earlier. The place was a mess, but it was otherwise quite clear to Allen what had happened there:

Our tents were soon pitched in the valley where Sitting Bull and his warriors had camped. Buffalo bones, elk heads and deer antlers were strewn over the valley and along the river front, while the bent-willow sweat-lodges were still standing, with the rounded pile of small boulders, just as they had been left by the red man. The earth still showed small trenches where the large, round tepees had stood, and the stakes and picket pins were still in the ground. After a careful survey of the valley we decided to cross the river and examine the battlefield.[8]

Allen probably wished he were elsewhere. "When our party gained the other side, a horrible sight met our eyes. Each soldier, who with Custer had sacrificed his life, yet lay where he had fallen on that ill-fated day. Each move that was then made could be read by us as from the page of an open book." We cannot today expect political correctness of Allen, who had held all the prejudices of the classic frontiersman: "We paused and counted the remains of seventy-six who fell to win Montana from the savage. Continuing, we came to the place where the survivors of the first attack had endeavored to regain the hill and escape by the route through which they had entered this death valley. Here lay the bodies of fifty or sixty men and horses."[9]

Allen's reconstruction of the fight is in places incorrect; we know this now, based on a century and a half of literature-scholarship and archaeology. He posited, for instance, a single battle line for the Sioux and Cheyenne, but we know today that no such single line existed (they were not fighting in the First World War). While his theoretical reconstruction might be a bit off, however, we have no reason to doubt what he said he saw. "We returned from the field sick at heart, but, after a restful night we concluded to pass another day there, as many points of interest had not been seen. We started early, determined to make the rounds of the…line occupied by the enemy. On the edge of Dry Creek," which emptied

into the Little Bighorn from the east, "on the ridge and in the cou-
lee, we found thousands of cartridge shells lying in piles, each pile
showing clearly where each warrior was situated. From these points
almost the whole battlefield could be seen, and the savages under
cover could pour in a deadly fire without exposing themselves. We
made the round of the entire firing line, finding empty shells by the
thousand."[10] Allen called this just one of many fighting positions.

"After the firing line had been thoroughly examined, we returned to the scene of battle. Here we found the triangle of dead
men showing three distinct movements under a terrific fire from
three sides, each soldier lying just where he had fallen, each with a
small amount of earth thrown over him, with his head protruding
from one end of the grave and his feet from the other. One very noticeable feature presented itself to me, the boot tops had been cut
from the dead." A common occurrence, one noted by a number of
observers around the frontier over time. The boot leather was too
useful to pass up. "Their skulls in many instances had been crushed
and shot with pistol bullets after being killed. Scalps had been tak-
en.... The horror of the slaughter seemed greater to us than we
had before realized. That such a massacre was possible has been the
wonder of all who have seen the battlefield."[11] Allen reproduced a
photograph of the purported spot where Custer fell, decorated at
that time by the skeletal remains of two or three horses.

This is what Billy Hofer saw, a scene most people would turn
away from—and a scene that countless thousands of historians and
Little Bighorn buffs would give anything to have seen. He had no
good excuse to be there. He was merely sightseeing...but what a
sight it was. One thing the West provided was an endless supply
of astonishing sights. That was a major source of its allure for Billy
Hofer, especially when compared to small-town New England.

A crucial point for the reader to take away is that this was a land
at war, and the war was not over. Sitting Bull had slipped over the
border into Canada in May 1877, and Crazy Horse surrendered
shortly afterward, bringing to an end the major fighting over the

Black Hills—but that was only one phase of the fighting. Still, amid the mayhem, one accidental but happy meeting took place. Billy described it in the biography he sent to Horace Albright:

> After crossing the river, a cousin and I, we left the party we had come from the Black Hills with and made arrangements to travel with a party from Helena, Montana, on their way to Baker Battle ground on the Yellowstone with a team to Hoskin's [and] McGurl's camp. We traveled across the country to the Yellowstone, arriving after two days, on a ferry to Hoskin's and McGurl's Station. Found quite a number camped about. That evening a Mackinaw came down the river, and aboard as passenger was P. W. Norris, second superintendent of Yellowstone National Park. We had heard stories of this place and had read N. P. Langford[']s account of the Washburn party trip in Scribner's Magazine.
>
> When we left the Baker battle ground to go up the river with the Helena party of three men we learned more about the park, but none of the party had visited there. We had made up our minds to see it as soon as possible. While at Hoskin's and McGurl's the first mail rider came through from Bozeman to Miles City. They were just establishing a route. Mail had come any old way up to this time by Mackinaws and teams. We heard too of the Nez Perces outbreak, and before two days the mail riders brought news of Gibbon's fight on the Big Horn.[12]

It was a primitive landscape. Phenomena as mundane as the arrival of the mail remained memorable decades later in the accounts of settlers. Travel was by horse, team, or Mackinaw, a kind of sailboat that was a hangover from the fur trading era.

Omar Hoskins and Thomas McGirl—Billy often had to spell by memory alone—opened a trading post at what is now Huntley,

Montana.[13] Working together, these two men operated the biggest civilized place in the area. It is a measure of how primitive this part of the Yellowstone valley was at that date that "Baker Battle ground," the major destination of Billy and his new friends from Helena, did not appear on any map and went by a dozen names, some of them bizarre: Baker's Battle Ground, Baker's battleground, Baker Battle Ground, Baker's Ground, Baker Ground, and so on. It remains maddeningly confusing today.

According to a comprehensive encyclopedia listing every combat between native people and the various armed forces of the United States, on August 14, 1872, Maj. Eugene M. Baker led a 370-man column east down the Yellowstone valley. At the point where Pryor Creek entered the Yellowstone, he fought an inconclusive skirmish with the Sioux and Cheyenne; the skirmish is usually known, to the extent that it is known, as "Pryor's Fork."[14] Pryor Creek entered the river at Huntley, where Hoskins and McGirl would set up their trading post. A major attraction of "Baker Battle ground" for Billy and the others may have been a rumor that Sitting Bull had ridden at the head of the Sioux.[15]

And yet, as sparsely settled as this territory was, what we can think of as "Hofer's Luck" suddenly came into play. He met, at Hoskins and McGirl's, the one person in the world he most needed to meet: Philetus Norris. The second Superintendent of Yellowstone National Park, Norris was the first person to physically occupy that post and bring to it a genuine, long-term interest in Yellowstone. He was also a great evangelist for the place and would employ Billy once he got there. Having read the description in *Scribner's*, Billy was primed. It was at this moment that it became inevitable that T. E. Hofer and Yellowstone NP would come together soon.

Even though he was superintendent, however, Norris was not really "in charge" of the park. At that moment, other people— native people—were looking after it. As Billy noted, in his short autobiography:

We reached the point where Billings is now, or a little below, when we saw a Mackinaw with a party who were to put in a saw mill, not far from the Grant Marsh Cottonwood tree, the highest point a steamer ever reached on the Yellowstone, and here we heard more about the Nez Perces. There were six of us in the party, well armed and able to take care of ourselves.

We saw no Indians at all except a few [C]rows. We reached Benson's Landing, two or three miles below where Livingston now stands, where we found men building mackinaws, to run supplies down the river to Miles City. The Helena party had been over all this route before, and could tell us about the country. We left the river here and crossed Bozeman Pass to Fort Ellis, not through Rocky Canyon, but over the hills to the north, and over the same trail that Lewis & Clark, explorers, had traveled many years before, and one which had been used by Indians and game for ages.

At Bozeman we learned of the Nez Perces making for Henry Lake, and of the government assembling a pack train to go to Howard and for other commands. It was a busy time. Jack Baronett came into Bozeman with sixty [C]row scouts. Wagon trains were sent out a few days after we reached Bozeman with supplies for Howard's command to reach him at Henry Lake. Tried to get employment as a bull whacker, but not knowing anything about the work, was turned down. Could not get any encouragement about a trip to the park, and as news came in about Indians in the park, did not want to tackle a trip there then.

Later the news came of the capture of the Cowan party, killing of two men and burning of the Henderson ranch, and not knowing anything about the country had to stay in Bozeman.[16]

He moved out of one war zone and into another. Grant Marsh was perhaps the most famous riverboat pilot in the country at this date. Trained by a then-retired fellow pilot, a writer who published under the pen name Mark Twain, he had recently made headlines evacuating the wounded from the Little Bighorn by riverboat under nearly impossible circumstances.

Then next year's war intruded. In June, 1877, multiple bands of Nez Perce left their reservation in the Pacific Northwest and fled roughly eastward, trying to get away from the Army.[17] They had already fought a series of skirmishes and outright battles. "It was a busy time" indeed: the Army had multiple units in the field under the command of Brigadier General Oliver O. Howard, all trying to either catch or cut off the Nez Perce, a task considerably complicated by the fact that no one knew where they were going, including, regularly, the Nez Perce themselves. The confident belief Billy encountered in Bozeman—that the hostiles were "making for" Henry's Lake in Idaho[18]— gives us today an approximate date for his arrival, in mid-August 1877, when Howard was in the vicinity of Henry's Lake and expecting to corral the Nez Perce there.[19]

Instead, the tribe veered west into Yellowstone National Park, entering near the present location of West Yellowstone, Montana,[20] and leaving through a pass near the present Northeast Entrance. During this period, poor Billy kept getting close to Wonderland, but then historical events would conspire to keep him out. He was not worried about the Crow, a name which he appeared to treat as a nickname (and correctly—their own name for their tribe is, approximately, the Absaroka). They were ancient enemies of the Sioux and were in general friendly to the Army and to non-Indian travelers. Note, however, that Billy and his party were also armed to the teeth.

We can confirm the rough date of Billy's arrival in Bozeman from the appearance of another Yellowstone celebrity, Collins J. "Yellowstone Jack" Baronett, who owned a toll bridge over the Yellowstone River inside the park beginning in 1871. On August

31, Baronett accompanied one of the arms of the military octopus groping for the Nez Perce, leaving Ft. Ellis and travelling with a force under Lieutenant Gustavus C. Doane to the north entrance of the park. Billy mentioned the Henderson ranch, which sat astride the road to the north entrance. A scouting party of Nez Perce had burned it down[21] and killed a tourist at the nearby Mammoth Hot Springs just as Doane and Baronett were arriving on the thirty-first.[22] The Nez Perce later used Baronett's bridge and, being pursued by troops, were so unkind as to burn it down after they had crossed it. Billy had been correct. This was not the year to go randomly exploring in Yellowstone National Park.

And a third war was about to intrude. As Billy explained later:

> Soon after reaching Bozeman I met and became acquainted with the first superintendent of the Yellowstone National Park, N. P. Langford, then bank examiner for Montana. Mr. Langford was a most enthusiastic friend of the park, and a noble, kindly gentleman, whose friendship was sincere and true. Of the many friends I have made and had in the park, I have lost none that I miss more. Carried mail to Spring Hill and Central Park, clerked in [the] N. P. Hotel and did odd jobs until '78, when my cousin got a job with a party going through the park. Later went with a team carrying some guns and ammunition to settlers on the Upper Yellowstone. Jim Alexander drove this team and was well acquainted with the park and country. We only got as far as Mammoth Hot Springs. I and a few acquaintance[s] had purchased a pony. I bought [their] share of it, my first horse. This I named Belshazzar because he was king of any herd he was with. He was from the "Hoop Up" country, Canada,[23] probably stolen from the Indians by white men. Part of the Bannock [I]ndians had broken out and were making a dash through the park. Ten Doy, and his sub chiefs were friendly, and were escorted through the country

via Bozeman, Fort Ellis and out to the Buffalo country for a big hunt. The Bannock outbreak was only a small affair, but it was not healthy to travel in the park during that season.[24]

Even under adverse circumstances, Hofer's Luck kept intruding. He found himself stuck in Bozeman for the winter— and who should be there to make friends with but Nathaniel Langford, first superintendent of Yellowstone National Park and, as noted, one of its early explorers. Their friendship gives us a glimpse of a phenomenon that we have seen already and will see again, and often: of Billy's capacity to move among radically different social classes. His own humble origins made no difference. He could still approach one of the more prominent businessmen in the region and make him a close friend. He did so even though circumstances forced him back to the kind of miscellaneous employment he took (as did nearly everyone else) when his larger plans were frustrated. He worked as a clerk—the "N. P. Hotel" was the hotel run by the Northern Pacific Railroad—and he again delivered the mail, this time to the outlying settlements of Spring Hill and Central Park, a job which at times may have required skis.

Then, in 1878, the Bannock tribe broke out of their reservation at Fort Hall, Idaho, and the Army had another episode of robust crowd-control on its hands, again led by General Howard. The fighting took place outside the park, but uncomfortably close to it, and the Bannock had a tradition of traveling through the park to reach an area in Montana, near present-day Billings, where the buffalo hunting remained good even as the larger continental herd was disappearing. For generations after this, Yellowstone tour guides even identified a single route as the "Bannock Trail" through the park, although recent research suggests that the Bannock hunters followed multiple routes.[25] Chief Tendoy of the Lemhi Shoshone, in Idaho, had fought the Nez Perce and stayed friendly to whites when the Bannock revolted and was rewarded with just such a hunt.[26]

During 1878, although his cousin traveled through the park, Billy only reached Mammoth Hot Springs, a mere five miles from the northern boundary.[27] It is worth noting that the cargo was arms and ammunition. This place was not yet anything like the tourist resort it would become. But at last, the next year, the magic moment arrived for Billy: "In '79 I picked up a green horn for company, and with a saddle horse each and one pack horse, struck out for the Yellowstone Park via Mammoth Hot Springs and Tower Creek."[28] On this trip, he covered much of what would become the park's road system. He met military men and frontiersmen almost exclusively, but not many of those. Yellowstone remained anarchic, a beautiful, genuinely awe-inspiring no-man's-land.

But I have been using the word "Yellowstone" freely and vaguely, as is common. What do we mean by "Yellowstone"? Most often, today, we are referring to the world's first national park, a block of 2.1 million acres carved out of the Northern Rockies and centered on the northwest corner of Wyoming, with strips of Montana and Idaho along the sides. It is the center of what we today call the Greater Yellowstone Ecosystem, about twenty million acres running up and down the spine of the Rockies. The park is most famous for Old Faithful Geyser, the Grand Canyon of the Yellowstone, and its wildlife, especially what zoologists call megafauna, the larger animals such as elk, bison, and bears, that routinely turn up right next to the roads.

Everything about Yellowstone, however, is contradictory, surprising, unexpected, or just bizarre. The name itself is the source of much baloney. People today often assume it refers to the walls of the Grand Canyon of the Yellowstone, where the dominant rhyolite rock runs through shades of red that in most places are a kind of "yellow." The problem with that assumption is this: the Yellowstone River went by that name long before anyone speaking a European language ever saw that canyon (the name probably originates from the sandstone cliffs near the distant junction where the Yellowstone enters the Missouri River, or from similar cliffs at present Billings, Montana[29]). The place is constantly throwing that kind of curve ball, to visitors and employees alike. Just when you think you understand it, it turns out that the opposite is true.

Humans moved in as the glaciers receded ten thousand years ago, but the place is so isolated and the terrain so rugged that no known mountain man saw it until John Colter penetrated its formidable defenses in 1806-1808. Prospectors and trappers knew it, but the broader public only heard about what they would soon come to call "Wonderland" after the Civil War, when a series of exploring expeditions brought back photographs, artwork, maps, and descriptions that resulted—with surprising speed, actually— in the bill establishing Yellowstone National Park that landed on President Ulysses S. Grant's desk in 1872.[30]

Yellowstone thus became the first national park in the world— but certainly not the first wilderness park. Aristocrats have of course been setting aside tracts of wild land for their own recreation almost since there have been aristocrats, and there was even a precedent for the U.S. government doing so: in 1864, it had deeded Yosemite Valley and the nearby Mariposa Grove of sequoia trees to the state of California as a permanent out-holding, although Yosemite would not become a national park until 1890. But while the traditional wild-land enclosures controlled by aristocrats and royalty have always had an obvious purpose—they were places to hunt—the modern, government-run wilderness park was a new thing in the world, and historians have long puzzled over the motives of their founders. Legal scholar Joseph Sax comments that "What exactly was meant to be accomplished by these unprecedented reservations is a mystery that will never be fully solved."[31] One early advocate for the parks, J. Horace McFarland, threw up his hands in trying to figure it out. "The parks have just happened," he complained in 1911. "They are not the result of such an overlooking of the national domain as would, or ought to, result in a coordinated system."[32]

One explanation popular for generations among some university professors sees the parks as a capitalist conspiracy: the railroads pushed buttons behind the scenes to get politicians to make parks so that the railroads could haul tourists there and put them up in their hotels. The idea is good as far as it goes—the Northern Pacific would profit greatly from Yellowstone (note that they were among Billy's first employers in the region)—but it gets the chain of causality backwards. Why did the Northern Pacific want to build a line to that place exactly? For all their power, they could not force people to enjoy the destination. The place had to do that for them.

One explanation that works well—for Yellowstone especially—is historian Alfred Runte's idea that the parks resulted from what he called "monumentalism" or "cultural nationalism":

> America's incentive for the national park idea lay in the persistence of a painfully felt desire for time-honored traditions in the United States. For decades the nation had suffered the embarrassment of a dearth of recognized cultural achievements. Unlike established, European countries, which traced their origins far back into antiquity, the United States lacked a long artistic and literary heritage.... In response to constant barbs about these deficiencies from Old World critics and New World apologists, by the 1860s many thoughtful Americans had embraced the wonderlands of the West as replacements for man-made marks of achievement.[33]

A moment's thought shows that Runte is correct (think how many Castle Rocks and Cathedral Peaks there are in North America). Like all academic explanations, however, it is bloodless. The early explorers of Yellowstone did regularly compare it to cultural monuments of the Old World. What the explanation misses is how utterly surprised they were by what they saw there.

In letter after letter, diary after diary, book after book, they pile on the superlatives: *stunning, gorgeous, dazzling, magnificent, exqui-*

site, et cetera ad infinitum. A thesaurus maker could put together a long entry for "beautiful" from that early literature alone. We know today that Yellowstone National Park sits on top of a plume of magma of stupendous size, one that regularly causes stupendous volcanic eruptions and that at present drives the world's premier collection of what the rangers call "thermal features"—geysers, hot springs, mud pots, and steam vents. It was these thermal features that most captured the fancy of the first generation of park explorers, along with the most stupendous of the other natural wonders, like the Grand Canyon of the Yellowstone. Later generations would take a closer interest in the animals. The park boundaries were drawn originally to try to contain all the thermal features, but this act created—largely as a side effect—a bastion large enough to protect habitat adequate to keep large animals alive while they were being gunned down elsewhere. As we have noted, when Billy arrived in Greater Yellowstone, he arrived in what was essentially a war zone. Despite the change in combatants every year, the war stayed the same: it was a war between the modern world and the Neolithic. The railroads were carrying the new industrialized United States westward, and both the native peoples and the animals that supported them would have to make way. Billy watched it happen, and he did not approve; he liked the West wild. In Yellowstone National Park, he had found a place where it would, to a certain degree, stay that way.

Yellowstone, then and now, takes some percentage of its visitors and captures them. It grabbed Billy. It grabbed me, too. When my life revolved around Yellowstone National Park in the 1980s and 1990s, I lived on a few thousand dollars a year, under circumstances that were routinely grim, and I was in heaven. That pattern is largely invariable even in the twenty-first century. Every year today, thousands of seasonal employees arrive to work in the park. A few are criminals and lunatics, and more still are there merely to work, with no interest in the world outside the hotel or store. A large minority—I was one—become addicted. As I noted, some become so thoroughly addicted that they will do anything necessary to stay—and they then face a trade-off that is more dreadful than you may think, because in almost every case, a decision to stay is a decision to live beyond the margins. My friends who are still there are also still forced to flip burgers and clean hotel rooms when the necessity arises. They decided to confront one of the rock-bottom realities of the place: you can stay, but it is hard to have a normal life there. A house, a spouse, kids, a career, those are normally out of the reach of the "parkie," as such people call themselves. I was not willing to go that far, so I felt I had to leave.

Billy *was* willing to make those sacrifices. What happened to him was therefore not unusual; he was simply part of what was perhaps the first generation of people to discover that they were willing to sacrifice everything to stay in this place. For Billy, it was surely that first trip, in 1879, that "set the hook." He saw the entire park, slowed by the primitive conditions for travelers— likely a plus, in his point of view. He traveled to Mammoth Hot Springs, then east to Tower Fall, where he met William Pickett, the man Billy took sailing when he built his boat the next year and possibly his first paying customer in the park. He then moved on to the Grand Canyon, where he fell in with a military party escorted by a company of the Second Cavalry—a reminder of how dangerous the region remained. He needed the safety of a military party to traverse it. They visited Mud Volcano and Yellowstone Lake, then took the road General Howard had built while chasing the Nez Perce two years earlier, which carried them with relative ease to the Lower Geyser Basin. After visiting the Upper Geyser Basin—home of Old Faithful Geyser—they left the military party and moved on to Gibbon Meadows, where they met Philetus Norris, the superintendent, and the soldier and scout Luther "Yellowstone" Kelly, a frontier celebrity. Billy probably saw something of himself in both men. He then traveled on to Mammoth Hot Springs and so to Bozeman—but not home. At some point during that trip, "home" for Billy became Yellow-

stone National Park. He ended his narrative of this crucial year
with an odd memory:

> On this trip through the Yellowstone National Park I was
> much struck with the damage fire had done and was doing
> to the timber and to the beauty of the park and resolved
> to put out all my camp fires, and not only did I do that
> carefully, but put out many others I found left by careless
> campers. It was years before any important steps were taken
> to prevent fires. All expeditions were in the habit of build-
> ing great camp fires at night and leaving them smouldering
> when they left camp in the morning.[34]

In spite of Smokey Bear's well-known warnings, many ecologists
and foresters have changed their minds about wildfire. They recognize today that fire is actually a necessary part of the cycle of life in
a forest. The more common attitude during the nineteenth century
regarded a forest fire as pure evil.[35] However, the average, vagabond
frontiersman, which is what Billy had been for years, would probably not have cared one way or another.

And yet he was concerned. He was not, of course, worried about
the economic impact of fire. He was worried about "beauty."

Yellowstone had grabbed him, and would never let go.

CHAPTER THREE

The Joys of Wonderland

The Yellowstone of 1879 was, however, different from ours, in many ways unrecognizably so. It was of course a primitive place. It was also, it seems, snowier. It may have been, in fact probably was, colder (a cold year is not necessarily a snowy year). What is certain from Billy's descriptions, and some other data we have, is that the snow reached depths we have not seen since perhaps the 1920s. It was during this period that the now-old joke was still new, that there are three seasons in Yellowstone: July, August, and Winter.

From our perspective today, reaching the most famous parts of Yellowstone has been relatively easy for a long time, first by railroad and stagecoach, then by motor vehicle. Again, Billy's pen tells us what it used to be like. Further, climate change has become a contentious political issue, of course, and the assertion that the winters were harder in the nineteenth-century requires proof. Billy has it. Whatever your opinion might be of global warming, Billy's writing provides abundant evidence that the snow was deep in old Yellowstone.[1] Here is an example.

When he wrote of his aborted trip across Yellowstone Lake in 1880, William Pickett blurred a crucial part of the story: "As early in the spring as the snows would allow, T. Elwood Hofer…and his cousin of the same name, fought their way through the snows and located near our present camp, determined to build a sailboat." In the autobiographical notes that he wrote for George Bird Grinnell and sent finally to Horace Albright, Billy gave us the rest of the story. It turns out that building the sailboat and surviving the storm was nothing to him. The real ordeal lay in simply getting there, as Billy explained to Albright:

> During the winter of '79 and '80 got my tools and materials together and early in the spring of '80 packed up and started for the lake via Mt. Washburn. The snow was pretty well gon[e] on the north side, but getting around the mountains on the Canyon side we found the country covered very deep. We climbed the summit of Washburn on the 21st of June, and could see Yellowstone lake half covered with ice. It was open only in the main part. After three days we got as far afoot as the Hot Springs now known as the Ink Pots. Snow was over five feet deep in the timber and only a few ridges were bare. The Hayden Valley ridges were swept clear, so we returned to the Mammoth Hot Springs, leaving some of our packs at a cache north of Washburn.[2]

It is hard to overstate how surreal this scene is when read by a person accustomed to early twenty-first century Yellowstone. We do not expect this nearly arctic landscape, not at so late a date in the year.

First, we should clarify Billy's route, and at this point the reader who knows Yellowstone needs to make a special effort to forget what the modern park looks like. The figure-eight road-system that today is the most distinctive human mark on the landscape, the Grand Loop, is really a creation of the early twentieth century. In 1880, only a handful of roads had been "built," following routes that would often surprise us. The park was traversed mainly by trails. He crossed first what we today call the "northern range," the cluster of wide valleys and sagebrush flats across the top of the park that stood around 6,000 feet above sea level, and so lost their snow first. By an unspecified route, he reached Mount Washburn, near Canyon. If he was riding Belshazzar, the horse must have been toting skis or snowshoes—Billy vastly preferred skis, for their speed—because this 10,200-foot peak could not otherwise be climbed so early in the year. Still moving roughly south, he reached Washburn Hot Springs, at about 8,400 feet. We can be certain these were the Washburn Hot Springs because this group, near the Canyon rim, today includes an Inkpot Spring and a Devil's Inkstand (a number of springs here have petroleum in them[3]). He at last decided conditions were not right for a trip to the lake and so cut west through the open Hayden Valley.

What is surreal to us as we read Billy's account today is the snow and the ice on Yellowstone Lake. Snow in standing timber, at 8400 feet on June 21, would not be an unusual sight in Yellowstone today, even snow five feet deep. The summer had not yet really begun, even though Billy happened to climb Mount Washburn on the summer solstice. After a wet winter, the drifts can still run to five feet at Canyon in June. This was, however, Billy's ninth year in the West. He was a long way from being a greenhorn. The trip from Mount Washburn to Washburn Hot Springs should have been an afternoon stroll, not a three-day ordeal. Strangest of all is his description of Yellowstone Lake, which nowadays might be half-covered by ice on April 21. It has not known ice to that extent on June 21 in living memory.

It got even weirder for Billy and his cousin:

> We had a very rough trip to Norris, and reached Gibbon Meadows on the 4th of July. Here a party came in with a mail sack, said they came from Virginia City and had a contract to carry mail to Mammoth Hot Springs. That was about all the mail that ever came through I understand. They had three or four letters in the sack. A few trips were

made when the route was abandoned. I remember the horses were branded "G" and "S". I think Gilmore and Saulsbury.[4] Elk were everywhere; a band of several hundred crossed the meadow that evening. Everything was afloat.

Next day we met Taswel [Tazewell] Woody and two other trappers, who had been trying to get to Yellowstone lake and Upper Yellowstone on a trapping expedition, but getting their horses mired so many times on Nez Perces Creek (then called East Fire Hole), they gave it up and were returning. They tried to get us to turn back, but as the conditions were so much worse any other way, we kept on, and reached the Yellowstone lake on the 7th of July.[5]

Again, the primitive conditions—and a mail sack with "three or four letters" in it remained so memorable an event that Billy recalled it as he sketched his life story, decades later.

Tazewell Woody was at this time one of the most experienced frontiersmen in the region, famous all over the West for an incident in which he and two companions defeated a war party of "1000 Sioux." The story was, at least, accurate if we dispense with the number.[6] That Tazewell Woody himself could not penetrate as far as Yellowstone Lake in late June and early July—that Tazewell Woody tried to get Billy Hofer to give up attempting to reach the lake from Gibbon Meadows, during the first week of summer—these things make it clear that conditions then were more like the Canadian Arctic than present-day Yellowstone. The elk were in Gibbon Meadows in such large numbers because, then and now, when snow fills the surrounding mountains, elk descend to lower elevations; they cluster in large herds for protection in meadows wide enough to accommodate their numbers and where they can find forage under the snow.

The grip of winter was at least breaking. "Everything was afloat," Billy noted, because the snow had turned Gibbon Meadows into a lake, which would be normal after a winter so fierce that it kept him from reaching Yellowstone Lake until July 7.

And yet he accepted the climate as normal for a place like this and did not regard this year as exceptional in any way. Over and over, in Billy's writing, we find these scenes. Here is another example: when Billy taught Emerson Hough to ski in mid-March 1894, they finished by making a downhill run from Mammoth Hot Springs to the Boiling River[7], a drop from 6200 to 5600 feet down what is today, in mid-March, an arid, nearly treeless slope of sage, rabbitbrush, cactus, and dust. When told of this feat, twenty-first century residents of the area—people who know Yellowstone and who even know of Billy Hofer and are aware that he was a reliable observer[8]—react by opening their mouths and shaking their heads. Except under freakish circumstances, this stretch of terrain has, year after year, not had enough snow on it to ski in mid-March in living memory and well beyond.

Snow and mud or not, Thomas Elwood Hofer set foot, on July 7, 1880, on the shore of Yellowstone Lake, and went to work, with his cousin, on his boat. When Pickett arrived, Billy at last began his paying career as an all-purpose expert on all-things-Yellowstone.[9]

July 7, 1880 was a long time ago, however, and Yellowstone might as well have been in a galaxy far, far away. The records of the period—like all periods—are confused, and the histories that result can amplify the confusion if we are not careful. Happily, enough records remain that the facts can be sorted out; learning Billy's story is actually not like searching for Jimmy Hoffa or D. B. Cooper. Furthermore, with Billy, a careful search of the records regularly reveals delightful surprises. Looking closely at 1880, for instance, reveals that Billy and his cousin, during that short summer, actually finished not one, but two large sailboats.

We know that William Pickett chartered the first boat, constructed by the Hofer family starting about July 7. It was finished, Pickett recalled, by the time he arrived. Billy and his cousin had taken over the earth-roofed cabin built by the pioneer businessman on the lake, Eugene S. Topping, who had constructed the cabin and a boat of his own in 1874, although he gave it up after three summers. The point on the lake where his cabin stood is today still called Topping Point, and it was home to the Hofers during this brief period.[10] They even used the same primitive saw pit. Understanding what they did there, however, requires a brief look at historical maritime-architecture.

The boat that the Hofers constructed for Pickett was a highly specific type, a sharpie,[11] a boat invented in New Haven, Connecticut and permanently associated with Billy's hometown, although variants appeared in many other places. It was a working boat, built for the oyster trade in two sizes, a 26 to 28-foot version that carried 75 to 100 bushels of oysters, or a 35 to 36-foot version that could handle up to 175 bushels—a substantial vessel.[12] Recall that Pickett said that his boat was "30 to 35 feet in length." The Hofers' first boat was therefore one of the larger kind. It had to be, because Pickett told us that the vessel carried eight men, a dog, and their guns, all "comfortably stowed away…The boat was not at all overloaded."[13]

Another VIP sailed Yellowstone Lake in summer 1880, however: Philetus Norris, the park superintendent. Every year, the superintendent was required to write a report on the previous year's doings in Yellowstone for the Secretary of the Interior, and his reconnaissance of Yellowstone Lake occupied a lengthy portion of the report for 1880. Norris treated the affair as quite a drama: "With the Explorer, made of green, whipsawed lumber, and which soon proved unseaworthy, my own navigation of this lake was made with two companions, Capt. Jack Davis and Mr. W.H. Parker. Suffice it to say, that after a voyage of ten or twelve days, and after encountering many mishaps and dangers, being once beached and fairly frozen in, we succeeded in circumnavigating the main lake and most of its bays and fingers; and with the first craft navigated by white men I ascended Pelican Creek, the Upper Yellowstone, and other streams to their rapids."[14] Even though Norris had already covered the journey, he returned elsewhere in the report and added more drama: he "ascended the Yellowstone River to its lake, and in a small, unsafe craft, called the Explorer, made the tour of the latter and its islands. We also ascended Pelican Creek and the Upper Yellowstone River to their rapids. After encountering several gales, one severe snow-storm, and a shipwreck, I ascended Mount Chittenden and other peaks of the range, crossed two passes… and returned to the foot of the lake and falls."[15] Despite the trouble the boat had caused him, Norris had gone so far as to name Explorer's Creek in its honor.[16]

To the extent that they have looked into the matter, historians have usually assumed that there was only one boat on Yellowstone Lake in 1880. There are, however, nagging discrepancies between various accounts of what happened on the lake in 1880: descriptions of the boat and what came of it do not line up. Reading deeper into Norris's report, things begin to click: "The Explorer, so called by my own party, was built by the Hoffer Brothers [sic], at Toppin's Point [sic], during the summer of 1880, and was some 20 feet long, 6 feet wide, and 2 ½ feet deep. Loggy and clumsy, it required skillful management and ceaseless labor to keep her in order; but with her I succeeded in exploring the lake and its near tributaries to the rapids. Finally, however, she was wrecked, and I left her battered hulk near the point where she was built."[17]

That clarifies matters, despite Norris's typos.[18] For Pickett, the Hofers built a full-size 35-foot sharpie; it was afloat for years before it took its ride of the Valkyries down the Yellowstone River and over the Falls (that must have been quite a sight). Later, the cousins built a second, much smaller boat for Norris, which was beaten to matchwood and sunk at the end of its first voyage. Since both vessels came to grief—recall that Pickett ended his sailing trip with a stove-in hull—we might doubt the cousins' boat building skills. Two other factors came to their defense. A real sharpie was made of white pine and oak, of which there was none on the shore of Yellowstone Lake, only, as noted, the wrong kinds of pine, spruce, and fir.

Further, a sharpie has little freeboard—the space between the water and the gunwales. In old photographs, a heavily loaded sharpie might show a few inches of freeboard. Descriptions of the boat in action, in its original context, make it clear why: "Sharpies originated on the Connecticut shore of Long Island Sound as a refinement responsive to both changing needs and advancing technology. Tongers"—oyster harvesters, so named for the tongs they used—"had to travel farther away for oysters as the beds near home became exhausted and they needed better sailing boats.... When working the oyster beds in well-protected harbors and bays, the sharpie was anchored by poles [at the] aft and forward ends, and was steadied with a bushel basket hanging off the stern. The tonger stood on the side deck working with 12- to 15-foot tongs—scissor style—to gather a load and drop it into the boat. Up to 100 bushels of oysters could be tonged by one man in one day."[19]

That design was fine for the sheltered water of New Haven Harbor, or the inlets of Long Island Sound (nowhere does the Connecticut coast face the open North Atlantic—Rhode Island is in the way). It was not so fine in a mid-afternoon Yellowstone Lake typhoon, where a loaded sharpie would broach and founder instantly, except in the hands of an expert. It may be that the Hofers were intimately familiar with a boat design that was just wrong for the high Rockies.

Norris said nothing about who actually sailed the boat. He called his companions, Jack Davis and W.H. Parker, "excellent navigators,"[20] and the word "navigator" could simply have meant "sailor" in 1880.[21] They might have sailed the boat—although they would have been taking an unfamiliar craft over an unfamiliar and dangerous body of water. Or Norris might have sailed the vessel. However, Philetus Norris, as the reader can tell from the brief passages quoted here, had a taste for melodrama; if he had been at the tiller, he likely would have told us about it. The wise thing to do would have been to take one or both of the Hofer cousins as pilots. We can only speculate about what happened in this particular instance. Perhaps the Hofers were busy elsewhere. Perhaps the matter merely slipped Norris's mind. In this case, it was a minor affair, but this kind of high adventure was the first instance of what would, from this date forward, be a normal phenomenon in Billy's life.

From 1880 on, Billy would spend every summer and an occasional winter in guiding Yellowstone VIPs. The many publications in which he made appearances revealed one reason Hofer is today so largely forgotten, or dimly remembered not as Thomas Elwood Hofer, accomplished naturalist, but as Uncle Billy, comic raconteur and frontier eccentric. Some authors refused to do more than mention him and would routinely leave him out entirely from descriptions of scenes or whole expeditions during which we know, from other sources, that Billy was a constant companion and teacher. Other authors could not get enough of him. In their accounts, Billy dominated page after page. And the difference was stark: in one book, Billy was a ghost hovering behind every page, but never named. In another, he was half John Muir and half Rooster Cogburn, a performer regularly on stage and talking.

A perfect matched-set of authors illustrating the problem is George Bird Grinnell and Emerson Hough. Grinnell wrote over thirty books (the exact total depends on how we define "book"), but as we will shortly see, Billy was virtually absent from them. Hough was about as productive as Grinnell, and Hough inserted Billy into his work given any excuse at all. The difference lay in the nature of a given book or article, and the circumstances of Billy's life dictated that he would likely appear in two kinds of writing: serious descriptions of the West written for a small audience of intellectuals, and outdoor travel books written for the largest possible public. Grinnell belonged to the former group; Hough belonged very much to the latter.

In general, the "serious" books were written by men who wanted to be taken in earnest as scientific observers, but who were fighting multiple and exhausting battles at once. They often represented fields of knowledge that were not yet even recognized as "fields," or else were widely mistrusted. Take biology as a general example, today among the most successful and colossal of scientific pursuits. Its founding document, however—Charles Darwin's *On the Origin of Species*—hit the shelves when Billy was ten, so that even when he was older, the average person would often regard biology just as that crazy thing the Englishman with the beard was using as his personal highway to Hell. Further, authors working in the West, even if they found out the hard way, would eventually learn that local guides did not always tell the truth. Thus, putting a guide into a serious book of science was sometimes not a good idea.

The writers of travel and hunting books, however, loved their guides. We note today that Billy's life (1849-1933) mostly overlaps that of Mark Twain (1835-1910), and sure enough, the nineteenth-century public loved funny stories about the frontier—and about frontier eccentrics. The guides themselves were professional entertainers already, if for a small audience. There were plenty of strong silent types in the guiding business, but the average guide knew that he would do better in life and commerce if he could provide entertainment around the campfire. Much of the tradition of the Western tall tale owes itself to generations of hunting guides telling funny stories to their clients, some of whom turned out to be journalists or dime novelists who took those stories and put them on the page word for word. They might even credit the source, namely that guide back in Montana Territory. Or they might not. As noted, Billy did not have to make up tall tales. Yellowstone was and remains today stranger than fiction and more entertaining. Like other guides, he told his clients stories around the campfire, but Billy, to his credit, seems to have stayed with just the true stories.

In retrospect, the whole situation can seem honestly unjust—but it was the way things went in their era. The online libraries Project Gutenberg and the Hathi Trust have together digitized every word George Bird Grinnell wrote, in book form; the project today is complete. In the process of writing a history of the Boone and Crockett Club, one historian examined the "Jack" books that

Grinnell wrote for young readers, books that took the fictional Jack Danvers, a pale greenhorn youth from the East, and ran him through adventures on the frontier that looked very much like adventures Grinnell experienced himself. This historian concluded that Billy is "written into" the books,[22] but the digital copies today reveal that, by name, Billy appears in only one sentence of one Jack book.[23] In all of Grinnell's other books, Billy appeared in only three volumes and was given significant space in only two.[24]

His near-disappearance in all those other books stands in striking contrast to the otherwise close friendship the two men shared, easily visible in the hundreds of thousands of words of correspondence they exchanged over decades. What was going on here? It was something very like plagiarism, but it happened to every serious Old West guide. Along with tall tales and fun at the expense of the dude clients, the guide also imparted great knowledge about the West, and some of those Eastern dudes then assembled that knowledge into books. The Easterners did not have to worry about getting caught stealing knowledge or advice. Their guides often could not read the books anyway, and plenty of other barriers— physical distance is only one—stood between the worlds of the literary East and the primitive West.

However it happened, Billy thereby took another step into obscurity. If every serious book in which he was involved gave him full credit for his contributions, the name *Hofer* would appear today on thousands of pages where it is presently just a shadow visible only to the expert.

Summer 1880 was the only season during which the Hofer cousins tried to live as tour-boat captains. Billy never mentioned his cousin in any published document written after 1880, and in fact, his cousin remains something of a mystery. We know only that his name was C.E. Hofer—the *Bozeman Avant Courier*[25] confirmed this name—and he and Billy were together for a time in the late 1870s and 1880.

We have one other intriguing mention of C.E. Hofer, in a letter

Billy wrote after the turn of the century: they had been planning on spending at least part of 1879 prospecting and trapping in Jackson Hole. "In August 79 my cousin and I planed [*sic*] to go to Jacksons Hole to winter[,] trapping and prospecting a bit. We were to join a Jerry Goodwin who had spent a winter or two there." Goodwin's advice apparently put an end to the Hofers' trip: "Goodwin said we would have to kill our meat early when the elk were passing through as none but a few old bulls ever wintered there. That he had cut some hay for his horses one fall traveling. Elk cleaned it up on their way through."[26] Those elk would have been passing through in the autumn, or earlier. By August, given how quickly autumn passes in the Greater Yellowstone area, it was too late for the trip in 1879.

Hiram Chittenden's short biography of Billy makes it clear why the boat business on the shore of Yellowstone Lake did not pay: there was no money to be made because there was no money physically present on the shore.[27] Business was in fact comically slow, and again, for the person who knows twenty-first century Yellowstone National Park, Billy's memories are surreal. During all of the summer of 1880 at Yellowstone Lake, he saw only the Pickett party, the Norris party, a pair of Oxford professors and their guide, a "Mr. Jordan," "one man from Bozeman," and "two other men, I have forgotten their names."[28] That was all of the visitors he saw, in the middle of what is today the busiest section of the lakeshore, with dozens of businesses, miles of paved roads, and millions of people every year.

Getting beached in fact turned out to be a blessing. In a landscape so lightly populated, Billy could never succeed by tying himself to a single location, even one as vast as Yellowstone Lake—which, in addition to its isolation, was also frozen over most of the year. He needed to be mobile, and he needed to build a reputation in order to continue making a living as a guide.

An opportunity presented itself soon enough: "Next year, 1881, I went out as packer for Col. W. D. Pickett on a bear hunt." Here

again was the same Pickett[29] who had been the Hofers' first paying client, and one might at first wonder why Pickett was so eager
to secure the services of the man who had almost drowned him.
However, things were coming together to set a pattern that Billy
followed for decades and that served him well indeed. He was an
outgoing, garrulous person who had friends and friendly acquaintances by the hundreds. He had, in 1881, entered his tenth year
in the West; he was now an old hand and had the skills he needed. Among those hundreds of acquaintances, he would regularly
encounter wealthy men of leisure who were headed off to have a
look at the new national park—a process requiring weeks of arduous travel—and Billy would offer his services, both his skills as a
frontiersman and, increasingly over the years, his knowledge of the
place. In time, word of mouth would provide him with his clients
in Yellowstone, many of whom would keep him both paid and
regionally famous.

Ultimately, a feedback loop developed. Upscale East Coast outdoorsmen made the trip to Greater Yellowstone and fell under
Billy's care. Once home, they wrote the whole grand adventure up
for various magazines. The adventures happened in summer; the
stories tended to run during the winter. The railroad baron, the
gentleman of leisure, the ambitious "natural philosopher"—they
read about Billy's adventures, they cursed the winter weather where
they were located, and they dreamed, and longed to go there. *And
it isn't just a vacation*, they thought: *It's how this guy lives.* That
longing drew them toward Yellowstone, and Billy's outfitting service, like a magnet.

Over a century later, it can still arise in the right kind of reader,
dreaming about the life Billy was leading…with the reader very
much aware that he or she is not leading that kind of life, but desperately wants to.

Billy's greatest challenge, in the early 1880s, was actually a pleasant one: he needed to "learn Yellowstone," to come to know the
entire park and the surrounding terrain in all its seasons and all

its many hidden places. That process takes a lifetime even today, when Greater Yellowstone has been thoroughly explored, if not thoroughly understood, and is if anything too readily accessible. Billy would be learning a place about which little had been published and which few people knew at all.

CHAPTER FOUR

Making a Living

Billy Hofer's relationship with Pickett remains instructive today, because it demonstrates another of Billy's advantages: he learned quickly from his clients, and some of his clients had a great deal to teach. His status as a packer would normally make Billy merely an employee, but the two plainly hit it off: "Col. Pickett was a famous hunter and an old school southern gentleman," Billy recalled, "one whom it was a pleasure to know."[1]

Pickett was indeed a Southern gentleman. The "Colonel" attached to his name was not an honorific like so many; instead, that had been his actual rank in the Confederate States Army. He was an engineer, and that accounts for the unusual and remarkably useful lessons he offered as part of the job: "Before starting, during the spring," Billy continued, "I had done a good deal of work for the Colonel, shooting for trajectories, using all sorts of rifles, and [I] learned more about rifles and the action of bullets than is usually the fortune of the average guide and hunter. Col. Pickett surely made a scientific test of the then modern rifle."[2] Pickett represented only one example of how Billy learned, client by client, taking something from each one.

Pickett's own memories of the 1881 hunt stand as the nearest thing to a typical "job" description for Billy during this period, and they are also a useful vignette of wilderness travel in the last years of the frontier. "In the spring of 1881," Pickett recalled, "I determined to spend the summer and fall of that year among the mountains bordering the Big Horn Basin on the west, between Clark's Fork and the Grey Bull River." At that time, Pickett lived in Bozeman during the winter, so Billy—whose annual pattern now was to winter in Bozeman and spend the (relatively) warm months working in Greater Yellowstone—was a neighbor. "I secured two excellent old-timers, each an expert packer, wholly reliable and full of resource. These were T. Elwood Hofer, as packer and horse wrangler, and Le Grand Corey, as campkeeper." Pickett offered only praise for the "educated and reliable" Billy.[3] Narrating the start of their trip, he gave us a glimpse of Billy at work, with an engineer's eye for detail:

> We crossed the Yellowstone May 5, swimming the horses at Benson's Landing, and crossing the baggage and men on a ferry. We went up to the edge of the mountains on Mission Creek, and soon after crossing, Hofer killed an elk for meat. In place of his own rifle, Hofer was carrying one of mine—a .40-90 Sharps business rifle. I had furnished 225-grain hollow-pointed ball. The cartridges were loaded with 100 grains C. & H. powder. At short range the effect of this bullet was apparently as killing as my .45-caliber. The elk was killed with one shot in the lungs, the base of the bullet lodging against the ribs of the side opposite to where it entered.
>
> From that time until June 15, I hunted along the foothills of the mountains bordering the Yellowstone Valley on the south as far east as Clark's Fork of the Yellowstone, a distance of about seventy-five miles. Though we did not find many bears, we had a very pleasant time, and greatly enjoyed the freedom from the confinement of winter quarters in a Montana climate.[4]

Ah, the pleasures of Nature: the sunshine, the freedom, the well-ventilated elk—Pickett was clearly ecstatic. Recall that when the Nez Perce were headed in his general direction, in 1877, Billy was not worried, being "well armed and able to take care of ourselves." He was in this way nothing like John Muir. He knew his way around some serious weapons—he was a good shot—and he was not shy about using them, if not on humans.

Without getting too deeply into the technicalities of rifle design and ballistics, Pickett was essentially running an informal field study with a relatively new technology, the "express" bullet; Billy's work with Pickett during the spring was likely part of this study. The express bullet was simply a rifle bullet with empty space down the middle of the round from the nose back—that is, a hollow-point round. It was, as engineers say, an "elegant" design, because this one alteration gave multiple advantages: it lightened the bullet, providing a higher velocity, while at the same time essentially exploding inside the victim when it struck home.

These were pretty big bullets, too. In the United States, caliber was then always measured in fractions of inches and other traditional English measures (there were no millimeters in the Old West). Billy's weapon threw a bullet four-tenths of an inch wide—.40—while Pickett, who was quite literally loaded for bear, fired a .45, but thought Billy's weapon just as powerful and destructive. We would today normally associate ".45" with a handgun, but no one would mistake Pickett's weapon for a handgun. Furthermore, no matter what their other properties, and even though the bullets had been partly hollowed, these were generous helpings of lead. To provide some context, the U.S. heavy machine gun of the Second World War, still in use today—the Browning M2, the famous "Ma Deuce"—fired a .50 caliber round. To a civilian today, such bullets do not look like bullets, but small artillery rounds.[5]

Today's wilderness travelers are rarely allowed the kind of freedom that Pickett's party took for granted. They in fact embodied the precise opposite of the modern wilderness ethic, as captured in

the old Sierra Club motto: Take Only Photographs, Leave Only
Footprints. It is not that they lacked any ethic at all; their ethic,
as we will see, was simply the opposite of the normal beliefs of,
say, the kind of people who like to hike today. The environmental
situation in the West—at that time far along in its commercial
slaughter of animals—was already starting to change. Billy would
be part of the change and would even help to drive and shape it. He
did not know it, but he was getting started when he found himself
putting out fires, his own and others', during his first trips through
Yellowstone National Park. Conservation was becoming a force in
American life—but only just barely.

There was not going to be any conservation happening on this
1881 trip. This part of the West was very much still the wild frontier. The party crossed the Yellowstone River downstream from
present-day Livingston, Montana, headed south (Benson's Landing was a small settlement four miles east of modern Livingston,
now vanished[6]). The men ranged among the flatlands, foothills,
and mountains to the south, wandering at will over a landscape
that is still there: drive Interstate 90 east from Bozeman to Billings, look out of the car to the right, imagine the ranches are not
there, and you will see that landscape—meadows in front of forested mountains that grow ever higher and more jagged as the eye
ranges southward. (Yellowstone National Park is, of course, down
there, forty or fifty miles due south).

The Clark's Fork of the Yellowstone, which flows into the Yellowstone River just upstream from Billings at Laurel, in present-
day Montana, made up the east "boundary" of their wanderings.
The lived on deer and elk and a single grizzly bear[7] that they killed
for its lard, and because Pickett could not pass a grizzly without
shooting it. Approaching the Clark's Fork, Pickett veered roughly southeast and entered the Crow Indian Reservation. Because
they were generally friendly to the U.S. and fought the Sioux, the
Crow were allowed, for a time, a substantially larger reservation
than other Plains tribes. When Pickett and his little crew entered

the reservation, it was so large that it ran inside the north border and wrapped around the northeast corner of Yellowstone National Park, the boundaries of which were themselves much more simple, the park being a plain rectangle stamped on the map.[8] As they moved southeast and entered the Crow reservation, Pickett first asked to enter: "I always asked permission of the agent, believing this courtesy due him."[9] Clearly, Pickett believed in doing at least some things right; he would prove later to be reckless at times. At some point, they passed into Wyoming Territory. Their route does not appear to have penetrated Yellowstone, but veered in that direction, and if Pickett had decided to go there instead, hunting was still perfectly legal inside the national park.

They did quickly meet a party of the locals, and we learned of other skills Billy possessed, along with his colleague Corey:

> In the latter part of June, just before the noon meal, a small party of Crow Indians appeared at camp. One of them was the son of a Crow named Little Face, whom I had several times met. Hofer and Corey, who could talk good Crow and make a few signs, learned that the son of Little Face had just married and was now on his bridal trip. It was therefore decided to give the party a meal of fat elk, dried fruit and whatever luxuries the camp afforded. Since in mountain life there are no rooms to which guests may be invited, and the only living room is around the camp-fire under the broad canopy of heaven, all gathered there and watched the cook beginning the operations of the meal. As time passed, the Indians talked pleasantly among themselves. They were evidently hungry and were gratified at the prospect of breaking their fast.

> The various cooking operations went on, the bread was baked and the fruit stewed, and finally came the frying of the meat, which would thus be steaming hot when served.

> Corey filled the frying-pan with thick slices of elk and

an abundance of bear lard, and from over the fire an aroma grateful to a hungry man began to rise. This odor soon attracted the attention of the Indians, whose countenances, after some little talk, seemed to express despair, a combination of grief at the loss of their dinner and of dread of some impending evil. As they talked they became more and more excited, until at last they arose as if to go away, and of this an explanation was asked. With some difficulty and the help of many signs, we were given to understand that the cause of this change of feeling was the smell of the bear lard. They could not—dared not—eat anything cooked in bear's grease, and were about to go away. They had detected the dreaded odor at once. We explained to them that we knew nothing of their belief, and if they would wait for a little time, meat would be cooked for them uncontaminated.[10]

The Great Plains tribes spoke a bewildering array of languages and developed a manual sign talk that linguists today call Plains Indian Sign Language. Versatile and flexible, with an astonishingly large vocabulary, it made possible communication between tribes speaking languages that did not share a single common word. Billy could make himself understood in "the signs," although on this occasion, Corey helped. More surprisingly, Billy spoke some Crow, enough to sort out, with Corey, this rather complex matter: a meeting of strangers in the wilderness that turned into a wedding feast, then into a cultural catastrophe for metaphysical reasons that could barely be comprehended by the whites who were present, followed by reconciliation and a return to harmony. Pickett was as good as his word, serving up some unappetizing dry elk with which the hungry Crow were perfectly happy. So Billy, in addition to his other talents, could offer clients his skills as a translator, a diplomat, and even a cultural attaché, namely a wedding planner.

As the men continued to travel roughly south by east, they eventually hit a natural barrier and another adventure: "On June 15,"

Pickett continued, "we had come to within a few miles of Clark's Fork of the Yellowstone, and camped on a fine trout stream called Moose Creek."[11] In a footnote, Grinnell identified this watercourse as "Bennett's Creek," and it still carries the name Bennett Creek. In all that follows, the reader should keep in mind that this was a marginal little watercourse—Pickett called it a "trout stream," and Grinnell went further, calling it a "little stream,"[12] the sort of creek that dries out in September. But this was 1881, and here again we find more evidence that the local, spring snow was deeper then. Pickett took one look and made a decision: "It was necessary to raft our property across this stream, which was high from the melting snows of the mountains, and a raft was constructed in a situation suitable for poling it into the current and drifting with it to a suitable landing point on the opposite shore."[13]

Colonel Pickett did nothing by half measures. In his memoirs, he wrote that a raft built for his expedition the next year, in 1882—which Billy missed, because he already had too much other guiding work—was identical, and he described this vessel: "The weight of the outfit to be floated was fully 1,200 pounds, and it was therefore necessary to find the required dead logs up the river, to snake them to the water by the saddle horn and float them down to the place where the raft was to be built. The logs must then be lashed together with picket ropes, a platform arranged on top to store the bulky baggage, and finally the things secured so that no accident would tend to loosen or throw them overboard. The whole work occupied four or five days' time."[14] Because he was the sailor and boat builder in the party, the raft would have been Billy's affair, although I like to imagine Pickett standing over him, studying a sheath of blueprints and rubbing his chin, the Gustave Eiffel of the wild frontier.

Yet even the resulting dreadnought did not impress the audience that appeared as they were getting ready to launch, namely a second, larger party of Crow who were friendly, as usual, but pronounced the raft "no good" and left to try a crossing where the water should have reached only halfway up their ponies' sides. Pickett rode up later to check on their progress and found chaos, Bennett Creek "full of men and women, pack animals and loose horses all mixed up. Men and women swimming and yelling, and some of the horses swimming." That was the result when they forded with the people and packs. Crossing the dismounted horse herd, they were attempting the impossible:

> A woman mounted on one pony was leading a mare with colt following, and when all was ready, she started into the water, the other horses following, being pushed on and urged by the Indians. Just before reaching the opposite bank, some of the mares turned back for their colts that were nickering. At once they began to mill, turning around and around and being carried down into deep water. The only thing to do was to get back again on the same side to make another trip. They did this three or four times, but finally gave it up, not crossing the horses until the next morning when the river was lower.[15]

The river would indeed have been lower because June was normally the month of most rapid snowmelt[16]—a time when the sun pounds the higher elevations, and at such northerly latitudes, full dark lasts only about five hours—which was nevertheless enough of a break in the melt to temper the creek's mayhem and allow the horses to cross. Pickett, at any rate, was not going to subject his rifles and ammunition to any such treatment, and he returned to Billy's raft. Finding a safe place to launch it required some reconnaissance, but Billy and Corey "soon returned, reporting a better point down below. The pack horses were carefully unloaded at the point we were to start from, the raft was launched, with Hofer and Corey on it, and I went to a point below, where I could catch a rope thrown to me. A safe landing was made, and before dark all our belongings had been ferried over and we were in a snug camp. The horses had been driven into the water and forced to swim across."[17]

Obviously, it was quite an affair, just to get across "little" Bennett Creek. Again, it is a scene seemingly calculated to leave people who know twenty-first century Yellowstone with their mouths open. From accounts like this, one begins to conclude that there really was more snow then, although quantifying how much is a different matter—and this time, it was the day *after* the summer solstice.

There followed a long idyll: "From this day, June 22, to August 19, we were camped on and about Sheep Mountain, the easternmost spur reaching out to the plains of the Shoshoni group of mountains. The easternmost peak of this end is Heart Mountain, said to have received its name from the resemblance of this peak to a heart. It is the dividing mountain between the waters of Clark's Fork on the north and Stinking River on the south." Some of the names have changed, but we can easily locate ourselves on the twenty-first century landscape from this description. Heart Mountain is about ten miles north of Cody, Wyoming. West of the city is the present Buffalo Bill Reservoir, which traps the north and south forks of the Shoshone River ("Shoshone" being the more common present-day spelling of "Shoshoni," a name ubiquitous all over the landscape in Wyoming and Idaho, where it retains the "i" spelling). "Stinking River" or "Stinking Water River" was the old name for the Shoshone River, and between the two forks—today, the two branches of the reservoir—rose a broad plateau that was Sheep Mountain.[18] "On these mountains," Pickett continued, "we had three different camps, the highest being at an elevation of about 8,200 feet. On the mountains there was a large band of cow elk with their young and enough young bulls and mountain sheep to give us camp meat."[19]

Billy was busy. Bringing in the sheep and elk for their kitchen would have been his responsibility, while Pickett concentrated on the grizzly bears. Billy would have helped with the latter, too, but

Corey was the more experienced tracker. Both were busy in early August with a frontier version of an errand: "it was necessary for Hofer and Corey to go with the pack train for a supply of provisions sufficient to last for the next three months. These supplies were to have been delivered at the Crow Agency by bull team from Bozeman. They left on the 5th of August and returned nine days later, on the afternoon of the 14th."[20] "Provisions" were the normal, nongame foodstuffs (available only in towns) that were carried by virtually all horseback parties at that time: flour, sugar, salt, coffee, beans, vegetables, canned fruits, bacon (for flavoring), ham, and other domestic meats, but not game-meats.

As noted, however, this landscape of near-absolute freedom of movement and action was already changing, as settlers moved into it:

> After the boys returned, we went down from these mountains, intending to cross the two forks of Stinking River and then to follow around the foot of the mountains toward Grey Bull country. We followed down the mountain by the trail along Rattle Snake Creek, and on August 22 camped on Carter's Creek, about two miles above the Carter Ranch. Here Captain Belknap visited me. He had just brought into this basin a thousand cows and located a ranch on the south fork. About the same time, Colonel Carter, from Fort Bridger, brought in about the same number of cattle under the management of his relative, Dr. Carter.
>
> At this time the only other cattleman located on the west side of the Big Horn Basin was Otto Franc. He had settled on Grey Bull River, six miles above the mouth of Wood River. He drove into the basin in 1879 several thousand head of cattle from the Madison Valley, Montana, going by a roundabout way through the South Pass of the Rocky Mountains.
>
> From August 25 to October 30 we were about the foothills of the mountains on the west as far as the point

where Grey Bull River comes out on to the plains through its last cañon, near the mouth of Buffalo Fork. Our principal camps were at the forks of the Meeteetse Creek, and on the Buffalo Fork, near the point where it unites with the Grey Bull River. On Rock Creek there were other camps where we remained for shorter periods. These two months were, on the whole, the pleasantest, and from the sportsman's standpoint, the most successful of all [my] years spent among the Rocky Mountains.[21]

There was a terrible irony in scenes like this one. First, we need some orientation, and again, the names have changed, but the locations are plain: the party headed generally east by south, descending the Sheep Mountain massif by Rattlesnake Creek, which entered the North Fork of the Shoshone, from the north. Carter Creek entered the South Fork nearby, from the opposite direction (and some of Pickett's campsites are today underneath Buffalo Bill Reservoir). The men were leaving the high mountains and entering the Bighorn Basin, drained by the Bighorn River, and its famous relative, the Little Bighorn. The Bighorn flowed roughly north to debouch into the Yellowstone River in Montana Territory; both the Shoshone River and, to the south, the Greybull River were tributaries.

Cattle ranches were replacing the open range.[22] Pickett did not disapprove. Reading his account between the lines, he appears to have been shopping for his own ranch. In 1883, on May 30, he moved into a cattle ranch he founded on the Greybull River, near his 1881 camp on Meeteetse Creek. Otto Franc, six miles away, would be his neighbor. He lived there most of the rest of his life.[23]

So they ravaged the land they loved, a process that was going on all over the West. Animals from prairie dogs and bobcats to wolves and lions and bison and scores of others had to die to make the range available for cows. Pickett had taken on the grizzlies as his own personal project. During 1881, he killed 23 of them; of these, he claimed to have felled 17 with a single shot each.[24] Other kinds of animals would die to feed the very employees killing them. The Crow, friendly or not, were going to have to settle down, too. The cattlemen would get rich, of course (until the winter of 1886-1887 wiped them out). The native meadows would make way for alfalfa and nonnative weeds and so on—all a familiar and depressing story to us, today, but it still conceals at its heart a mystery. Why could they not see what they were doing? The standard explanation has always stated that nineteenth-century people believed natural resources to be unlimited. In this case, the explanation, in my opinion, fails. Pickett was not a stupid man, and he was extraordinarily good at math. Could he not see that in a few years, he would have killed everything but the cattle, and that shooting whiskey bottles would just not be the same?

Billy *could* see it, one of the many qualities that made him so exceptional. Perhaps he had not seen it at this early date, but he ultimately would. We know so because, as his circle of friends expanded to include men powerful enough to help, he would repeatedly do what he could to keep the West wild. Part of his education, during the 1870s and the first half of the 1880s, included an exceptional lesson: that the West was not invincible. It likely helped that Yellowstone National Park was there, standing as a reminder of what had been lost, or was going fast (remember his spontaneously putting out those fires in the Yellowstone forest duff). We can guess that the work he was doing during this period, while it taught him both the geographical landscape and the skills he needed to make a living on it, also had a potentially painful edge: they made him an agent in the destruction. At the same time, we should note one point in Pickett's favor, at least in honesty. He styled himself an assassin of bears and was proud to be such—and everyone in Montana at that date, except the native people, would have approved wholeheartedly. A bear was just an unusually big varmint, and besides, grizzlies were dangerous, too.

Nevertheless, when the opportunities began to present themselves, Billy would do what he could to make himself the opposite—a man who valued his unfettered environment. The conservation movement, as it gathered strength, would be not a threat, but a solution. We do not know what he thought of bears at this date, as he was working for Pickett. Just a few years later, however, in June 1887, he wrote the following in *Forest and Stream*. He was visiting the old Marshall's Hotel, at the Lower Geyser Basin in Yellowstone National Park:

> On the morning of the 25th a large yellow-faced grizzly bear came within 250yds. of the hotel here; he came from the Queen's Laundry Basin, crossed the Fire Hole and meadows within sight of the house, walking leisurely along, now and then stopping to feed on an ant heap, then entered some dead timber where he rolled logs over for grubs, hunted mice and beetles, but paying no attention to the carcass of a dead horse which he walked around. He was probably in delicate health and could eat only choice food. He would pick up a bit of sod with his foot, and after critically examining it, eat some root, then drop the sod and walk on in rather a zigzag course. Several times he came toward the hotel as though with the intention of making us a visit. We watched him through field glasses until out of sight in the timber on Nez Perce Creek. We then went out and measured his tracks, the hind foot not counting; claws were 8in. long. Judging from that he would weigh from 500 to 550lbs. at least, possibly more.[25]

Whatever he was thinking at the time, at Marshall's Hotel, the tone of that passage does not in any way suggest hatred for grizzlies. Nor was the animal much of a terror.

Pickett did the bulk of his grizzly hunting for the year during September and October, 1881, killing nineteen bears,[26] which must have kept everyone busy. Colonel Pickett finally blew retreat:

"After spending a few days at Captain Belknap's Ranch, I set out for my winter quarters at Bozeman, Montana, following around the foothills of the mountains." He wanted to avoid his experiences of the previous year, when during the trip home in the autumn, he experienced a full month of temperatures between 25 and 40 degrees below zero. "This year, therefore," wrote Pickett, "we started for Bozeman about November 1, crossing the Stinking Water on the lodge pole trail, just below the lower cañon. Thence we went by Crow Agency and Benson's Landing, reaching Bozeman December 3, 1881."

Not every year was an arctic catastrophe. In this particular year, "winter" arrived on September 4 with a six-inch snowfall—mild weather, for the region—and throughout the ride home, "The weather was pleasant," and "the direct route had not yet been obstructed by snow."[27] There exists a town today named Crow Agency…but that is not the way they went, because that town did not yet exist. The place named "Crow Agency" was the headquarters of the reservation and moved multiple times as the reservation shrank. The "Crow Agency" of that era was at present-day Absarokee, Montana, midway between the mountains and the Yellowstone River. The mountains, seen on a large-scale map, here formed a kind of bulge pointed northward. To get home, Pickett needed to follow a rough semicircle, north toward Crow Agency, then west toward Bozeman, all the while trying to cut the semicircle short by pushing higher into the foothills, with some success: the "direct route" was open.

In general, Billy's life went this way for the next several years: active in the field from the spring melt until the weather forced a stop, typically in October or November. Billy was not as immobilized during the winter as other people, because he could ski. Nearly everyone else simply hunkered down; in the words of one historian, even the native people of the region spent the winter "as close to hibernation as a people could get."[28] The job with Pickett was perfect for this phase of Billy's life, when he still had lessons to absorb—and Pickett was a good schoolmaster, a gentleman, yes, but with more than a trace of obsessive compulsive disorder that may have become a positive trait, in an unsettled and often dangerous environment. We should pause to at least accord a little respect to what they had just pulled off: they had gone on a camping trip that lasted, without a real break, for seven months. That is a long time to go without a proper bath, or the various improvisations that nineteenth-century Montanans used for toilet paper.

Pickett's future lay with the cattle business in Wyoming, however, and Billy's lay in and around the new national park. Then and now, tying your life to Yellowstone meant taking whatever work came along, and Billy was playing that game during an era when the work often had to be invented by the worker. So during 1882, Billy developed other temporary solutions. One solution, for at least a season, lay in the approach of the single force that more than anything would change Yellowstone from the remote wilderness Billy had explored in 1879 to the international tourist-hub it has become today. That force was—cue the ominous music from *Jaws*— the railroads.

The Northern Pacific began building in Minnesota in 1870, its goal the ocean in the Pacific Northwest. The basic route was completed and had its golden-spike ceremony in 1883. From the earliest years of the national park, it was obvious that the Northern Pacific would eventually in some way "serve" it. The major questions were in what way and how much. As it entered the Greater Yellowstone area, once the core line was completed, it followed the Yellowstone River upstream through Billings to Livingston and from there over Bozeman Pass to Bozeman and the Gallatin River valley, and thus past Billy's home. As noted, he had already worked at the Northern Pacific hotel in Bozeman. Now, he turned to the NP again.

A number of questions hovered over the entire operation as the railroad line crept nearer to the park. A relatively minor one was which route it would follow toward the park: the line could either turn south at Livingston to follow the Yellowstone River to the park's north boundary, or it could turn at the Gallatin River and run south to meet the Madison River and enter the park at or near the present location of West Yellowstone, Montana.

Billy had taken his earnings and invested them, as he recalled in his autobiographical notes: "Next year [1882] I went into partnership with a man named Nelson,[29] and we started a pack train to Cooke City, a newly named mining camp."[30] His choice of words, "newly named," helps us locate the event in time. Cooke City is today a tourist town five miles outside the present Northeast Entrance to the park, a former mining camp where men had been digging gold since before the national park was established. It was christened "Cooke City" on February 1, 1882, in a not well camouflaged effort to flatter Jay Cooke of the Northern Pacific (NP) and win for Cooke City a railroad of its own.[31] It never got one. (Livingston and Billings were named in honor of NP nabobs also. The list could be lengthened.) The trips to Cooke City must have been arduous, and hauling beans and whiskey to the denizens of a gold camp was not Billy's career goal. However, it was paying work that kept him in the park: the route to Cooke City was a wagon road that crossed the northern range of the park, hacked out of the landscape by the prospectors themselves before the park existed.[32] A pack train, further, could be repurposed in any number of ways.

So Billy helped decide which way the railroad would go: "Our pack train was busy during the summer with a survey party under a Mr. [M.G.] Grant, locating a railroad through the park, and in the autumn with the same party locating a route up the Gallatin from Bozeman, but this route was abandoned for the one from Livingston, but never completed further than to Gardiner, for no railroads were permitted to enter the park."[33] Mr. Grant—no relation to the former president—was identified by park historian Aubrey Haines as "Location Engineer Grant."[34] The surveys of the branch lines southward were, for whatever reason, not the cause of much local excitement—the railroad itself, marching into Montana, was the real focus of delight—but the *Bozeman Avant Courier* did report on the completion of Grant's survey from Benson's Landing to the park on April 27, 1882.[35] The survey team then kept going.

Hofer and Nelson would not have played a sophisticated role in the project, instead hauling supplies to Mr. Grant as he worked his way up the Yellowstone, the Gallatin, and, interestingly, also laid out "a railroad through the park," although Billy did not specify the route. We do, however, have one source that tells us where exactly Hofer and Nelson spent much of that summer. Later in the 1880s, George Wood Wingate wrote a travel book, *Through the Yellowstone Park on Horseback*, and his publisher enclosed with each volume— hidden in a pocket inside the back cover—a tourists' map of Yellowstone. The map was dated 1882 and credited, at the top, to "Carl J. Hals and A. Rydstrom, Civil Engineers." Both men were topographers who helped Grant run the Northern Pacific line through the park—both, in fact, have features named for them in the park[36]—suggesting that the map was a promotional gift from the railroad. It included the entire length of the proposed line through the park. Those few copies of the map, in those few books, are today among the last traces of Grant's ghost railroad line.[37]

Hofer and Nelson actually had their hands full: the route ran the entire length of the park from north to south. It crossed the boundary near the present-day North Entrance and for the most part followed the corridor of the twenty-first century roads, south through Mammoth and Norris to the Lower Geyser Basin. It left Yellowstone Lake and the canyon alone; they were to be served by stagecoach roads and trails. Once they departed the Lower Geyser Basin, however, Grant and his topographers made a move that can be outright startling to a person looking at that map today. The route plunged out of the modern road corridor and into what is today deep backcountry, skirting closely along the south shore of Shoshone Lake, then continuing to hug the water past Lewis Lake and along the Lewis River to exit the park near the present-day

South Entrance—but having followed a route along the opposite shore from the twenty-first century roads. Building a railroad along that line, especially from the Lower Geyser Basin to the South Entrance, would have caused a great deal of destruction that the park happily escaped. For Shoshone Lake to have been thus abused would have been tragic. Shoshone Lake—another of Yellowstone's countless rarities—is today believed to be the largest lake in the Lower 48 states that is not reached by any road. It would have lost this status when the park was new, had the railroad come to be.

Since there was no formal plan in place to build a branch line that actually ran through the park, Grant's survey within its boundaries must have been an informal effort executed at the request of any number of parties: the Northern Pacific, the U.S. government, capitalists local, national, and international, all of the above, or someone else. This attempt was among the first of many to try to run rails through the park. In the end, the branch line from Livingston would stop at Cinnabar, Montana Territory, the official first train arriving there on September 1, 1883. Eventually, the end-of-track arrived three miles farther on, at Gardiner, astride the North Entrance, where it finally stopped for good. Billy would live for many years in both towns.[38]

About a decade later, Billy would do everything in his then-considerable power to keep any trains from getting any closer to Yellowstone than they already were. Indeed, he would render crucial assistance to a political campaign which actually destroyed a railroad that threatened the park. So by working for the Northern Pacific, he was in the same position he was in with Pickett: the only way to make a living was by helping to indirectly destroy the place. If, by this point, he was feeling pangs of conscience, he constantly had recourse to the psychological defense that most of us fall back on regularly: "A little bit won't hurt."

In this case, however, we should arguably take a more sophisticated view. The railroads have, in histories of the national parks, been so often treated as villains that it is difficult to recall that, in the early 1880s, such a view would have been decidedly in the minority. Historian Paul Schullery has speculated that "if a poll had been taken of Americans in 1880, asking if railroads should be run to the major attractions in Yellowstone, an overwhelming majority would have said yes. To them the railroad was the very soul of the future; what could be wrong with swift, efficient travel around Wonderland?"[39] Further, "In its development of the park's tourist trade the [Northern Pacific], an aggressive and extraordinarily powerful American corporation, followed the business impulses of the day and the example of almost every other resort area in America. The railroad long attempted to lay track clear to the geyser basins.... It's hard to imagine these railroads in the park today without wincing, and even then there were quite a few people who did not think the park needed so much improvement." The resistance that the railroads met "must have surprised them."[40] It came from important legislators and journalists. One nexus of resistance where such people came together was George Bird Grinnell's decade-old weekly newspaper, one that would play a determinative role in Billy's life from then on—namely *Forest and Stream*.

Just a little over five months before that first train rolled into Cinnabar, the most unobtrusive of announcements graced the back pages of this newspaper. The ad was perhaps two column inches in size. "SPORTSMEN & TOURISTS," it shouted, but there the raucousness ended, and the ornate curlicues of mid-Victorian prose took over, showing that the schoolteachers in Billy's Connecticut still had an influence:

> The undersigned guides and packers wish to make arrangements with parties for the coming season. Those who wish to visit the Yellowstone National Park, or make a hunting trip for buffalo, Elk, Deer, Antelope, Mountain Sheep or Bear, and fish some of the finest trout streams of this section, should secure everything necessary in advance, thus saving time and trouble on arrival here. Saddle and pack

animals, and all camp equipage furnished. For full information and terms, address....HOFER & NELSON, Bozeman,
Gallatin Co., M. T., Care Walter Cooper, Gun Store.[41]

From this little ad, one can almost feel the wild frontier!

The phrase "saving time and trouble" could be translated: "If
you show up unprepared, just asking around for help, you will be
robbed and left on the prairie to die." Hofer and Nelson had been
in business for a year, and yet they had no mailing address. Neither
did Cooper's gun store, which was not on a named street, it seems,
and the store itself did not even have a name. And yet these "directions" were adequate to get the mail delivered.

Elsewhere among those back pages, cluttered like an old garage,
we could have found the Publisher's Department, which included the following piece of opinion from the editors: "WESTERN
GUIDES. — Attention is called to the card of Messrs. Hofer &
Nelson, of Bozeman, Mont." That they have displayed the energy
to advertise in this particular journal "is to be taken as presumptive
evidence of their ability as guides."[42]

It is, for us, always amusing to see a couple of nineteenth-century Montana heathen addressed as *Messieurs*. Nor did this sentence
represent the best piece of logical deduction about Hofer ever to
be found in this publication. It was a rare and isolated lapse; much
better was to come, because this was only Billy's first appearance in
Forest and Stream.

CHAPTER FIVE

Forest and Stream (and Ice, and Snow)

Forest and Stream and *Field and Stream* would have been even easier to confuse if the former had survived—the Great Depression killed *Forest and Stream*, and *Field and Stream* bought the remains.[1] The confusion today is sad. The elder publication—through much of its history, more newspaper than magazine—was not just a hook-and-bullet advertising organ, like nearly every other publication of that sort. It had higher ambitions, and it arguably achieved them.

Founded in 1873 by Charles Hallock, the periodical took on many of the key qualities it would display for the next fifty-four years when George Bird Grinnell took over as editor in 1876. Born in New York, Grinnell finished a bachelor's degree at Yale in 1870, and in 1880 he became one of the early candidates to finish a new kind of degree, a Ph.D. Originally a zoologist and later an important anthropologist and historian, he had his own life changed forever when he joined Captain William Ludlow in 1875 on a U.S. Army reconnaissance of the new national park.

Grinnell was officially the naturalist and paleontologist of the expedition. The report he prepared made clear from the start his true path and did so at the strikingly early date of June 1, 1876.

That much was evident in the introduction to his report, addressed to Ludlow. Grinnell may have felt an odd pang as he wrote it, sitting in a comfortable room back East, because he was supposed to be in the West at that moment: he had declined an opportunity to join George Armstrong Custer on the general's latest outing. It was twenty-four days later that the Seventh Cavalry crashed into the Little Bighorn valley. Grinnell's report of course had nothing to do with the coming catastrophe, but the two were of a piece. To Grinnell, the forced neutralization of the West had become downright stupid, and with the optimism of youth—it would have required optimism, at that date—Grinnell set out to help put a stop to it:

> It may not be out of place here [strictly speaking, it was], to call your attention to the terrible destruction of large game, for the hides alone, which is constantly going on in those portions of Montana and Wyoming through which we passed. Buffalo, elk, mule-deer, and antelope are being slaughtered by thousands each year, without regard to age or sex, and at all seasons. Of the vast majority of the animals killed, the hide only is taken. Females of all these species are as eagerly pursued in the spring, when just about to bring forth their young, as at any other time.
>
> It is estimated that during the winter of 1874-'75 not less than 3,000 elk were killed for their hides alone in the valley of the Yellowstone.... The Territories referred to have game laws, but, of course, they are imperfect, and cannot, in the present condition of the country, be enforced. Much, however, might be done to prevent the reckless destruction of the animals to which I have referred, by the officers stationed on the frontier....[2]

He meant specifically U.S. Army officers, and he would get his wish in 1886, when the Army took over administration of Yellowstone National Park. It may have been precocious for a young man just out of school to lay an entire national conservation policy at the feet of his boss, Captain Ludlow, a policy that was antimatter to the whole present way of doing things, but in spite of what was about to happen to Custer, the Indian Wars were effectively over. The Army was soon going to be out of work. To use present-day military jargon, they needed a new operational doctrine—a job, that is. It can be argued that Grinnell gave them one, an open-ended mission that, from their point view, might never cease. Even though Ludlow could do little about it, Grinnell's intent here—akin to lifting a torch—was smart. That young man, in those few lines, also launched a career for himself as a conservationist that would occupy him for decades, with Billy as a major ally. It is a common belief today that, apart from a few visionaries like John Muir, environmentalism is a creature of the 1960s. That belief is false. What we call "environmentalism" was a feeble force in 1876, but it was already alive.

Grinnell's thoughts alone show that it was. His letter to Ludlow even identified allies, in the West: "The general feeling of the better class of frontiersmen, guides, hunters, and settlers, is strongly against those who are engaged in this work of butchery, and all, I think, would be glad to have this wholesale and short-sighted slaughter put a stop to."

What we call *environmentalism*, they called *conservation*, and their language can confuse us in other ways as well. The word "sportsman" has lost the glow it once had. Today, it suffers from the considerable handicap that it cannot be politically neutered: "sportsperson" does not work, and "sport," as a label for an individual, means something else entirely. Further, to call fishing and especially hunting "sport" puts killing on the same level as golf. However, in the later nineteenth century, "sportsman" did not mean "frivolous killer." It was the opposite of "market hunter," and was a label worn with pride. It designated a gentleman who was not in it for money and so could be expected to follow at least some ethical rules, as gentlemen—some ladies were involved, too— were supposed to do in the rest of life. An analogy would be the modern Olympics, where the old rule that athletes had to be pure amateurs had the effect of keeping bar-fighters out and was designed to do just that. That was snobbery, but they engendered a more family-friendly Olympiad that way. Similarly, amateur sportsmen could be expected to leave a few animals alive when the day's shooting was done.

An important work of scholarship on this issue is John Reiger's *American Sportsmen and the Origins of Conservation*.[3] The book explains a mystery that today rarely gets the attention it should: how did Theodore Roosevelt, when he became president, get away with the radical conservation measures he took? We celebrate him for it now, but at the time, creating millions of acres of national forest and national monument with a wave of his hand had an arrogance about it. Why did the electorate of that day put up with it? Because the way had been prepared for him by decades of conservation effort by sportsmen. Here is Reiger:

> What I have called "the code of the sportsman," which regulated behavior in the field and the taking of game to ensure its survival into the future, began as an aristocratic set of rules in Europe, particularly England, and was later adopted by the American upper classes, at least partly to separate themselves from the "common" hunter and fisherman. Thus, the conservation creed that evolved out of the code of the sportsman also had its origins in an elite world view, at least before 1901, when the main time period covered by this book ends. But the twentieth century witnessed a continuous "trickling down" of these conservation principles, to the point where they are now part of the thinking of millions of contemporary hunters and anglers.[4]

He reported that his own students told him, at his campus in rural Ohio, that folks out in the countryside, with no education beyond high school, practiced good sporting ethics without knowing "how much their thinking derives from what was originally the world view of a relatively small, elite group of Americans."[5] This was the sort of activity that professors today normally denounce as cultural imperialism, but Reiger approved of it, and I approve, and so do many others.

Grinnell was certainly happy with it. Long before his Ph.D. was finished, he took the helm of *Forest and Stream* and went on the offensive, ranging far and wide but with a special place in his heart for the place that had changed his life, Yellowstone National Park, which was being subjected to such depraved abuse.[6]

No source has yet turned up for us today that records how Billy Hofer and George Grinnell met, but given the grip Yellowstone had on both, given that Billy was now there nearly full time, and given the similarity of their temperaments, a friendship was inevitable, and it was surely born in the park. For a few years in the mid-1880s, Billy did enter one of those periods—happily, the last—during which his movements were and are difficult to track. We know what he was doing. In summer 1882, along with the railroad surveys, "I guided my first party through the park, Gen. Brooke and party. The N. P. was completed past Bozeman, and tourists were flocking in. I was busy every summer with parties on trips."[7] From then on, he would have his hands full doing what he had been aiming to do: spending as much time as possible working in the park itself.

Our problem today is that the only one keeping track of Billy's activities, during this period, was Billy. The "Gen. Brooke" he referred to demonstrated the kind of trouble that developed. Summer 1882 happened to be the year when, it seemed, the whole U.S. Army descended for the season on Yellowstone, led by the Civil War notable Philip Sheridan. In their annual reports, the early park superintendents often included a section on VIPs who turned up in Yellowstone that year, and in the list for 1882, the soldiers—including the military escorts—outnumbered the civilians.[8] The list includes only those about whom the superintendent knew, and "Gen. Brooke" slipped through the net. Unless General Brooke's rank was like Colonel Sanders'—which seems vanishingly unlikely—then he earned the rank in the Civil War, as did all general officers during these years, or at least those still spry enough to chase Billy Hofer around Yellowstone. This person could only have been U.S. Gen. John Rutter Brooke, because the rebels had no general named Brooke (or any variant spelling), and the only other candidate for us is William T.H. Brooks, who died in 1870.[9]

John Brooke had a long, interesting career, seeing much violence in the Civil War, serving afterward in the West and even remaining in uniform long enough to fight the Spanish in 1898. He was among the last surviving Civil War generals when he finally died in 1926.

That such a prominent soldier could slip through like that unreported suggests how popular the new park was with the Army, which was filled with outdoorsmen (the cavalry especially). Officers stationed in the West could visit Yellowstone more easily than the average New Yorker or European. That Brooke chose Billy Hofer also suggests to us that Billy's reputation was already both high and spreading fast.

Because by this point in his story, Billy had truly arrived in Yellowstone, and his movements, by the later 1880s, are today not especially difficult to track, this would be the place to note one reason—peculiar to the folkways of Yellowstone itself—that Billy tends to disappear from histories about the park. A number of observers have commented on the process by which he has become "lost" to us. The historian Paul Schullery, in one of the more thorough biographical sketches anyone has ever written about Billy—in his book *Yellowstone's Ski Pioneers*, appropriately—gave voice to one cause that others have invoked: "He rarely worked for the government, which may be one reason why his formal record is so slight; operating as an independent guide, trapper…and small-time concessioner, he was usually only on the edge of park administration, however central he may have been in park adventures."[10] Schullery might have added a fact of everyday life in Yellowstone, and one that Schullery himself, a longtime resident of the region, has noted. Writing of the tendency of the children of concession company managers to marry the children of rangers—and the corruption or other problems that might imply—he calls it "all but unavoidable in a place like Yellowstone.... Besides being a national park, an international symbol, and a great regional cash factory, Yellowstone has also long been a very small, very isolated human community."[11] Historians today approach someone like Hofer expecting correspondence to routinely exist between him and the various officers of the federal government who ran the park during his time there. We expect, during periods of crisis or other excitement, to find a paper avalanche. Why is it absent for Billy?

We forget how isolated and insular Yellowstone is, and how small its human settlements remain today; it was even smaller in Billy's day. Almost as soon as it existed to receive him, Billy moved to Gardiner; the park's managers were at Mammoth Hot Springs. Ridden energetically by a cavalryman, a horse could cover the distance between the two places in about thirty minutes. Gardiner people and Mammoth people saw each other nearly every day back then, and still do. The mental atmosphere, then and now, sometimes gets downright claustrophobic. Any information a park official wanted to impart to Billy, he could impart over lunch. Also, not too long after Billy arrived, so did a new gadget: the telephone (the first lines went up in the park in 1886). The vast bulk of "official" communication between the officials and Billy was oral. Its remnants were carried off on the wind—and then, only when both sides were available to talk. Billy spent a lot of time away on business, and his business took him to places no form of communication could reach.

Once Billy and Grinnell connected, and once Grinnell discovered that Billy could write, *Forest and Stream* would serve as a diary tracking much of Billy's life in Yellowstone. We must look closely at both the diary and the relationship between the men. The best way to do that is to look at the first major meeting of the two: Billy's epic 1887 ski and his almost equally epic record of the event.

Again, 1887 was the year that set the records. It did not *almost* destroy the Western cattle business; it *did* destroy it, if only temporarily. By an outstanding piece of bad timing, a U.S. Army officer who had achieved some success as an Arctic explorer, Frederick Schwatka, attempted a much-publicized "exploration" of the wintertime park beginning on January 5 of the fatal year, sponsored by the *New York World*. He and most of his party ended having gotten no farther than a couple of miles past Norris, maybe 25 miles of the 200 necessary. The rest of the press, including *Forest and Stream*, had a great deal of fun at his expense: "we proffer to the New York *World* our sympathy," *Forest and Stream* crowed, followed by a long session of *schadenfreude*.[12] The *New York Herald* called it a "great 'faking' party," and quoted Billy, who called the affair "humbug."[13]

Schwatka was defeated by the unprecedented weather, yes, but he also chose bad equipment, and he became seriously ill. One member of his party was F. Jay Haynes, at this time the official photographer for the Northern Pacific Railroad and later, for decades, the unofficial "Official Photographer" of Yellowstone National Park. In better shape than the rest, he recruited a few other diehards, and they completed the circuit—but not until misjudging the weather and nearly getting themselves killed in a blizzard on the north face of Mount Washburn.[14]

One historian has seen something more than just deadly slapstick in these events: "Hofer and other experienced civilian scouts proved," Jeffrey Meyer wrote, "to be valuable mentors to the tenderfoot skiing soldiers of Yellowstone. Where many of Schwatka's and Haynes' exploits in 1887 provided valuable cautionary tales on what not to do, Hofer provided a model of how safe and efficient winter travel on skis should be undertaken. With the accrued knowledge of the seasoned guides and skiers, the Army learned the tactics of the poachers and the skills of skiing necessary to pursue them." After all, only a few of the soldiers—mostly Scandinavian and other Northern European immigrants from the Upper Midwest—actually showed up in Yellowstone already knowing how to ski. "The learning curve was steep, but the efforts soon bore some fruit. The first arrest of poachers by the Army occurred in April 1887 at Norris. The Army's determination to patrol the park's extensive boundaries from poaching incursions throughout the winter established skiing as a necessity for the job. Dramatic ski adventures, along with the monotony of winter life housed in snow bound cabins, began unfolding each winter in Yellowstone as soldiers went about their work."[15]

To another question we have occasionally considered—whether it was more snowy in Billy's Yellowstone than our own—1887 must be treated as an outlier, a freak event so extreme as not to prove anything one way or the other. Still...can you imagine Winter 1887 happening today?

The publicity surrounding these events influenced Grinnell in his decision to dispatch Billy on his winter mission. That the request came from Grinnell is clear from the editorial note that ran just before the series did. It was unsigned, but was clearly Grinnell's work. Any alterations to the original—and this goes for any older document quoted in this book—will only appear inside brackets herein and then only sparingly. The many, many variant spellings common during Billy's lifetime have been allowed to stand, with a [sic] used only when needed for the sake of clarity. This is how Grinnell introduced Billy Hofer:

> NEXT week we shall begin the publication of the report
> of the special commissioner intrusted by the FOREST
> AND STREAM with the difficult and dangerous duty of
> making the tour of the National Park in winter. The attrac-
> tions of this wonderland in summer are well known, but
> until now no man has beheld its winter glories—glories in

many ways more striking and strange than those of the summer time.

Our commissioner had our full confidence and was pinned down by no definite directions, but we instructed him, if it were possible, to visit the various Geyser Basins, the Yellowstone Lake and the Falls, and to report on their winter character. He was also to look out carefully for game, and above all to see if he could discover any bison or signs of them in the park.

His trip has been in all respects successful. All the principal localities of interest were visited by him, and the marvellous effects of the frost are described in his report. After leaving the Upper Geyser Basin, the crest of the Rocky Mountains—the Continental Divide—was crossed in a blinding snow storm in which it was impossible to travel except by compass, for all landmarks were hidden by the flying snow, and the wind whipping about among the peaks, came, as it seemed, from half a dozen different quarters at the same time….

With the modesty of a brave man our commissioner speaks lightly of the perils and hardships undergone on the trip. There are few men who know what such a trip means; a journey of over 200 miles on snowshoes, through a country whose features are all changed by the deep snow, in a temperature often 60° below the freezing point, and where provisions and blankets have to be carried on the travelers' backs.

Our correspondent has done his work bravely and well, as we knew he would when we selected him for the work. There has been no bluster about him, no long-winded dissertations about what he was going to do. His journey accomplished, he tells his story in a simple, quiet manner of the old-fashioned mountain man.[16]

Approaching anything in *Forest and Stream*, particularly any-thing written by Grinnell and Billy in concert, it is best to take care and not allow yourself to be fooled, in this case by the tone of these paragraphs, by degrees officious and grandiloquent. The passage reeks of arrogance in the face of the absurd challenges it throws down and the equally absurd praises it sings, but understand that the intended tone, throughout the entire series, was a low-key, self-deprecating humor that in fact characterized the publication itself and plainly had to do with the personalities involved.

The tone reflected Grinnell's nature and happily that of many of his authors and readers as well, including Billy. *Forest and Stream* was not sending a "special commissioner" because it imagined itself to be a shadow government with super-secret agents to keep an eye on things. Grinnell was setting Billy's trip up as a parody of a real government investigation—rather like the overblown Schwatka affair—this time played for laughs, but ultimately with a serious purpose. Much that happened in *Forest and Stream* was written for laughs—precisely because the journal was filled with otherwise deadly serious information and opinion about the fate of the wild-life of the West. Grinnell knew that he could not fill the journal with deadly serious information and opinion and nothing but that. So every issue was also filled with practical hook-and-bullet advice, and every issue was fun to read, because it was funny.

Grinnell had other tricks up his sleeve. A technical term from filmmaking is useful to understand what was happening here. The "MacGuffin," a term Alfred Hitchcock is thought to have invented, is a device in a script that sets the plot in motion, but only appears to be important; once it has done its work, it recedes, and the char-acters may even forget its existence. Think of the transit papers in *Casablanca*: inherently absurd (magic papers that allow the bearer to flit around the globe, no matter what the Nazis think), we never see them and eventually forget about them.

From the start, environmental politics have been full of Mac-Guffins, for instance, members of a tiny endangered species that puts a stop to a giant industrial project. There may be thousands of such examples. Here, the MacGuffin was more substantial. Yellowstone National Park was not originally established to protect the animals: instead it protected the geysers, canyons, waterfalls, and other geologic special effects. Grinnell was using that geology as a gigantic MacGuffin. Billy would give the journal's readership a mental postcard of the geysers in winter and at the same time collect the information Grinnell really cared about: the health of the wildlife and its habitat.

Grinnell's experience in Yellowstone was extensive enough that he had learned what everyone learns about Yellowstone eventually: that the park in warm weather was not the real park. Most of the year, it was an icebox, and understanding the health of the wildlife meant getting a look—and publicizing that look—at how the wildlife fared when Yellowstone returned to its natural, normal deep freeze. It was a look that virtually no one had yet taken.

And it served another purpose to which Grinnell would return again and again for years: by showing the life of the park when it was at its most vulnerable, he highlighted the need to protect it from disruption little or large, from an individual poacher to an entire railroad. In the following week's issue, when Billy began his actual report, Grinnell offered another short introduction: "The interesting relation of what he did and what he saw will be read with pleasure by that very large portion of the public who have followed the history of the Park and have noted the many attempts by various individuals and corporations to obtain possession of this reservation which belongs by law to the nation."[17] Grinnell would spend decades trying, with considerable success, to strengthen the legal bastions around the park.

Billy may have been amused to be designated a Special Commissioner and picked up his new office with some wry enthusiasm, reporting from Mammoth Hot Springs in a letter dated March 7 and published exactly a month later: "*Editor Forest and Stream.*—Having completed the midwinter snowshoe expedition through the

National Park undertaken at the instance of the FOREST AND STREAM, and as a special commissioner of that journal, I submit herewith my report of the trip."[18]

Few people know it, but he had already made a lengthy ski during this fatal winter, one that may perhaps have served partly as a trial run for the "Winter in Wonderland" voyage. On New Year's Day, 1887, the *Livingston Enterprise* reported that "Elwood Hofer gives an interesting account of his recent snowshoeing expedition to the National Park in search of stray horses. He started with a pack of seventy-five pounds, including blankets and three days' rations. On one occasion he slid noiselessly into a band of elk, among which were some of the finest and largest bulls and cows he had ever seen. These antlered monarchs of the mountains were pasturing with Indian ponies on the most friendly terms." At least one of the horses refused to leave the elk, and the *Enterprise* depicted the entire errand as an unhappy bother that Billy endured with aplomb. It even left him philosophical: "Billy Hofer is an old and experienced mountaineer and rather enjoys spending a night now and then with the wolves in winter and the tourists in summer. He says: 'All solid comfort comes to him only who can compare the good, the better and the best. A snowy bed is poetically good, a bed of down is theoretically better, but a spring bed at the Cottage hotel, after one of China Jim's good suppers, is superlatively best.'"[19]

Assuming that the *Enterprise* got the weight of his pack correct, seventy-five pounds was too great a load for the kind of marathon he and Tansey would undertake; their packs represented some careful winnowing. Billy devoted a great deal of space to his preparations, as made sense, given how few people had done what he had, although he believed more would in the future: "The outfit I thought necessary to take with us included an Indian lodge for shelter while camping out," he began his description of his gear. By "Indian lodge," he meant the characteristic conical structure of the Plains tribes, the one we usually call a teepee. "This was 10ft.

in diameter on the ground, made of heavy sheeting, and weighed complete, 7½lbs."[20]

Grinnell's graphic artists included a pair of illustrations of the lodge, assembled and looking monstrous.[21] To a twenty-first century person, it at first looks impossible. How could all that weigh just 7½ pounds?

We forget that Billy had a major and unexpected advantage precisely because his lodge was not made by LL Bean. The single dominant tree in Yellowstone was and is the lodgepole pine. In the poor soil that covers much of the region, they often grow a mere twenty feet tall, beanpole straight, with surprisingly little foliage. They could scarcely be improved on as poles to support lodges... and hence the name. Billy did not need poles from LL Bean. He had millions of free ones from which to take his pick.

He continued with his description of his gear, all of it chosen carefully by himself, some of it manufactured carefully by himself, the whole making a personal kit that had been shaped and perfected by at least a dozen years' practice, since he had begun his "snowshoe" career skiing the mail in Colorado in 1875. This was advice on how to proceed from one of the world's great skiers. Along with the lodge, he included:

> A small chopping hatchet, handle and all, 2½lbs. A pocket knife for each of us, two sheath knives and one revolver between us, a small .38-cal. Smith & Wesson— carried for fear of an accident. I could use it to build a fire or kill small game if we ran out of provisions. Then there were a small compass, a package of small screws of various sizes under 1½in. to mend broken snowshoes, and two miner's candles[22] each. We took a change of underclothing and socks, which were also to be used for extra clothing in extreme cold weather. Each had a pint cup. I took from here 5lbs. of sugar, 1lb. of best black tea, salt, 1,000 matches, ½lb. extract of beef, 2lbs. condensed soup. Bedding and

provisions for the camping out part of our trip I intended to get at the Upper Geyser Basin.

Billy and Jack Tansey could count on some resupply on the trail ahead. By this date, there were plenty of structures in the park, some of them substantial and valuable enough to require winter keepers. Some items of supply, however, had to be carried from the start:

> Clothing for a winter's trip through the mountains is one of the most difficult things to decide on, as it is very important that one should have sufficient, and still not be burdened with superfluous or useless garments. I used next to my body a fine undershirt, then an antelope skin—short sleeveless—shirt Indian dressed, a California flannel shirt, a woolen overshirt, vest and buckskin jumper; for my legs a pair of mission drawers, pantaloons and canvas overalls; for my feet fine cotton socks, calf boots and arctic overshoes, with canvas leggings tied on with buckskin strings. I used a common white felt hat, and for cold weather I had a jersey cloth hood and mask to draw down over my face, with two silk handkerchiefs to tie around my neck in windy weather, and smoked spectacles to protect my eyes from snow blindness.

Antelope skin, flannel, wool, buckskin, canvas, cotton, felt, silk—ad copywriters did not bother to use the term we see every day, "all natural ingredients," because they knew nothing else. No matter how heavy or inadequate his gear was, Billy was restricted to what nature provided. That rule of course extended to the men's most important items of gear:

> I had gloves and leather mittens for my hands, and I used long snowshoes—"skeys" or Norwegian—made of red fir, 9ft. long, 1in. thick, 4in. wide in the middle, tapering

to 3¾in. at the front, and 2¾in. at the back end. Fourteen
inches of the front was thinned down to ½in., steamed and
bent up so that the end was 8in. off the ground. The tops of
the shoes are beveled off, to allow the snow to slide off readily. The shoes were saturated with melted beeswax, candles,
linseed oil of equal parts, with a little rosin to harden the
mixture; this preparation was put on the shoes after first
heating them before an open fire. The bottoms were heated
enough to scorch them a little. After allowing them to cool,
I put a coat of shellac on the tops to keep melted snow from
wetting the wood. Measuring from the front end of the
shoe back 4ft., I put on a hard wood cross piece or cleat,
4in. long, 5/6in. wide, 1½in. thick, thinned down to ½in.
in the middle to allow the foot to fit in well. The projec-
tions assist the foot in guiding the shoe. Two inches in front
of the cross piece, two pieces of leather 4in. wide and 3in.
long were well fastened with screws to the side of the shoe
in a groove as deep as the leather was thick, so that nothing
should project beyond the side of the shoe. These pieces
were laced together to fit the foot. They came over the toe
and well back on the instep. The latter must not interfere
with the easy movement of the foot while walking.[23]

Articles in *Forest and Stream* were always, for the readership,
partly wish fulfillment and partly rudimentary guidebook. A minority of readers might actually want to try these things out; those
sentences about the ski measurements read like instructions because they were. Always, at the very least, a writer working for *Forest and Stream* could expect his readers to be daydreaming about
changing places with him. Skis were so new to Americans that we
not only needed a definition and pronunciation guide; the graphic
artists also provided a picture.

That is how outdoor travel was conducted by a world-class expert in 1887, perhaps one of the few such experts in the U.S. at that

time. And to think: not one bit of this stuff had been field tested by *Outside Magazine*.

In another one of his self-portraits with the plate-glass-negative camera given to him by Forest and Stream *magazine, here is Hofer eating a meal at home in his cabin, with cheesecake pictures on the wall.* COURTESY OF BRIGHAM YOUNG UNIVERSITY.

CHAPTER SIX

A Walk in the Park

Hofer and Tansey left Gardiner on February 12 and took it easy the first day, climbing the long hills to Mammoth Hot Springs, then to Swan Lake Flat. In the short piece that introduced the series on March 31, Grinnell had written that "but little game was seen" before the two reached the Hayden Valley, and he meant game that his readers might, in their imaginations, shoot. Fish and animals, the two saw constantly. Billy's reports are filled with them—but not just as lists. He included information about behavior and habitat, and more. When a sighting was beyond his knowledge as a naturalist, he had Grinnell to back him up in the magazine. Often, the scenes in Billy's descriptions matched exactly what we would see in the same places in twenty-first century Yellowstone. In a way that is fascinating—and, again, surreal—they often did not.

Given the animals they met, their trip up the Gardner River[1] falls for us into the "charming" category: there are the same cutthroat trout in the same deep holes in the Gardner, the same bighorn sheep that plop down in the road and stop traffic today, in the exact same places. The two skiers did not, at least, get stuck in a traffic jam. But Billy also made the following observation: "Water wrens [*Cinclus.—ED.*], queer little birds, were dashing in and out of the water seeking their food; they would sit on a rock, bob up and down a few times, then with a squeak dash into the water and out of sight, popping up in an unexpected place." Along the same stretch of the Gardner River today where the sheep routinely stop traffic, the twenty-first century visitor will find plenty of these birds, not wrens, but ouzels, or American dippers. They are easy to spot because, while they are small and slate gray and nothing spectacular to look at, that bobbing action is eye-catchingly distinctive; they then dive into the river and forage along the bottom, as if the water were not there. They were John Muir's favorite bird—it seems odd that he had a single favorite, but he did—because they confronted the most fearsome environments with such cheerful fearlessness.[2] Grinnell stepped in to correctly identify the genus as *Cinclus*. In spite of the name, American dipper, these individuals were almost certainly *Cinclus mexicana*.[3]

Arriving at the Cottage Hotel at Mammoth Hot Springs, they discovered that Pete Nelson, the park mailman, had been missing for two weeks and was presumed dead. Probably taken aback by this, they were additionally delayed for a day by a snowstorm, then skied first to one of Schwatka's old camps, then on to Norris, where they spent the night at the recently completed and empty hotel there. This pace was almost painfully deliberate for Billy, who would normally have traveled a minimum of fifty miles south after two days of skiing quickly by himself. Schullery has logically speculated that Billy was letting Tansey get accustomed to the skis.[4] When Billy guided Emerson Hough over the same trail in 1894, they covered the same distances over the same approximate periods of time, and Hough was just as new to skiing when they started. Acclimatization to the thin mountain air was also an issue. Billy appears to have worked out a detailed system for teaching people how to ski, making him, in addition to his other firsts, perhaps the nation's first professional ski instructor (he was, after all, getting paid for this by *Forest and Stream*).

Tansey took to the skis quickly enough, although the two men did not fall into a routine; what they got instead were surprises. Billy tried to be careful and "objective" in his reporting, but regularly let his personality slip into the narrative. The two were crossing Swan Lake Flat when he turned to look toward the distant Electric Peak. "All the high ridges exposed to the west wind were blown free from snow, and on them were several bands of elk feeding, I counted up to 120 in all; only four of them were old bulls; they were off to one side. The elk were in small bands of ten and fifteen; it was a beautiful sight. I could not resist the temptation to shout, and I gave one *whoo-pee!* I think every elk heard it and started for higher ground." Thoughtful skiers often avoid that sort of behavior today, because it stresses the already-hungry elk. It would not be surprising to learn that Billy was aware of that and just could not help himself.

The surprises could be pleasant, like the encounter with the elk, or they could remind us of what could go wrong. From the start, the two met a surprising number of travelers on the trail ("I began to think the woods were full of people," Billy commented). One was the missing mailman, Pete Nelson, who told a story that Billy related as an example of the kind of trouble that could develop for even the most experienced skier, and with what speed. When they met him, Billy reported:

> He had been very sick from a wetting he received in the Gibbon River on his way out. He had to cross on a log, at the further end of which there was a large snowdrift, in which he tried to beat a foothold with his snowshoe pole, when suddenly the whole drift gave away, knocking him off the log into the river, where the water was four feet deep. The snow rolled over him, and kept him under water for quite a while. When he finally got out, his matches were wet, so he could not build a fire to dry himself. He was six miles from Norris and twelve miles from the Lower Basin Hotel. He concluded to go on to the Geyser Basin. His

clothing soon froze like armor. He was hardly able to move. About half a mile further on, at the Beryl Hot Springs, he warmed up and thawed out his stiffened garments. Then by moving fast he kept warm; went on the next day to the Upper Basin, and there was taken sick from the effects of his wetting and exposure. This accounted for his being out in the Park so much longer than usual. We were glad to learn of his escape, for Pete Nelson is a good, reliable man and a first-class snowshoer.

Nelson was first class indeed. He also regularly repaired the park phone network, and for a period in the 1890s, the park superintendent had a rule: no one was allowed to travel alone by ski—except Snowshoe Pete, as he was then known. He was the only exception, thus surely lifting him to the rank Hofer assigned him: "first class."[5]

Or the surprises could be absurd, or hilarious. The next morning, a member of the growing party of travelers noticed a bottle twelve feet up a tree, above the level of the snow, perhaps five feet deep in that spot. Climbing to retrieve it, they discovered it to be an empty bottle of Fine Old McBrayer Whiskey. Written on the label, in the white space between the distiller's printing, they found, in uneven handwriting that read like a message from Captain Scott of the Antarctic, "Schwatka / Jan. 7 / Thermometer –51° / Placed on the level of the snow." Billy was mildly, very mildly perplexed as to how the bottle got there. He knew that, on this part of the road on January 7, the snow had still only been three feet deep, even here in 1887. "As there was nothing in the bottle but air I concluded that the whole thing was a misstatement and that the high winds had blown and lodged the bottle in the tree.... Strange things happen in the Park."

Billy peeled off the label for a souvenir. Grinnell made a photographic reproduction of it and ran it as a mock-serious illustration. Poor Schwatka. Grinnell's readership exploded in hilarity at his expense. The correspondence from the readers turned into an exer-

cise in citizen science, attempting to explain the latest Yellowstone
mystery, the 12-foot-high bottle. In the April 14 issue, Grinnell
gave the results:

> For example, a correspondent who has devoted a great
> deal of anxious thought to the subject of the bottle in the
> tree, advances the ingenious theory that at the time it was
> put in position twelve feet above the level of the snow, the
> whole [Schwatka] party was elevated to that extent. This
> might account for the inscription on the label, and if the
> hypothesis be correct it opens up a series of interesting ques-
> tions as to the possibilities of 'Fine Old McBrayer.' If this
> fluid possess such lifting power as suggested, it will naturally
> attract the attention of aeronauts, those who go up in the air
> in balloons.[6]

Billy spent February 16 taking an extended tour of Norris Geyser Basin and writing it up in fulfillment of one of Grinnell's re-
quests, that he bring back an account of the geyser basins in winter.
By this point in the history of the park, the thermal features were
no longer the stark-raving novelty they had been. Hundreds of descriptions had been published,[7] enough that a kind of literary genre
had come into existence, the Visit to the Geysers, involving a great
deal of purple prose and multiple metaphors invoking Hell. Billy
in fact knew that this very sort of thing was expected of him, but he
gave it his personal stamp. As Schullery noted, the result resembled
less the conventional geyser visit than something out of Edgar Allan Poe, and Billy's prose made it seem that way:

> A heavy fog hung over the country, with a light snow. As
> I approached the Basin, I was startled by the resemblances
> to men and animals the ice-laden trees showed, as, standing
> sentinel duty on each side of the road, they appeared to be
> watching our approach. Everything was loaded down with

steam frozen as it had drifted from the geysers. There were
fantastic forms of men and women looking into the pools.
Up the road were seen hogs, rabbits, mules, elephants, leop-
ards, tigers, cats and dogs; animals of all kinds and shapes,
creatures that outside of the Park nothing but a disordered
mind could conjure up. All were in white, but often with
dark eyes, ears and mouth, or limbs or faces, where the deep
green of the pines showed through the white ice. Now and
then a bough free from frost projected through the ice to
form the plume of a soldier or the ears of a mule or rabbit.
Again there appeared the form of a woman holding a child,
bending over it as if to protect it from the wintry blast. Others there were with groups of children gathered about them,
all in white, as though just escaping from their burning
homes; and it wanted but the red glow of a sunset to make
the illusion complete; the steam looked like smoke, while
the confused sounds of the geysers resembled the burning
and crackling of flames and the crash of falling buildings.
I was alone with all this mysterious, ghostly band, and I
confess to a strange sensation amid these weird surroundings
as I descended into the basin through the fog.[8]

Toward the end, it is less like Edgar Allan Poe than something the
world had not yet seen: an air raid. Or something the world and
Billy had seen: the 1871 Chicago fire.

Having given Grinnell one of the major reports he had asked
for, Hofer now gave him another, a wildlife sighting well worth
saving:

Wolverine and lynx tracks were seen every few rods; one
can follow with his eyes the attempts of the lynx to catch
rabbit for his dinner. They never make many jumps, only
about three; if they miss a rabbit then they give it up and
try another. These rabbits can make as long a jump as a

lynx, and can outrun a lynx on the snow. When a rabbit hides in the snow he is unsafe. I noticed places where a lynx had been diving for a rabbit; into his hole he would go, the rabbit getting away from it and making for another place to hide, only to have the lynx down on him again; and so it went on until the rabbit was overtaken by the lynx. A little blood stain showed where the hunt had ended. A lynx sinks but little in the snow, its very large feet prevent its light body from sinking much more than a rabbit.[9]

Schullery also called attention to this scene because it is one of a number of observational nuggets in Billy's series, and there have been developments since Schullery wrote that only strengthen his point. The "rabbits" were actually snowshoe hares, common at Norris, then and now. Wolverines, however, are rare today in Yellowstone, and the lynx is the nearest thing to a ghost. The animal Billy spoke of here is the Canada lynx, *Lynx canadensis*. An intensive survey, conducted inside the park between 2001 and 2004, found just four lynxes.[10] In 2007 and again in 2010, lynxes showed up in the park wearing radio collars. Yellowstone's tracking ace, Gardiner-based biologist Jim Halfpenny, believes these animals wandered from a site in Colorado where wildlife authorities are restoring the lynx population.[11] Yellowstone's own population is minuscule. Since these were not the only lynx tracks Billy would find during his trip—he found many—they suggest a change in population, although it takes a great many such sightings to draw anything like a conclusion.[12]

Billy and Tansey left for the Lower Geyser Basin at 3 a.m. on February 17 (Billy commonly started a ski in darkness, for the firmer, less sticky snow that the cold provided—and hence the need for miners' candles). They weathered a blizzard and the avalanche zone in the Gibbon River canyon, which had almost undone Snowshoe Pete, but where Billy, as we have seen, decided there was "no danger here at all." They arrived, that evening at 6:00, at the Lower

Geyser Basin hotel (the former "Marshall's Hotel," also known as the Firehole Hotel).

They visited with the J.H. Dean family, friends of Billy of course, who were winter-keeping the hotel. The weather was so bad that Dean wrote the *Livingston Enterprise* just to declare how bad it was: "for the past nineteen days," he reported in a letter dated February 5, "the wind has been blowing a gale and the snow drifting mountains high. Indeed, I have never witnessed such storms, nor have I ever read of any to equal what we have had here."[13] Billy spent the 18th building a new pair of skis for Tansey, from scratch, another sight you will not often see in the park today. The pair had now arrived at the lower edge of the most extensive and spectacular geyser fields in the park and surely the world, the aggregate collection that lines the Firehole River starting far upstream at Lone Star Geyser, then running through the Upper, Middle, and Lower geyser basins and innumerable smaller side basins and individual features. Today, most attention is focused on the Upper Geyser Basin, where Old Faithful Geyser is the star and a not-so-small village has grown up to support the intense traffic. During the 1880s, more attention focused on the Middle and Lower basins, where there were some spectacular performers during this period.[14]

Here was plenty of the kind of visual entertainment that Grinnell wanted, so once Tansey's skis were done, Billy went out and got it, touring all the major features, if in no great rush. As he did so, he continued to make the observations he had all along. Dean had been keeping weather statistics, some of which Billy reproduced, with a focus on the snowfall: "a total of 153in. or 12ft. 9in., a very respectable amount of snow" had fallen since October, "considering that March and April are very snowy months, some years as much falling in these two months as in all the others put together." The result, around the hotel, was the kind of entombment that remains a striking feature of the region, during those years when the skies open up: "The snow was drifted around the buildings in immense piles. This hotel is the only one at all exposed to the wind, the others are sheltered either by timber or hills. Around each building on three sides would be a narrow space, the snow drifted in perpendicular walls. On the other or north side it will be piled up against the building 7 and 8ft. deep."[15]

The whole "Winter in Wonderland" series is filled with vignettes of life in the midwinter park during this era, a time during which the place was changing quickly: it was no longer as deserted as it had been when Billy first knew it. The telephone network was in place, for instance, although it was a constant struggle to keep the lines up during the winter. "On the 20th, a bright cold morning, the thermometer reading –21, we started from the Upper Basin," Billy reported. "As the telephone wire was down we took a piece to repair it, expecting to find it broken where it passes over a hot spring where, when it is very cold, the wire gets heavily loaded with frost from the steam." On the way, they made another sighting that flirts with the surreal, for the Yellowstone enthusiast today:

> Soon after crossing the Fire Hole River, I saw a very large lynx. I called Jack's attention to him and he thought it was a lion until he saw there was no long tail. A little further on we came to a place where the lynx had watched our approach. Wishing to know more about us he had crossed the road and was passing to the windward of us when I saw him. He was grayish on his back, had reddish gray sides and light gray belly—a Canadian lynx and a very large animal of its kind. Its track measured 4in. wide and 6in. long. It did not stop long in sight, but soon disappeared in the timber. I gave a cat-like call, hoping to stop it, which I did, but it was behind some brush and out of sight. Here it stayed a moment and then trotted on.

The lynx had just walked right out in front of him. Today, you will look for decades before you see one. And they would find more lynx tracks later in the day.

But it was not all wild savagery: as noted, Yellowstone was changing. Tansey and Billy's purpose, after all, was partly to fix the telephone line. They next ran into the Roake family, from Old Faithful, on skis and running the same errand that Billy and Tansey were, looking for the line break. The story now took an amiably domestic turn, and Billy showed us family life at the Upper Geyser Basin during the worst winter ever.

It turned out not to be so bad. James Roake skied up, winter keeper of the hotel at the Upper Geyser Basin, "and his son Willie, a 12-year old boy, both out on snowshoes, the boy being able to do his ten miles in a day with anyone." They had already repaired the break and, knowing that the Special Commissioner from *Forest and Stream* and party were along the line somewhere, they had come to find them. Headed for the Upper Geyser Basin, they met 14-year-old Bert Roake, also on skis. Arriving at the basin, they skied up to the Roake home:

> Mr. Roake and his family were living in the loghouse in front of the hotel, which they had fixed up for the winter. We soon came in sight of a stove-pipe above a bank of snow which showed where the cabin was. We could just see the top of the house when we got on the same level with it. The snow through this section had settled considerably, as was shown by little mounds 2ft. high around every tree, bush and stump; still, on a level, there was 7ft. of snow. Soon an object came up out of the snow which proved to be another son of Mr. Roake, Harry, a little fellow seven years old, and soon a little girl four years old popped up out of the entrance to the cabin to tell us that the telephone was all right. We soon descended into the cabin, and were surrounded by these children, whose nearest neighbors were ten miles away—too far for a call except over the telephone, which they all use. Sending to Mr. and Mrs. Dean word of our arrival, we were soon sitting down to a good meal, and, as

this was to be our last stopping place before striking out for the forests and streams, and lakes and rivers of the Shoshone and Yellowstone country, we made the most of it....

The evening we spent with Mr. and Mrs. Roake's happy family. All the children know how to play chess, an unusual thing in the mountains. Even the four-year-old Topsy played two games. I left my king exposed to see if she would notice it, which she did, mating me at once.[16]

But this would be the last of the domestic bliss for a while. Billy and Tansey spent a leisurely two days looking at the thermal features, then, fortified by eight pounds of oatmeal biscuits provided by Mrs. Roake to fill out their food supply—their packs now 25 pounds, mostly food—they hit the trail again on February 23.

They now had to tackle the Continental Divide. One of Yellowstone's millions of oddities, the divide crosses the southern part of the park in such a way that travelers moving on a west-east axis normally have to cross it multiple times. The weather drew a bead on them immediately: "Soon after leaving the Fire Hole River it began to snow, hiding the sun, so that we had to travel by guess work, as all signs of a trail and most of the land marks were hid."[17] Firehole River water runs into the Madison, then the Missouri, then the Mississippi. They were now making for Shoshone Lake, which feeds the Snake and ultimately Columbia Rivers. Slowed by the snowfall, they set up Billy's "Indian lodge" for the first time and reached Shoshone Lake the next day. Still moving east, headed for Yellowstone Lake, they crossed the Divide again (Yellowstone River water mingles with Firehole River water in the Missouri River). The weather was now, however, truly acting like 1887. As they left Shoshone Lake,

We went into a grove of timber, made a fire and lunched. The snow here was very deep. I could not reach bottom with my 7-foot pole. The absence of all game, the impos-

sibility of seeing anything—for the falling snow shut out the
mountains—made this a very desolate country. Shoulder-
ing our packs we struck out in an easterly direction, until
we found a water course which I wished to follow up to the
summit of the divide. At length we reached the top—a high
country, somewhat level with groves and openings. Here for
the first time I had to use the compass; the wind and snow
came from so many ways at once.[18]

Billy wanted to reach Yellowstone Lake. There were only a few
places in the entire "Winter in Wonderland" series in which Billy
revealed a trace of anxiety. Here was one: the weather had turned
on him, and he wanted very much to get away from this baffling
landscape and onto the security of the known: Yellowstone Lake.
Tansey was, however, not strong enough to reach the lake before
nightfall. They broke out the teepee again and made it to the shore
after a cold morning spent trying to dry out from the storm.

The weather gave them only occasional breaks. They toured the
thermal area at West Thumb, then cut across the Thumb itself—
across that bay of the lake, skiing on the frozen lake itself with
its several feet of snow on top of the ice—to reach a point on the
Thumb's northern shore at the outlet to the main body of the lake.
After a search, Billy found solid ice again, thermals having melted
some of it, and they started skiing across the frozen surface of Yellowstone Lake. The weather attacked again:

The wind had been increasing all the morning, and was
now blowing a gale from the west-southwest. As this was
offshore, we did not feel it until well out on the lake. Clouds
of snow were flying in the air and along the surface of the
ice. We could see only a short distance ahead in a horizon-
tal line, but looking up we could see the bluffs and timber
for some distance. We had as yet seen no game on the lake
shore, except a few ducks in the warm water. After passing

Bluff Point we saw what we at first took to be animals. They were 250yds. from the shore, and the flying clouds of snow would make them come and go, appear and disappear as though they were running around. We soon found they were stumps of upturned trees on a little rocky island.[19] Owing to the storm and the flying *poudre,* everything we saw changed thus. We would see a point ahead, then it would be entirely hid for a long time, then would suddenly show up again, now near, and then would move off until out of sight again.

Nor could even the ice itself be trusted, even once they were well away from the shoreline thermal areas. The farther they went, the creepier it got:

> Every few rods I sounded the depth of snow, which was from 8in. to 2ft. When far out from shore I once ran the pole into 6in. of water under 8in. of dry snow. Going on further I struck more water. I had not felt the ice under the water and did not like to stop until I was off this kind of ground, so next time I tried the snow I used considerable force and pushed the small end of the pole through a foot of dry snow and a foot of water and snow down to solid ice. This was all I cared for. I did not mind the water on the ice as long as there was dry snow enough to keep my shoes out of it. Jack was some distance behind me and had been watching my movements, and was naturally somewhat interested. He would try every hole I did with like results, and he said his hair stood up when I did not strike ice through the water. Soon the ice was again dry under the snow, then it became again wet. When we wanted a drink of water all we had to do was to feel down until we found it on the ice, then clear a place away and dip it up. I think the ice was broken into great cakes, the weight of snow sinking the cakes in places enough to have the water come on top.

The two men passed another night in the lodge, then traveled alternately over timber and lake ice toward the point at which the Yellowstone River leaves the lake. The weather combined with the ice conditions to make life ever creepier while they were skiing the lake. Billy had thought he had felt the ice heaving in West Thumb. Now it left no doubt: "Soon we were out in the main part of the lake once more. Again I felt the raising and falling I noticed on the west arm; the further out we went the more I noticed it. I stopped and waited until Jack came up, and asked him if he noticed the motion. He said he did, but at first thought it was something wrong with himself. Before getting to the outlet I found the undulations increased still more. I expected to hear some noise as the ice rose and fell, but the wind drowned it if there was any."

At two o'clock in the afternoon of the 26th, they reached the cabin at Topping Point where Billy and his cousin had launched their first Yellowstone venture seven years earlier. Finding it full of snow and nearly invisible, they continued north on the wagon road. He had already provided his employer with plenty, but now Billy gave editor Grinnell what he really wanted. After lunch at Mud Volcano, the pair skied north into the vast open rolling meadow that is Hayden Valley. Here, they began to find the kind of animals, and in the kind of quantities, that sent a thrill through the average *Forest and Stream* reader.

They found elk in the valley, then skied on to the small, primitive hotel at Canyon—it was buried, but they spotted the roof, and a smoking stovepipe. The smoking stovepipe was a crucial navigation beacon, during this era. They first made what was now a familiar sighting: "Following the river down we entered the timber below Alum Creek; here was more lynx sign; they had run all over the country. I could see where they evidently had their quarters, as, from under overturned trees and other places, on the steep side hills their trails lead, the snow all patted down around them. These lynxes are large enough to kill a young elk, which I am quite sure they do, as there is a great number of them."[20] There are countless animals in the "Winter in Wonderland" series, and I have given extended attention to the lynx because it is a clear instance of Billy's observations revealing an important change over the past century and a half. At this point, given the evidence Billy provided, we have to conclude that there were significantly more lynx in the park then than now.

Billy got the news from Canyon, and soon after they arrived, the indestructible Pete Nelson skied in. The park phone lines were now up, and the news went out that Hofer and Tansey were alive. People around the region were wondering, given the weather. The two then spent four days at Canyon, counting the animals and looking at the sights. A special feature of the larger waterfalls in Yellowstone is the ice cone that forms across the falls during a cold winter, spray freezing from the sides to eventually join in the middle and completely cover the still-flowing water beneath. The average *Forest and Stream* reader had not seen that, so Billy gave them a word-picture, although on this instance he may have overdone it. During their era, there were no guardrails, and "safe" was a matter of entirely personal judgment. He skied to the brink of the Lower Falls of the Yellowstone River, 300-plus-feet tall and raging like a madman:[21]

> The ice on the river projected 15ft. out over the falls, curving down on the outer edge until out of sight. Going near the brink the most beautiful frost work in the whole park was to be seen. Words could never describe this grand sight. On the south side the whole precipice from the river up and away around for hundreds of feet was one mass of ice and frost work.
>
> Up for about 200ft. from the river, the ice was in the form of gigantic icicles from 1ft. to 200ft. long. Above this the ice was more like a great bed of flowers, on edge masses of flowers, clusters, bunches and bouquets, projecting out from the rest; globular-shaped pendant clusters of

ice, the surface covered with pearly frostwork like frozen
dew drops, or the iridescent formation of the geysers, for
100 and 200ft. more. All this was not without color. The
flowers were delicately shaded from a dark straw color to
white, the icicles a faint blue, green and yellow. The whole
of the cliff was overhung with a fringe of icicles from the top
almost pure white. The top of the cliff and timber back of
it was coated with fine ice that glittered as the sun shone on
it from over the edge of the cañon above. Two dead trees,
whose ice-coated tops were in the sunshine, looked like electric lights, they were so bright. The sun striking the other
side of the highly colored cañon cast a golden glow over the
whole scene impossible to describe.

Going to the platform and venturing out as far as one
dared, I looked down to see the ice bridge formed across
the river. This reached up at least one-third of the height of
the falls, and was crescent-shaped, leaving an immense hole,
into which the water poured; below this bridge the river was
open.[22]

Where do we begin in analyzing this scene? First, Billy needed
specialized ice-climbing axes and then specialized ice-climbing
crampons. He might even have thought of a rope—although Tansey had no idea how to belay. But of course, except for the rope,
none of those things existed yet. Throughout the "Winter in Wonderland" series, Billy had been promising descriptions of what he
called, over and over, the "delicate frost work" characteristic of the
park waters in deep winter. It would be Grinnell's best "McGuf-
fin," and Billy did what was necessary to give Grinnell what he
needed.

Billy was not just providing entertainment, however. His editor
had a very serious purpose in mind. After all, Grinnell was among
the first to see Yellowstone in a new way, certainly not the very first,
but he was an important early voice arguing that this new kind of

place was not just a museum of oddities. They had not intended to, but when Congress and President Grant created Yellowstone National Park, in protecting the geology, they accidentally protected everything else. In 1872, no one noticed or cared. By 1887, Grinnell did not need his Yale Ph.D. to see that the landscapes and wildlife of North America had no future unless radical steps were taken. The systematic destruction of the continental bison herd is the best known example of the great slaughter, but every animal worth shooting was disappearing fast. Hunting inside the park had become illegal in 1883. Here, Grinnell knew, was a place where really large populations of really large animals—and everything else—might weather the general holocaust and be available to repopulate the surrounding landscape at some future date when, for reasons as yet unimagined, a sane balance could be restored.

Grinnell's plan ultimately worked. Although many were scarce, all the animals that Yellowstone had begun the nineteenth century with were still there when the twentieth dawned, and the twenty-first. For generations, game animals have been born and raised in the park, only to wander over the line into one of the massive national forests that border the park on every side, where they have become fair game for hunters, often well-heeled out-of-staters, to the delight of the local merchants. Animal populations that should have died out, did not, the grizzly bear and the bison most prominently. His idea caught on, and before long Grinnell had powerful allies, among them a future president. "What has been actually accomplished in the Yellowstone Park affords the best possible object-lesson as to the desirability and practicability of establishing such wilderness reserves," President Theodore Roosevelt wrote in 1905, after his presidential visit to Yellowstone. "This reserve is a natural breeding-ground and nursery for those stately and beautiful haunters of the wilds which have now vanished from so many of the great forests, the vast lonely plains, and the high mountain ranges, where they once abounded."[23]

Bison were near the top of Billy Hofer's list of animals that

Grinnell wanted him to watch for, but right alongside them were the elk, *Cervus canadensis*. Today, the International Union for the Conservation of Nature, the non-governmental organization that maintains the so-called "Red List" of species threatened with extinction, ranks the elk as a species of "Least Concern." There is no shortage today. It is fascinating to compare the situation now with that during the later nineteenth century, when the most informed observers assumed that the elk were just as doomed as the bison and for the same reason: indiscriminate, industrial-scale market hunting. If Yellowstone was going to serve as a nursery for game animals, Grinnell must have thought, the first step should logically be to send the most reliable local observer in to survey the populations and describe the habitat—and to do so, again, in an entertaining way and so win converts. That was Billy Hofer's task during this winter of 1886-1887.

Hofer and Tansey left Canyon on April 4, skiing north over Dunraven Pass to Pleasant Valley—close to the present-day Roosevelt Lodge and Tower Junction—where they put up at Yancey's. Uncle John Yancey, one of the fixtures of the park, operated a hotel there. An old friend to Billy, Yancey was glad to see the pair: "Here we learned people were discussing our trip," wrote Hofer, "some going so far as to say they never expected to see us again."[24] The most difficult part of the trip was indeed over. There remained only a (relatively) short ski-run[25] across the (relatively) mild northern range, and a warm welcome at Mammoth Hot Springs.

From the time they had arrived at Hayden Valley, Billy had been seeing more and more elk. On the north face of Mt. Washburn, they seemed to multiply, and Billy counted them as carefully as he could. Near the end of the "Winter in Wonderland" series, he gave the results: "We had made the round trip through the Park, as we intended to do when we started out, 160 miles on snowshoes. Counting in addition to this the side trips made, I traveled 225 miles." (Today's Connecticut, we might note in passing, is 110 miles wide at its widest). "We camped out six nights, suffered no hardships or privation, and withal had a most enjoyable time. To be sure, we made no wonderful discoveries, for there are none to be made; the Park is too well known for that. My purpose in going through the Park was to see its winter features and to learn something about the game there."[26]

He had a few surprises left to offer, where the park's animals were concerned. Crucially, he estimated actual numbers of elk and bison in the park during a time when no one else had, and thus his statements stand tall as the only near park-wide, early appraisal of these numbers:

> I can only give estimates in regard to the game. When it was possible I counted them, but still, one never sees all there are. To count all would require "a round up."
>
> On the ridges around the Washburne there are at least 150 elk; about the falls, 50; on Specimen Ridge and the section of the Park to the north, at least 2,000; on Black Tail, Lava, Elk and Lost creeks, and country north of Tower Creek, some 1,600; in the country between Mammoth Hot Springs and the Madison Mountains, some 500. I know nothing of the number on the west side of these mountains. On Alum Creek and the country across the river there are elk, but how many I do not know. Perhaps 200 would be a large estimate, though some people put it as high as 800. In the south end of the Park I do not think the elk winter, but come in very early in the spring. Not counting these, this would give us 4,500 elk in the Park this winter. A few of the best hunters, men who do not get excited when they see a hundred elk and say there are a thousand, think there are from 7,000 to 8,000: but I cannot think so, judging from the number I have counted in the country spoken of. One thing noticeable is the very small number of bulls older than two years old seen. On our trip not over fifteen were found. In one place where there were over a hundred cows and

calves, there were but five bulls, and this, too, in a country where I could see almost all the game. We may be sure that the bulls we saw are not all there are by a long way. Some of the reasons for this disproportion of bulls to cows are these: The bulls are killed in summer because they are the best meat up to the running season.[27] After that they are killed for their heads and horns for specimens. Then, too, a bull is easier to be found and approached than a cow, especially in the fall, for one sometimes goes up to a band of horses or a man on horseback just to see what they are, unless he has the wind of them.

Of bison I saw but thirty. I believe, however, that there are between 200 and 300 in the Park. Some people think there are not even fifty, as the high price paid for them, $50 to $75 for fine heads and hides, has induced hunters to kill them off and to take great risks of detection for the money offered.

So there were elk in the park, plenty of them, and as Billy freely admitted, his census was partial. That was the good news. Finding only thirty bison was unsettling. At this date, Billy still accepted the standard census figure of several hundred animals, but he would soon join the ranks of those who thought there were far fewer, because poaching was ever-present. Something would have to be done, and as events developed, Billy would be at the center of it.

CHAPTER SEVEN
National Park, National Limelight

The five lengthy installments—essentially a short book—that made up the "Winter in Wonderland" series had an immediacy about them that created the illusion that the adventure was happening as Billy wrote it. Of course, the actual journey was weeks in the past as the series ran, Billy writing from the warmth and comfort of home, in what was the only way he could have done it. So, even before his "Winter in Wonderland" series wrapped up, Billy commenced his regular column-writing work for *Forest and Stream*, which would continue, off and on, until 1920.

On April 21, in a story datelined Mammoth Hot Springs, he wrote in with the kind of park news that *Forest and Stream* readers wanted: the condition and location of the game animals, and the epic weather. He included a bit of news about the ice cone over the Lower Falls of the Yellowstone, the one onto which he had climbed. His readers would probably have already guessed that the cone was not the most stable platform from which to view the canyon. His news confirmed that guess: "All the great cliffs on each side of the upper and lower falls, which were so beautifully ornamented by frozen spray during the winter months, are now free from ice. When it commenced to go, great masses would fall into the cañon with a sound like distant thunder"—another heroic Yellowstone phenomenon that few had ever seen or heard.[1] The elk, blacktail deer, antelope, and mountain sheep were making the annual spring migration to higher ground, and so were no longer as visible as they had been (a phenomenon that frustrates the summer tourist to this day). Other animals were making the same shift, but he focused on what he had seen, or of which he had reliably heard.

Another article appeared on May 5, datelined Mammoth. The weather had turned nasty and some of the animals were reversing course back to lower elevations. The turn in the weather was, he noted, simply normal for this date (and probably this era): "We are having our spring snows now, making it very unpleasant for those who have to be out in them. They wet one through in a short time if not well clad; they come up very suddenly and sometimes last but a few minutes, at others developing into a blizzard which kills off many poor and weak animals of all kinds. Elk and other game that have struggled through a very severe winter will often die soon after one of these cold spring storms."[2] These articles covered a wide range of park matters: $20,000, for instance, was to be available on July 1 for an extensive summer road-building program. There had also been a spectacular case of poaching, for the details of which we will return.

Billy was normally reporting on the movement of animals specifically inside the park, but a *Forest and Stream* reader on his way to Montana or Wyoming to hunt would be grateful for any information about regional wildlife habits. He and Grinnell never followed a set schedule with articles like these, which nevertheless developed into an informal column that ran off and on for decades, news on conditions in Yellowstone from the one source that *Forest and Stream* readers could trust as much as anyone. They make repetitive reading today—the phrase "I saw elk," in some variant, must occur hundreds of times—but reading them all at once is to violate their spirit. They were news, appearing at intervals of weeks or months, and I suspect that the original readers, nearly all hunters, found them riveting.[3]

The two articles excerpted above can stand as representative of the content of Billy's shorter work. They made it clear that because of poachers, the weather, and the dead-end quality of the food under all that snow, if Yellowstone were to be a "natural breeding-ground and nursery for those stately and beautiful haunters of the wilds," it needed help. One of the great strengths of the working relationship between Grinnell and Hofer was that they looked at a problem and tended to see similar solutions.

Billy was already on board with the idea that Yellowstone should serve as an ongoing refuge and nursery. "I saw one band of mountain sheep several times," he reported of a group just outside the boundary, "each time a little nea[r]er to the great national game preserve, where they can live, have their young, grow fat and enjoy life until forced out by deep snows."[4] This marked the first occasion Billy had spoken of Yellowstone that way, as a "great national game preserve." The snow could not be controlled, but such travesties as the poaching could. In the future, working especially through *Forest and Stream* and his many contacts, Billy would strive to strengthen every kind of protection the park needed. So, to even greater effect, would Grinnell. Their enemies would be devious and almost pathologically persistent. Followed through *Forest and Stream*, park affairs could seem like one long, barely contained insurrection. This effect was inevitable. Because Yellowstone was the first national park, no one could quite say what its boundaries meant. No hunting, yes—but did that mean no fishing? No homesteading, yes—but did that mean no railroads? No collecting of specimens in the thermal areas, yes—but did that mean no collecting of arrowheads, elk antlers, not-especially-rare rocks, or common flowers? There were no precedents for these rules, if they were even going to become rules. Among others, Grinnell and his team set about helping to create and build them.

Already a local celebrity, the 1887 ski made Billy, in a modest way at least, a national celebrity. For instance, the *New York Herald*, then one of the nation's major newspapers, covered the journey at great length, reprinting large sections of "Winter in Wonderland" in a series that ran in the *Herald* in April and May, 1887.[5] A certain outdoorsy subset of newspaper readers in the more populous sections of the country were coming to recognize the name "Hofer" when it appeared in *Forest and Stream* and elsewhere. And Billy did not just report the news. Although "Winter in Wonderland" would be his longest single, written work, he would also produce lengthy features in which he described a major project he had taken on. These longer stories have a further advantage in that they often focused on a topic which had interested him for years and so help us today fill in his activities during his earliest years in the region, when the records are otherwise cloudy or scarce. And it was not all about the elk, of course. Few people today are aware of, for instance, the extraordinary impacts on the underwater world of the park. It would make sense that a man raised sailing sharpies in New Haven Harbor and Long Island Sound would take an interest in fish. Billy Hofer did not lose that interest when he wandered into the mountains and took equal interest in the new, underwater landscapes that he would encounter there. It began when he first heard of Two Ocean Pass early in his Yellowstone career and decided instantly to visit the place, despite its utter isolation. It was the fish that did it for him.

To understand Two Ocean Pass and the interest it held for him, we need to back up. Specifically, we need to back up 640,000 years, give or take ten thousand. Perhaps the single most important truth to understand about what we call Yellowstone is that it is in its infancy—geologically, that is. At the same time, while even the most distracted visitor can tell that the place is somehow volcanic, it does not look like a "volcano," or in places even like "the mountains." A typical Yellowstone landscape is a high, rolling, forested plateau, with nothing that looks like Mounts Vesuvius or Fuji. The reason is that, through much of the southern half of the park, the visitor is actually inside the volcano. It has erupted repeatedly, with the most recent major event having occurred 640,000 years ago—a mere twinkling, on an earth that is today believed to be 4.5 billion years old.

The ancient eruptions created what geologists call *calderas*, ultimately from the Latin for "cauldron," appropriately. We know today that the vast magma chamber under Greater Yellowstone periodically empties itself, the caldera collapses, then refills with primarily rhyolite lava flows that give us a landscape that, while it bubbles and steams, rarely looks like the volcanoes in science class. The violence of such an event leaves the thesaurus whimpering in inadequacy.

To provide a comparison, when Mount St. Helens exploded in Washington State in 1980, covering much of the West with ash, it ejected between one-quarter and one-half of a cubic mile of volcanic rock. During the first eruption in Greater Yellowstone, the earth ejected six hundred cubic miles of material. In effect, Yellowstone was Mount St. Helens multiplied over five thousand times, each St. Helens erupting at once.

And geologists say it will likely happen again. What we call "Yellowstone National Park" sits atop what those researchers rather cutely call a hotspot, a stationary spot in the earth's mantle that, as the continental plate rides over it, leaves a linear trail of eruptions. The phenomenon is easiest to see in action by looking at a map of Hawaii, where a similar hotspot drives the volcanoes. As the seafloor tracks over the hotspot, magma periodically issues forth to make a new island and, given time, a new tourist paradise. The Hawaiian magma is, however, basaltic, typical of a seafloor, and gasses trapped in the rock escape through the molten fluid in relative peace. The chemistry of the rock in Yellowstone is such that it holds those gasses until the rock can hold them no more and violence follows.[6]

The pioneering scientists whom Billy spent much of his life guiding had only the crudest understanding of these matters, and knowledge of the hotspot today comes ultimately from the twentieth-century revolution in plate tectonics. The hotspot, however, determined everything they saw, especially the earliest explorers, because Yellowstone is akin to a blackboard that is periodically wiped entirely clean.

That scouring was most obvious in the park's waters, which were substantially barren of fish when Billy arrived. Park Historian Aubrey Haines explained the situation. While fish were plentiful in places,

> On the other hand, the explorers of 1869 found the Lower Geyser Basin barren of fish, a condition they were inclined to attribute to some noxious effects of the locality, and the subsequent discovery that the drainage of the Gibbon River was likewise uninhabited by fish led to a belief that there was not much to be hoped for—fish-wise—in streams that were warmed by hot springs and chemically impregnated. Indeed, this empirical view of the barren waters in the western half of the park persisted even after it should have been obvious that the absence of fish was the result of the obstruction of stream channels by waterfalls.

The park's barren waters attracted no attention until 1889, when Captain F. A. Boutelle, who was an enthusiastic angler, initiated a program of stocking the barren streams and lakes. He reported:

> In passing through the Park I noticed with surprise the barrenness of most of the water of the Park. Besides the beautiful Shoshone and other smaller lakes there are hundreds of miles of as fine streams as any in existence without a fish of any kind. I have written Col. Marshall McDonald, U.S. Fish Commission, upon the subject, and have received letters from him manifesting a great interest....

McDonald visited the Park that summer and decided

upon a rudimentary program. This called for the immediate stocking of some streams (brook trout for Glen Creek and the Gardner River above its falls, rainbow trout for the Gibbon River above Virginia Cascades, Loch Leven [brown] trout for the Firehole River above Kepler Cascades, mountain white fish for Twin Lakes and the Yellowstone River between the lake and the falls, and blackspotted or "native" [cutthroat] trout for Lava Creek above its falls), and for a reconnaissance by David Starr Jordan as a basis for all future fish-planting activity.[7]

But in fact, there had been previous interest in the barren waters. Billy had, by 1889, explored all of them as part of his daily work, sorting barren waters from non-barren ones as places to take clients. One of his first appearances in *Forest and Stream* came of this exploration. A client caught a five pound "trout"—it would have to have been a Yellowstone cutthroat, at that date—in the Yellowstone River on February 24, 1886. A fish that big was thought at the time to be a record for the river, and when the client could not resist sending a paper pattern of the fish to *Forest and Stream*, Billy wrote in to witness it.[8] This small incident showed that he did not merely work as a packer for grizzly hunters. When the Fish Commission showed up, they fell quite naturally into his hands.

Again, Billy Hofer's interest in the aquatic life of the park began with his first full view of the place. Near the end of his long 1879 tour, recall, he had fallen in at Gibbon Meadows with Superintendent Norris and Luther "Yellowstone" Kelly. They and another guide whose name had slipped Billy's memory "were telling of Two Ocean Pass." "This interested me," he wrote, "and I treasured the same in my memory, intending some day to see it."[9]

Happily, that ambition would work together with his new "assignment." Again, the first Northern Pacific Railroad train arrived at Livingston in November, 1882, and the line reached Bozeman shortly afterward. In his reminiscences, Billy recalled what happened after the railroad reached Bozeman as the crucial moment for him: "The N. P. was completed past Bozeman, and tourists were flocking in. I was busy every summer with parties on trips."[10] The term "flocking" is today worth a smile from us in its context. The total annual number of visitors to the park is believed to have reached one thousand in 1880-1882, then five thousand from 1883-1887, and six thousand at the end of the decade.[11] These are obviously estimates, but by contrast, the number today looks set never to go below four million again. The net effect of this new work was that Billy was learning every hole and corner of the region.

A striking instance of how well he knew his way around even by 1884 occurred in "Winter in Wonderland," during one of the more ominous moments in the story, when Billy and Tansey were trying to fight their way over the Continental Divide and reach Yellowstone Lake in a snowstorm, the one that was so disorienting that Billy had to break out his compass for the first time. And yet he still had a sense of where he was: "now and then I saw a grove that looked familiar, though I had been through here but once, in 1884."[12] One major advantage he had was a nearly photographic memory for topography. A few more years of this, and Billy would have a map imprinted on his mind superior to anything in park headquarters or Washington, DC. He was even apologetic about using the compass. He felt as if he were being fussy and should have been able to do without.

It was also in 1884 that Billy made firm contact at last with George Bird Grinnell, actually on the ground in greater Yellowstone. Starting in January 1885, *Forest and Stream* began running a fifteen-part serial titled "Through Two Ocean Pass," the very place that had so sparked Billy's curiosity.[13] To be brief, Two Ocean Plateau is a substantial landform, covering a wide swath of the deep wilderness of the park's southeast corner. It is named for Two Ocean Pass, just south of the park, which may be Yellowstone's equivalent of Blackbeard's treasure or the Lost City of Z. As park Historian Lee Whittlesey explains: "Two Ocean

Pass is a marshy meadow where the waters of North Two Ocean Creek and South Two Ocean Creek divide and flow in two directions: one to the Atlantic Ocean via the Yellowstone River and one to the Pacific Ocean via the Snake River. There are a few other places in the world where this kind of division occurs, but the phenomenon is rare."[14]

Yet the mere mingling of waters is not what made Two Ocean Pass fascinating to Billy, so much so that he "treasured" the location in his memory and decided to visit it even as he heard Norris and Yellowstone Kelly describe it in Gibbon Meadows in 1879. The theory was that fish could swim from the Pacific slope to the Atlantic and vice versa through this mingling of waters. Such a find could do much to explain how fish had distributed themselves around North America after the last ice age, as well as possibly explaining how the cutthroat trout, a Pacific-waters fish, got into Yellowstone Lake, which drains to the Atlantic Ocean. No wonder Billy was fascinated.

So was George Bird Grinnell. In summer 1884, he joined Arnold Hague of the U.S. Geological Survey, who was continuing his long and productive career in Yellowstone, and they explored Two Ocean Pass from the south. One of the products was the article "Through Two-Ocean Pass," all fifteen parts of which are unsigned, but are plainly Grinnell's work; according to the journalistic convention, an unsigned article was the work of the editor, and by way of confirmation, the narrator opened the first installment by explaining that he had explored the park in 1875, which few people had done that year other than William Ludlow, with the young Grinnell in tow.

The series, a leisurely tour tens of thousands of words long, need not concern us greatly here, except for its very last paragraphs. Grinnell noted with some horror that the railroad was selling tickets that gave their holders only five days to see the park before they were due back at the railhead. The result was mere exhaustion and misery. Another option beckoned to the visitor: "If one desires to

go off from the traveled roads to climb the mountains, and penetrate the virgin forest, by all means let him hire a few animals and
a good packer who knows the country, and then branch out for
himself. All the streams abound in trout, and there is game in the
mountains without the Park. A man named Hofer makes a business of taking out parties in this way and has the name of a very
reliable and worthy person."[15]

Hague and Grinnell had not employed Billy during the Two
Ocean Pass trip (Grinnell specifically mentioned another man
working as packer), but they clearly had made contact. Given everything else he accomplished, it is easy to forget that one side of
Billy's business involved simply showing anglers the best waters and
what to do with them. They could do that in the deep backcountry
or they could stick closer to home, and it was this aspect of his
business that provided the greatest range of challenges, from severe
to none at all. Billy moved from Bozeman first to Cinnabar, then
to Gardiner, although we have seen what postal addresses were like
during this era, and we have no nice, single dates for his changes of
residence. He once told a reporter that "My home is in my hat."[16]
By the time he reached Gardiner, however, he would have been
able to stand outside and hit the Yellowstone River with a thrown
rock. One of the world's premier trout streams was located just in
front of his door. He spent his life surrounded by mountain water,
and he must have done a great deal of this sort of guiding, but stuck
to more dramatic topics when he wrote.

Nor did he ever forget Two Ocean Pass. He at last made the trip
to it with W. Hallett Phillips, a crucial figure in the history of the
park who, outside legal circles, is not remembered anything like
as well as he should be. In his well-known administrative history
of the park, Richard Bartlett gave him appropriate space: "Least
known of the park defenders was a prominent Washington lawyer named William Hallett Phillips. By the 1880s he was known
affectionately as 'Judge' to such notables as Henry and Charles
Francis Adams, Theodore Roosevelt, George Bird Grinnell, L. Q.

C. Lamar, John W. Noble, Arnold Hague, members of the Supreme Court, and many Congressmen including Senator Vest." Bartlett's list can serve as a rough-and-ready catalog of the most prominent friends of Yellowstone, a body that was still coming into existence, although the nascent movement had already produced some impressive friends. Senator George Graham Vest of Missouri was especially important. For years, he kept an eye out for potential threats to the park and acted with vigor when they could be stopped by the considerable means available to a U.S. Senator.

"Phillips was an ardent fly fisherman," Bartlett continued. "Possibly it was from a Yellowstone fishing trip that he became interested in the park. At least twice he traveled there as confidential agent for the secretary of interior."[17] Bartlett elsewhere called him a "special investigator"[18]—he was in Yellowstone to report on conditions without letting the locals know what he was doing. "One of his reports was published as a government document. More important than this, however, was his dedication to the proposition that the park must be made safe from poachers, aggressive concessionaires, and encroaching railroads…. Phillips was the unappointed and unofficial Washington agent for the loosely structured cabal that was determined to save the reservation."[19]

He was also close friends with Billy. We do not know when they met—it was surely one of those informal meetings in person that was not recorded on paper—but it likely happened during Phillips's first visit to the park as a spy, between July 26 and September 6, 1885. We can be certain that they hit it off, because they became friends for life. Phillips's report on his visit—the "government document" mentioned by Bartlett[20]—included a section on concessionaire contracts that was in places brutal, when dealing with a substandard concessionaire. He wanted some of them thrown out. It also, however, included the following application from the charmingly misspelled "Elmwood Hofer," whose official address was still Bozeman. We can blame the printers for "Elmwood"— they also had multiple spellings for the well-established "Bozeman" in the same document—but the typo helps further explain how "Thomas Elwood" became "Billy." Throughout his life, people mangled "Elwood" in astonishing ways. And, as Chittenden told us, "Elwood" was "too dude-ish" for the likes of Billy.

Phillips had the following to say about him:

> He applies for a lease at the Mammoth Hot Springs for a stable and corral.
>
> Mr. Hofer is the leading guide and outfitter in the Park, and I take pleasure in favorably recommending his application. His business is principally confined to outfitting camping parties for the trip through the Park, and furnishing horses. He is a man of high character and in every way worthy of the confidence of the Department. I recommend that a lease or license be given him for the purpose of enabling him to erect a stable and corral at the Mammoth Hot Springs near the present ice-house of the Park Improvement Company. Mr. Hofer should be required to furnish a survey of the site designated, and the amount of land embraced therein should not exceed 2 acres.[21]

So Billy was now "the leading guide in the park" (and Belshazzar the horse, if he was still among the living, had a home). At this early date, however, with so little traffic through the park, being the leading guide did not imply any great fame. Billy had already obtained his first lease in the park during March of the previous year. The *Enterprise* newspaper, in nearby Livingston, reported that the lease would go to "William Hofer." The editorial team was not yet aware that "Billy" was a nickname.[22]

The friendship with Phillips had some far-flung consequences not long afterward. On June 2, 1886, legislators introduced a bill into the Senate—among the first of many such attempts—to drive a railroad through the park. Senator Vest unlimbered his oratorical artillery and opened fire. *Forest and Stream* printed the bill and the debate verbatim.[23] Two of the more important witnesses were not present, but Vest read their testimony into the record:

> Now, let me read…a letter coming from a practical hunt-er and woodsman whose opinion and testimony is worth all the rhetoric and all the appeals that may be made in this Chamber within the next five hours. When in the Yellow-stone Park I made the acquaintance of Mr. Hofer, one of those men fast disappearing now from the frontier, who live in the forest—men who, like Daniel Boone and [Simon] Kenton, when their cattle mingled with those of a neighbor twenty-five miles distant, thought the towns and cities were encroaching upon the domain which they loved so well, and immediately moved further west. This man Hofer lives in the mountains. He knows by instinct almost equal to that of the animals themselves their habits. Here is his testimony in regard to the result of even the imperfect guardianship which we have been enabled under an act of Congress to put over this splendid park…. Mr. Hofer, writing to Mr. Hallett Phillips, says, speaking of the proposed railroad….[24]

That it was a monstrosity, of course, as Billy explained at length to the U.S. Senate itself, which must have been a heady experience even though he required Phillips and Vest as his intermediaries. His argument was one he would return to again and again, as we shall see in the next chapter: that any railroad would destroy the park bison, elk, and antelope herds.

Despite his geographic isolation and his relatively humble ori-gins, he now had allies who were on his side in these matters, in the highest places. And Senator Vest, in that speech, let drop the sur-prising news that he in fact knew Billy. It is not clear when exactly they met, but of course we know where: in Yellowstone. The park has always been its own greatest advocate, but Vest was obviously impressed with Billy, too.

Thomas Elwood Hofer really had arrived, and it is unsurprising, actually, that this (then) relatively unknown writer was given much of five issues of *Forest and Stream* during 1887 for "Winter in Wonderland," and would then become the journal's Yellowstone correspondent.

And it was with Phillips that he finally traveled to Two Ocean Pass. "One year not having any early parties in view, and wishing to visit the Two Ocean country," recalled Billy later, "I wrote my friend, W. Hallet Phillips of Washington, D. C. to join me on a trip. He did so and we made an extended trip through all the wilder part of the park, and which today [1926] remains very close to a state of nature. Only now and then has a tree been cut down, everything is as it was before the country was known."[25] We do not know when this first Two Ocean journey took place; "sometime in the 1880s" is our present, if feeble, best guess at the date. Phillips returned to the park in 1894, engaging Billy Hofer as guide, and became what Bartlett called the "acknowledged expedition leader"[26] of a kind of safari to the same area, with what had then become the usual parade of celebrities, aristocrats, and scientists, the most famous on this trip being Henry Adams, the political journalist best known today for his sardonic memoir *The Education of Henry Adams* (annoyed with his other companions, he paid his guide a backhanded compliment: "the guileless prattle of Billy Hofer alone taught the simple life").[27]

Bartlett described the rest of this rather ambitious trip: "Accompanying Adams was his close friend John Hay; Hay's son, Del; geologist Joseph Paxton Iddings; W. Hallett Phillips...and Yellowstone guide Billy Hofer. They traveled three or four hundred miles on horseback, much of the time camping in the Two Ocean Pass area. They fished and (south of the park boundary, we presume) hunted."[28] When Phillips died tragically young in a boating accident, three years later, the news must have been painful to Billy indeed.

That journey was in the future, however. Billy would later look back to 1882 and the arrival of Philetus Norris's replacement as park superintendent, Patrick Conger, as a crucial moment that helped move him down the right path—not that Conger himself was crucial, but his arrival marked a turn, in Billy's mind, toward the modern and forced him to adjust his approach to his work in what a proved an ideal manner: "Conger had been made superintendent and an army officer put in charge of improvements and ten assistant superintendents appointed as police. The first important road work was done by then Captain Dan C. Kingman, U. S. A. He built a road to Norris basin through what is now known as Golden Gate"—but also known as Kingman Pass, named after Kingman supervised its construction from 1883-1885.[29] He built "another from Norris to the Grand Canyon and one to the Yellowstone Lake."[30] It was the modern Grand Loop in its earliest infancy.

This relatively intense activity had an unexpected impact on Billy Hofer: "All this road building rather hurt my business, as my mode of travel was only with saddle and pack horses." However, travel on the roads, as Grinnell discovered in 1884, was for the suffering masses. Kingman's roadwork led Billy to specialize in the VIPs and scientists who could afford his backcountry services, and the problem dissolved, because "I had become better known and had all I could do every season, meeting some of the most learned people."[31]

While we know that he missed Arnold Hague and George Bird Grinnell's trip to Two Ocean Pass in 1884, we also know that Billy was working for Hague by 1885. We know this because Billy was present for one of the most spectacular and bizarre fatal accidents in the modern history of the park. It occurred on September 5, 1885. "Prof. Arnold Hague," Billy recalled, "came in with a party of the U. S. G. S. and spent several years on the survey. A Mr. A. Lamartin[e] built a boat and took it to the Yellowstone La[ke], which was used by some members of the survey. Once when Prof. Renshaw[e], a Mr. [M.D.] Scott and another was in the boat out in the lake it was struck by lightning. Two were rendered senseless and Mr. Scott was killed. Mr. Renshaw[e] was the first to recover and found himself lying at the bottom of the boat in a few inches of water. The boat had drifted ashore. Another one of the party recovered but Mr. Scott was dead. He was buried nearby where the cabin was that I lived in when I built my boat, and the grave was marked by a log pen. Later the body was removed and all traces of the grave have long since disappeared."[32]

Whittlesey gave this episode significant space in his wonderfully morbid classic *Death in Yellowstone*. The details match, with minor exceptions: Lamartine may only have found the boat, not constructed it, and there were two other unidentified men in the stern, one unharmed, one left "out of his head all night." The bolt had struck from an entirely cloudless sky. Then things got even weirder. When Scott's wallet was later examined, it contained "sixteen thousand dollars in cash and certificates," in 1885 dollars. Imagine a USGS geologist scrambling around the park today with a hammer in one hand and $10 million in his backpack. Scott's family arrived only seventeen days later, disinterred the body and returned it home to Illinois. One wonders if they were interested only in the body.[33]

In short, through the 1880s, in addition to everything else he was learning, Billy learned all he could about the waters of the park. Experiences like these paid off when, as Aubrey Haines noted, the U.S. Fish Commission took an interest in 1889 in the fishless waters in the park. As Billy recalled:

> I remember with pleasure guiding Dr. David Starr Jordan, Dr. G. K. Gilbert, Prof. Forbes, Prof. [Stephen] Linton, O. P. Jenkins and B. W. Evermann for the U. S. Fish Comission. When under Col. McDonald, whom I met, and who came at the request of Capt. A. Boutelle to study the then barren waters of the park. Under Capt. Boutelle all the barren streams were stocked with game fish, trout

and land locked salmon. The streams stocked were Glenn
Creek, all the branches of the Gardiner River above the falls,
and East Fork of the Gardiner, all the waters of the Gibbon
River above Virginia Cascades, and all the Fire Hole River,
(Upper Madison), including Nez Perce Creek, east fork Fire
Hole, and later all the waters of that branch of Snake River
draining the southwestern part of the park, including Shoshone and Lewis Lake, and on down the Canyon to where
the falls cut off the fish coming up from Jackson Lake.[34]

An immense, decades-long effort had just begun. Even in that
long, locational sentence directly above, Billy is summarizing an
immense operation, almost military in character, and it was only
the opening campaign for fish-stocking. The planting went on
for decades. Billy kept an eye on the results. Reporting how each
planted species was faring in specific stretches of water became a
regular feature of his park news "column" in *Forest and Stream*.
Some of the planted fish survived, some thrived, and some joined
the crew of the *Mary Celeste*, leaving behind only speculation about
their demise.

And frankly, it was good riddance to them, in the opinion of many
later park biologists. On this matter, twenty-first century people with
a little education in ecology have parted company with Billy, the scientists he guided, and really his whole generation. They believed that
they were "fixing" a problem with the park, when they stocked those
barren waters. Schullery has explained the problem (or at least one
major problem) involving the park's streams:

> Actually, they were anything but barren; they were home
> to a rich invertebrate fauna and to a flora whose diversity
> was probably heightened by the numerous geothermal
> sources, which introduced both heat and an assortment of
> chemicals into the streams. The Firehole River, which drains
> the park's most spectacular and famous geyser basins, looks

"almost as if short sections of many different streams from many different places were spliced together and the aquatic life within each was made to live near totally alien environments." For more than 10,000 years these unique aquatic habitats had been developing and tailoring life communities that responded to their strange and varying characteristics. But these life communities, though of great interest to naturalists, were judged insufficient to the needs of sport fishermen. Modern fly fishermen will enjoy Rudyard Kipling's condescending description of the Firehole in 1889 as "a warm and deadly river wherein no fish breed."[35]

So the "barren" communities were altered or destroyed in ways that may today be impossible to reconstruct. That was really only the start. Some of the species chosen were so wrong as to be comically wrong. Across vast stretches of the park, streams today are filled to exclusion by brook trout (*Salvelinus fontinalis*), transplanted from Eastern North America. Introduced to a body of water empty of other fish, the species tends to reproduce until, as resources are stretched, each individual shrinks in size. In Yellowstone today, an average "brookie" is seven inches long. The champion brook trout of a lifetime is nine inches long and fights like a shard of lettuce.

The newly planted fish also tended not to stay put. Others, while staying put, caused unexpected trouble, especially since not all the fish planted went into barren water. The brown trout (*Salmo trutta*), darling of fly anglers, has outcompeted—or likely will eventually—the native grayling and cutthroat that were previously the dominant native species in many watercourses. Among their other challenges, the fishery and aquatic science specialists in the park have a full-time job simply undoing the damage done by those early enthusiasts. The Yellowstone National Park Service has a policy statement that clarifies both some of today's challenges and how much attitudes have changed since Billy's day:

Approximately 48% of Yellowstone's waters were once fishless, and the stocking of non-native fishes by park managers has had profound ecological consequences. The more serious of these include displacement of intolerant natives such as westslope cutthroat trout (*O. clarki lewisi*) and Arctic grayling (*Thymallus arcticus*), hybridization of Yellowstone (*O. c. bouvieri*) and westslope cutthroat trout with each other and with non-native rainbow trout, and, most recently, predation of Yellowstone cutthroat trout by non-native lake trout. Over the years, management policies of the National Park Service have drastically changed to reflect new ecological insights. Subsistence use and harvest orientation once guided fisheries management. Now, maintenance of natural biotic associations or, where possible, restoration to pre-Euro-American conditions have emerged as primary goals. Eighteen fish species or subspecies currently are known to exist in Yellowstone National Park; 13 of these are considered native (they were known to exist in park waters prior to Euro-American settlement), and five are introduced (non-native or exotic).[36]

At the same time, we cannot expect that people born before the American Civil War would have acted in their day like twenty-first century professors of wildlife biology. In one of his news columns for *Forest and Stream*, Billy revealed what was simply a typical attitude of his era. He was reporting on fishing conditions, especially bait, in the Yellowstone River in late summer 1887:

> We have no angle worms in this country, but nature has kindly given us the salmon fly and the grasshopper. I have often noticed that when a "true sportsman" can't catch fish with artificial flies he will take very kindly to grasshoppers and salmon flies. One will often see a fisherman after a festive grasshopper, striking wildly at it with a hat profusely

ornamented with artificial flies. The Yellowstone River is unusually full of a fish, called here, "whitefish," "stone-rollers," "suckers," and by some "grayling." They are not grayling but a sucker-mouthed fish with a projecting nose for turning small boulders and digging into the ground. They are quite gamy, will take artificial flies or bait and will fight quite as hard as trout, but are not as good a table fish. They are very fond of trout eggs and other fish eggs, which their nose or bill enables them to get from the gravel where the trout have deposited them. May their number grow less.[37]

Grinnell again stepped in and corrected the identification: these were mountain whitefish, and Grinnell as usual supplied at least the genus, *Coregonus*. It took decades to learn the park, and Billy was still learning, although he was always honest when he did not have the exact answer. Yet note his desire here to eliminate the "bad" whitefish to benefit the "good" trout, even while the whitefish was every bit as native to the park—every bit a part of its network of life—as the bison and the grizzly bears. And of course I forgive him, especially because he had characteristically provided that image of the geared-up dude fly fisherman haplessly chasing grasshoppers and not even catching them, much less any fish.

A friend of mine who has worked in Greater Yellowstone for a half century once told me about some fairly shocking travesties he himself participated in, during the 1970s, but followed up his memory with a question: "Who knows what we're doing wrong now? In a lot of cases, we're doing things in the park that will seem just barbaric in a hundred years, and we have no way of knowing what they are." That much is worth considering, and most scientists today would agree with my friend.

None of the fish biologists Billy named, above, knew Yellowstone well enough to know where all the "barren" waters were, or how most easily to reach them. They certainly did not know every inch of Yellowstone's watercourses, the way Billy did. He had to show them where to put the fish. In fact, I suspect that sometimes he told them where to put the fish.

When Barton W. Evermann wrote up his 1891 reconnaissance of the park for the *Bulletin of the U.S. Fish Commission*, he included the following acknowledgement: "During this expedition we had as our guide Mr. Elwood Hofer, whose energy, intimate acquaintance with the region, and personal knowledge of the work already done by the Commission in the Park, made his services invaluable to us."[38] Nor was Evermann one of those scientists who failed to give credit where it was due. Billy appeared throughout Evermann's dense 57-page report, showing the way over the landscape, pointing out obscure watercourses, contributing to the Two Ocean Pass controversy and, most delightfully for him, checking to see if water was "barren" or not by breaking out his tackle. Often enough, his fishing rod doubled as a divining rod determining where the new fish would go. In this, as in so many things, what we find today in Yellowstone is a landscape that Billy Hofer helped create.

From a biological point of view, it is unfortunate that it should have worked out so poorly, but fish were only part of Billy Hofer's life and livelihood. Through the 1880s and 1890s and well into the twentieth century, he and his friends confronted not shortcomings that required fixing, but actual existential threats to the integrity or even the existence of Yellowstone National Park and especially its large wildlife. He and his friends fought back, and when he faced down these challenges, he had better luck. In fact, he would soon play a key role in yet another spectacular Yellowstone success.

Hofer lived in a cabin in Gardiner, Montana, just outside the park boundary. In this photo-graph, his cabin is on the side of the road closest to the Yellowstone River, the second building from the left. The water wagon is parked out front. The date of this photo is unknown, but the bridge was built in 1885. COURTESY OF BRIGHAM YOUNG UNIVERSITY.

CHAPTER EIGHT

A Natural Breeding-Ground and Nursery

Those columns of park news that Billy sent to *Forest and Stream* normally dealt with routine matters, though often they were vital matters to the journal's readership—the movement of animals, the passability of the roads, the state of the weather, and more. As Billy himself said, however, referring to Schwatka's allegedly magic whiskey bottle, "Strange things happen in the Park." Yes, strange and exciting things did indeed happen. In his report for the May 5, 1887, *Forest and Stream*, much of his column was consumed by an extraordinary bit of skullduggery.

After years of feckless and haphazard management by various civilian officials, some of them wonderful, some of them worthless, the nation had finally turned to the one force that was available, armed, mounted, monied, and thus capable of imposing order—the U.S. Army. Aubrey Haines narrated the crucial event: "In prompt compliance with Special Orders No. 79, Headquarters, Department of Dakota, issued at Fort Snelling, Minnesota, August 13, 1886, Captain Moses Harris marched the fifty men of Company M, First United States Cavalry, from Fort Custer, Montana Territory, to Mammoth Hot Springs, where they arrived on the evening of August 17. A tent

camp was established at the foot of the hot spring terraces, and the
captain assumed the duties of the superintendency on August 20,
1886."[1] Harris's title was in fact "Acting Superintendent," because
the Army's presence was supposed to be temporary. Instead, the soldiers stayed for thirty-two years. The tent camp at Mammoth gradually evolved into the buildings of Fort Yellowstone. One of the architectural treasures of the region, it serves as park headquarters to this
day. One of the first challenges Harris and his men faced was to try
to get a handle on the poaching of park wildlife. Billy's May 5, 1887
column gave some sense of what they were up against. It was bylined
from park headquarters at Mammoth:

> A few days ago Capt. Harris, acting superintendent of the
> Park, learned that a party living at Norris was engaged in
> hunting and trapping for furs. He immediately set to work
> to effect their arrest. Temporarily disabling the telephone
> wire between this point and Norris, which had recently
> been repaired, he cut off all chance of their being warned
> in time to hide any evidence of their guilt. Securing the ser-
> vices of Ed Wilson, one of the ex-assistant superintendents,
> the Captain started him out on the night of the 20th, with
> two soldiers, Sergeant Swain and one private.[2]

During the brief period at the start of its history when civilians
ran the park, and only for a portion of that (1882-1886), Yellowstone was "policed" by a small force of "assistant superintendents."
Wilson was one such who stayed on, becoming a civilian scout
working directly for the Army, without actually being a soldier.
Billy's narrative continued:

> They traveled on snowshoes. Arriving at the Gibbon,
> without making their presence known, they followed up
> different trails and secured the traps set for the capture of
> beaver and other fur-bearing animals.

They then arrested the parties, James and A. Kelly. James is one of the freighters snowed in at Norris with his teams. The other, Con Sheehan, left the Park in March, taking his horses out on the crust. In James's possession they found beaver and otter furs. After arresting him they took possession of his horses, harness, sleds, rifle, gun, traps, and all property belonging to him. Kelly, who is in charge of the hotel at Norris, was placed under arrest. To what extent he is implicated I could not learn. Leaving the soldier in charge they returned to the Hot Springs with James as a prisoner. He was turned over to Captain Harris.

It appears that James, on his last trip over the Grand Cañon, where he was engaged in hauling lumber, killed three elk. This was sometime in January. The snow getting too deep for the teams to work, he put in some of his time hunting small game and trapping.

It is reported that other parties are implicated in the killing of game. Who they are and what the extent of their depredations your correspondent has not learned. This arrest is the first one this season and shows that Captain Harris is doing everything possible to suppress all hunting or trapping in the Park. What action will be taken in the James case is not known, [but] at least his property will be confiscated.[3]

Hunting in the park had not been illegal for long (only four years), and it is eminently unlikely that the men involved, whatever embarrassment or annoyance they might have felt, would have also felt a sense of having done anything morally improper. We would be mistaken to think that really large numbers of people were disturbed by such events; game laws were then still an intrusion by distant authorities, running against the grain of deep local traditions, and the poacher was often seen as the local version of Robin Hood. The change described above, in which not-especially-wealthy rural people adopted an aristocratic fair-chase ethic, lay decades in the future.

And yet there was an element of treachery here that remains offensive to us well over a century later. These were park employees, if of the cruder sort, who might have been expected to care just a trace more about the place than the average game thief. They did not. And how brazen it was to run an entire trap line through Yellowstone National Park! From our vantage point, it begins to resemble organized crime, as if the "Five Families" had gotten their start by sending hit men to Norris to whack beaver and elk.

At the very least, the incident shows us vividly today what the park's defenders were then up against. Harris's men were vigorous, according to Billy. On June 23, he reported another violation: "Captain Harris's scout"—Ed Wilson—"is making it very interesting for the hunters and trappers who venture into the Park. One man who thought it unsafe to go in from Gardiner, tried it by going around over two hundred miles, and then found Wilson in camp as he drove across the line. He is out of the Park now, after contributing a pack horse, traps and outfit to the collection made by the superintendents."[4]

Billy did not just approve. He was delighted. But at the same time, that last sentence hints at the real problem. As in the earlier case, soldiers confiscated all the poacher's property, and he was kicked out of the park—but that was all. No law existed under which authorities could prosecute and jail poachers. They were simply turned loose. The Army did at least get to keep the horses, guns, and gear.

This outright silly situation would endure for seven more years to come. In the meantime, as the maturing national transportation network tangled the park more and more in its skein, and as more and more people both visited the park and settled in the region, the killing would intensify, especially because game was growing scarcer everywhere. The vast game "nursery" grew more and more tempting as the only place the poachers could even find the animals they wanted most, those whose hides and heads could be sold at absurdly high prices to taxidermists, whose own profits also call to mind the world of organized crime. Poaching in Yellowstone was the nineteenth-century equivalent of smuggling cocaine— without any of the risks, except the possible loss of your horse and gun.

Let us note, however, that Billy's standards were astonishingly strict when it came to park aesthetics. On September 22 of that year, he wrote in with no complaints about the animals, but including this observation: "The topographers connected with the Geological Survey"—the long-term surveying work that Arnold Hague was running—"whose special work this year has been to make surveys of the Geyser Basins and Mammoth Hot Springs, are camped at the Norris Basin, having completed the survey of the Upper and Lower Basins. The scale on which the work is being done will accurately show the situation of every geyser, spring and pool. These properly named and mapped out will do much to prevent the confusion of names so indiscriminately applied, and if enough of the maps are published, one can be placed in the hands of every visitor, doing away with the unsightly signs that now deface so many points of interest and remind one of advertisements, and the labeled objects in one of Mrs. Jarley's wax work shows," the last a minor character in Charles Dickens' *The Old Curiosity Shop*—again, Billy was a ravenous reader. Today, every visitor receives a map, but we will have to apologize about the signs, Billy: they are today as much a part of the park as the geysers behind them. A former chief law enforcement ranger once even wrote a celebration of them as a kind of folk art, the fine work of the park's master sign-maker.[5] But we note with fascination Billy's distaste for any intrusion onto the park landscape by any trace of humanity. The fish stocking was presumably proper because the fish, to most observers, were invisible.

The poachers were back again in the November 3 *Forest and Stream*, as Billy reported: "Recently Ed Wilson the scout brought in a man found killing elk in the southern part of the Park. His camp and stock was outside the Park, only his saddle horse and rifle was captured with him."[6] Given that confiscation was the only deterrent available, such a case represented only marginal success for park authorities. On November 10, Billy reported the intentional destruction by soldiers of a cabin on Hellroaring Creek that had been used by a party of poachers the winter before.[7] And so it went. In this effort, the boundary lines, intended to protect the reservation, became something of a curse, because the park was surrounded on every side by refuges for the enemy. The Army was fighting a low-key, relatively peaceful rehearsal for the challenges it would face in Vietnam eighty years later, when the Communist insurgents tried when possible to stay close to an international border that the Army could not cross.

Nonetheless, the effort to stop poaching, although difficult, was not doomed to failure. On February 20, 1890, Billy filed the following brief but remarkable census of the park wildlife. He had been intimate with the place for over ten years and had watched it change…in many ways for the better. He now penned a report on the changes. The headline writer at *Forest and Stream* threw up his hands and gave the story a blanket headline, "Lots of Big Game."[8] Billy was staying, perhaps just paying a visit—he did so often—at Yancey's Hotel, near the future Tower Junction. During this era, that was ground zero for the large and growing herds of elk:

> The effects of protection on the increase in number of all kinds of game animals in the Park has been very noticeable from year to year since 1883 [the year hunting in the park was outlawed]. At that date there were less than at any time in the history of the reservation. Up to '83 the slaughter of elk and other game had been very great, but from that time on the game has been carefully protected, until now the elk can be seen by hundreds, where once they were very scarce. Most of the game that now winters in the Park used to go to a less snowy region to pass the winter months. Especially

was this true of antelope and white and blacktail deer. Even now most of the deer leave the Park when the snow begins to get deep. The antelope remain on the reservation, but at the lower altitudes.

Another thing very noticeable is that the animals are showing less fear of man since they have learned that they have nothing to dread from his presence. Traveling about as I do through the Park during the winter months, I have paid considerable attention to the game, noticing its habits and doing all I could toward counting or making an estimate of number of animals here. From the window where I am writing these notes, I can see a large seven-point bull elk. He is lying down in the snow on a point of a hill, not over three hundred yards from the hotel. Another bull is down on the sidehill feeding where the snow is three feet deep. To get to the grass he is pawing the snow out of the way, and occasionally pushing it away by swinging his head from side to side. Men and teams are moving about, choppers are cutting trees for firewood only two hundred yards from these elk. There are seven bulls who have been camping on this hill for the past three weeks. When the sun comes out bright and clear they get in the shade to lie down. Dogs barking will only cause them to raise their heads for a look; they show no fear of anything they see or hear from the ranch.

At this point, we should note that the scene Billy described is another of the many, many scenes he saw that leave the twenty-first-century Yellowstone enthusiast with mouth open and head shaking. Yancey's is gone today except for its foundation, still visible where the hotel concessionaire holds its cookouts during the summer months. The modern road passes quite close by to the south and is plowed throughout the winter because it serves as the only access to the outside world for the small tourist town of Cooke City, Montana. So you can see all the terrain Billy described surveying from the hotel, and you can see it on the same day he was actually writing, February 1. You will probably see part of the park bison herd, much larger today than in Billy's era, although they often turn up as scattered individuals in that exact area, depending on their mood. You will see nothing like the following:

> From the hotel...we can see with field glasses hundreds of elk. Across the Yellowstone River there is a band of government animals, mules and horses. Two of the horses have bells on. Within a circuit of a mile about the horses are 300 elk; sometimes the elk are within 10yds. of the horses. They pay no attention to each other unless to seek companionship. I am inclined to think the bells attract the elk, at least the sound does not drive them away or alarm them. They appear to stay with the horses that have the bells on them.
>
> The mail carriers, freighters and travelers over the Mammoth Hot Springs and Cooke City road, see elk everywhere. From the time they leave the springs until they reach Soda Butte station, they are in sight of elk all the time. The elk are in bands from 25 to 50 and occasionally bands of 200, 300 and even 400 can be seen.
>
> The greatest number are seen on the north side of the Yellowstone and [Lamar] Rivers, or East Fork,[9] their favorite winter feeding ground. Specimen Ridge is covered with elk at times. As the wind blows the snow off the grass here, they congregate during the night and remain feeding until the sun comes out clear, when they go to the green timber to bed. Several hundred elk are wintering on and about Mt. Everts, one band of these, some 45, came off the mountain down to the flats at the junction of the Gardiner and Yellowstone rivers; they were within easy rifle shot of the town of Gardiner for hours, some lying down, others feeding about on the sweet sage. Antelope are on this flat every day. Men from the town often ride out among them on their

way over the "Turkey Pen" road. In one of these bands I counted 130 antelope, in others 80 and 63. Besides the antelope here, there is a band at Junction Butte and one in the Black Tail Creek country.

To clarify the locations, Billy was referring to places on the eastern side of the "northern range" mentioned earlier. He was essentially describing the animals that a traveler might see on the various roads and trails that ran from Gardiner and past Yancey's to terminate at Cooke City, although he only followed them as far as Soda Butte, an isolated thermal feature in the northeast corner of the park, where the Army had built a station to monitor traffic headed into the park through the Slough Creek/Lamar River corridor. Animals will inevitably congregate on the northern range in winter, if only because the elevations normally run about a thousand feet closer to sea level than is more common in the interior of the park. What surprises the reader today are the sheer numbers of elk Billy reported and their concentration in legions reminiscent of an African savannah, if we can ignore the snow.

And the increase showed no signs of slowing. On June 26, he reported that "The cow elk are having their calves. If the rate of increase goes on as it has the past five years the Park will soon be overrun with game."[10] The next year, on March 19, 1891, he produced what was—given the limitations imposed on an observer in the era before aircraft—probably the best overall population number for the elk herd inside the national park that we will ever get for that date: "I have tried to get an estimate from a great many people acquainted with the country as to the number of elk in the Park and vicinity. They claim all the way from 25,000 to 75,000, some as high as 100,000. Without a doubt there are not less than 25,000 elk on this reservation."[11]

By the date of the article above, surely, the Yellowstone elk were "saved." I do not wish to reprise here the controversies that have swirled around the park elk for nearly a century and a half; interested readers can have a look at James A. Pritchard's fine study *Preserving Yellowstone's Natural Conditions*, and if necessary, look at the bibliography and go from there.[12] In short, the elk population kept expanding until later generations of managers decided that there were too many, then decided that there were far too many, and for decades even culled the herd by shooting them in large numbers. The shooting ended in the late 1960s, but the controversy never did. It is unresolvable, because it is so often debated in such rudimentary terms, presented as a matter involving the relationship between a few species of big, photogenic grazing animals like elk versus a few species of predators and the weather, with humanity as the ultimate arbiter. But there may be millions of species in Greater Yellowstone. Turn over a buffalo chip, and you discover a universe. We forget about the bacteria, the molds, the algae, the rodents, the insects, and on and on and on. After a few more centuries of study, we may have some "understanding" of how every piece relates to every other. We have not yet even found all the pieces.[13]

This much is undeniable, however: only a few years earlier, observers on every side assumed the North American elk was going the way of the dodo. Now it most certainly was not. As troublesome to enforce as the park rules could be, Billy liked them because they could be made to work.

I would not want to leave the impression that Billy only cared about, and wrote about, big game. He could just as easily write the following, which appeared later, in July 1909: "I have said so much about game in the park that I fear you are getting tired of my mentioning it at all…. Last year I noticed the first sign of porcupines in the park for several years. Formerly there were thousands. Then one year they disappeared from all this country, but lately I have seen a little sign of where they had been feeding in winter. It will take many years to bring them back in anywhere near the number they used to be."[14] Here is another jaw-dropping moment: thousands of porcupines scrambling every which way would be a bizarre sight in Yellowstone today, where small, highly localized colonies of porcupines are known only to people who live there, who routinely cherish the knowledge of each location as a personal secret, sharing it only with friends. Billy followed up the thought in what turned out to be his second-to-last article in *Forest and Stream*, in June 1915:

> It is not necessary to have a hard winter and spring. Let the game become too numerous and crowded, and you will have some disease that will carry them off. There was a time some twenty or twenty-five years ago when porcupine were very thick and plenty all through the mountains and Park. In one ride toward evening south of the Park I counted 42 porcupine along the trail. They were everywhere, and their sign, too. Next year not a porcupine could be seen and it was years before I saw any sign in the Park or the mountains around it. Nothing but a disease could have wiped them out. No hard winter can discourage a porcupine; he can climb a tree and live off the bark of one for the whole winter.[15]

In fact, readers never knew what they were going to get from a Hofer column. His stories for *Forest and Stream* were a grab-bag; he was aware of that, and he had fun with it. He chose to finish a column from September, 1905, with a bit of such fun. Here is his second-to-last paragraph:

> I see many queer things in the way of animal actions, but don't like to tell about them. I notice that when I do the people I talk to look at me as though they doubted my word, and then I hear them say, "My, but he draws the long bow." But I must tell one incident that happened to me the other night in Gardiner. I was sleeping in my cabin with the door wide open. On my table were some sheets of "tanglefoot" fly paper and other things, letters, papers and magazines. Along

about 1 A. M. I awoke, hearing considerable noise among
the papers on my table and a squeaking noise, like that made
by a mouse when hurt. I lay listening for a while, wondering
what was the trouble. Then reaching for a match I struck it.
At the flash some animal on the table made a great clatter
and then remained still. I lit the lamp and looked at the
table. In a corner next to a cupboard and the wall was a small
hare, a cotton-tail. I stood looking at it for some time and
saw that it had been stuck on the fly paper.

The night was quite cool and the sticky stuff was not soft
enough to get in its deadly work. At the flash of the match
the frightened animal broke loose from the paper by its sud-
den start. I picked it up by its ears, carried it to the door and
turned it loose, and told it to fly, but not play a fly again. I
have had many visitors to my cabin of nights—porcupines
(years ago when they were numerous), mountain rats, birds,
bats and once a grouse. Fortunately, I never had a visit in
this cabin from the little black and white pussy that proves
so offensive.

By "pussy," he means a skunk, normally a rare visitor to Gardiner
(there have always been stray domestic cats). The story is all the
more appealing because, throughout its life and to this day, the
town of Gardiner has been infested by masses of the world's cutest
cottontails—cute, until they burrow under the chicken wire and
get into the garden.

In the last paragraph of the article, he turned to more savage
beasts. We should pause here to note that for decades, a major
Yellowstone pastime during summer evenings was watching the
kitchen staff at the local hotel take out the trash. Hordes of bears
would, at the magic hour, emerge from the woods and scarf up the
garbage—and yes, it was quite a show and at times a travesty:

I saw one man this summer who said he had been hurt

by a bear. I asked him how. He had a bad cut on his fore-
head. He said he and several others were watching the bears
eating slops at the Lake Outlet. A female grizzly with two
cubs was not very friendly. The cubs came on toward the
crowd and the old one came too. The crowd broke and ran.
Some went up trees. He ran against a tree, striking his head
against a dry limb. This knocked him out. His friend said
the bear came within ten feet of him, then went back. When
he came to his friend helped him to camp, dressed his cut,
and this was the way he was hurt by a bear.[16]

So Billy could have fun in print, as he could in actual life. There
remained, however, one crucial hole in the censuses of the big animals, a cause of irritation for him over a period of years, and it
came up regularly in *Forest and Stream*. He could not get a fix on
the bison population, and he wanted one badly; as he explained,
after the Army's civilian scout, Ed Wilson, discovered a group of
65 cows and calves that he had not expected to find, in June 1890,
"It was no novel sight to him to see a band of 50 to 100 elk, but the
buffalo are not so plenty, and they gladden an old-timer's eyes."[17]
The buffalo appeared in his 1890 article "Lots of Big Game," but
as the one species he could say nothing definite about and the one
that worried him the most:

As no particular effort has as yet been made to find
them, very few buffalo have been seen. One small band was
discovered from the hotel at Grand Cañon and one band
seen in Hayden Valley. They range away from any traveled
route in winter, and to see them one must make a snowshoe
trip with that object in view. Later in the winter they move
out to Specimen Ridge, and sometimes across East Fork to
Slough Creek. Others keep in and about the Lower Geyser
Basin. Elk are as numerous in the Swan Lake, Madison and
Gallatin basins as they are anywhere in the northern part

of the Park. They are plenty in Hayden and Pelican Creek valleys, on Mt. Washburn, [Mount] Holmes and the range extending to Electric Peak. They are everywhere. Their trails cross and follow the wagon roads; they have passed over thousands of acres of snow; they are about the soldiers' quarters on Soda Butte Creek. One old bull feeds on the waste hay thrown from the stable at the game keeper's cabin.[18]

Note the jump from buffalo to elk in the middle of the paragraph, the kind of thing his teachers in Connecticut might have landed on with a big red "AWK/ILLOGICAL." In fact, there was nothing "awk" about it: he was drawing a contrast between the extremes. The elk were so abundant as to verge on the comical—and that plentitude only served to call attention, for the practiced observer, to the bison that were missing.

In this context, "buffalo" and "bison" were the same thing. When European settlers first encountered these titans, the settlers reached, as they normally did, for an analogy with Old World animals, and as often happened, their analogy did not fit well. The bison of North America are not even related to the Old World buffalo, the water buffalo of Southeast Asia, say, or the Cape buffalo of Africa. They do not even look alike. In this book, I have followed the normal practice of letting nineteenth-century people call them buffalo (to call a buffalo chip a "bison chip" is beyond pedantic), while referring to the species in general, and as it exists today, by their proper name, *Bison bison*. They are among the characteristic animals of Yellowstone, to many the very symbol of the place; when it came time to design a logo, the National Park Service chose the Yellowstone bison as the one animal to place on center stage, by putting it onto the stylized arrowhead that represents the service. Grizzly bears and wolves take down the younger, older, and more vulnerable animals, but were it not for the weather and the invention of the rifle, the bull bison, 2,000 pounds when full grown, capable of running 35 mph and tossing a human like a rag doll, might be as close to indestructible as an animal can get. Appropriately, the species is among the few mammals that appear never to develop cancer.

The Yellowstone bison herd, numbering between three and five thousand today, is made up of the descendants of the last wild herd on the continent. Through the 1880s and into the 1890s, Billy pursued any rumor he heard about bison, but their numbers gradually fell. Mary Meagher, long the National Park Service's Yellowstone bison expert, combed the old records and found that the low reached twenty-three individuals in 1902, although as always, the count missed a few.[19] It requires little speculation to guess what effect this decline had on Billy, as a purely emotional matter ("they gladden an old-timer's eyes"). When he traveled to Colorado in the 1870s, he would have seen the old continental herd—it had once numbered at least 25 million—when it still possessed some of the breathtaking glory the earliest pioneers had known.

Oddly, amid this holocaust, a trace of localized optimism was not irrational. The central plains lost their bison first, because that is where the railroads arrived first. In Montana, really large herds, numbering in the hundreds of thousands, persisted well into the 1880s. The technology slowed the slaughter, because hides and other bison products (like pickled tongue, which enjoyed a brief vogue) could make the first part of the trip to Midwestern and Eastern markets only by steamboat. The numbers were truly extraordinary. The Bozeman *Avant Courier* reported in 1881 that 100,000 hides would be shipped from Montana Territory that year,[20] and the last bison hides to leave Montana would not depart until 1884. Only the next year did the shipments stop for good. Further, the unofficial headquarters was Bozeman, which became the capital of the local slaughter. Bozeman was bounded on three sides by what we now call the Greater Yellowstone Ecosystem. Did it not make sense (people like Billy might have reasoned) that at least some groups of animals from this vast assemblage should have

backed into the mountains and away from the hail of lead—backed
into the mountains and found refuge in the park?

Still, the decline continued, and it was not a sad thing. It was a
horrifying thing, and Billy Hofer was beginning to try to do something about it. The first step was just to get a sense of where the
animals were and how many were left in the park and its immediate surroundings. He was no closer to even an adequate guess at
the bison population when he produced that estimate of the total
number of elk in March 1891. For the bison, he was forced to
fall back on what he usually avoided with care: the Conventional
Wisdom, which was normally wrong. When he gave a count, it
was normally what he himself had seen combined with what such
trustworthy voices as Ed Wilson, Pete Nelson, Tazewell Woody
and the like could add. The old timers made up an informal survey
team, one that in this case had failed:

> I am unable to give all [an] accurate estimate of the num-
> ber of buffalo in the Park. Last summer several bands were
> seen with from one to eighteen calves. It would be necessary
> to make an extended snowshoe trip over a greater portion
> of the Park in order to see most of the buffalo or arrive at a
> definite estimate as to numbers. If they have not been driven
> from the Park there ought to be not less than 400 on the
> National Reserve, this allowing for a very small increase and
> more than natural loss. They are so wild and unmanage-
> able that the greatest caution is necessary to get a glimpse of
> them in the timber, where they usually spend most of their
> time.
>
>   I learn that very few buffalo have been seen in the
> Hayden Valley, where usually quite a band spends the win-
> ter, owing probably to quite extensive fires which burned
> their winter feed.[21]

Billy lost an important ally, in what proved to be a shocking manner, on July 27, 1891. Ed Wilson, perhaps the most accomplished of the civilian Army scouts—he had been in the park since 1885 and was such a zealous enemy of the poachers that he was even keeping an eye on the more roguish soldiers—had fallen in love with the youngest daughter of one of the park's hotel keepers. She did not love him back.

They called it Wonderland, and living there sounded like a dream come true; however, as I can personally testify, the life can turn so lonely and the routine so grinding as to become unendurable. Wilson climbed a hill above Mammoth with a bottle of morphine and poisoned himself. His body did not turn up until a year later.[22]

At least the bison caught a break, a huge one. Wilson was replaced by Felix Burgess, a man who was a scarce commodity: a ready-made old-timer. Haines called him "a tough veteran of the Indian Wars in the Southwest." He "was employed as a regular scout following the disappearance of Ed Wilson in July 1891 (the date of his commission as deputy U.S. marshal for the park is September 1, 1891). When his service terminated is unknown, but it was after April 19, 1899."[23] It was a crucial period, and Burgess played a crucial role in the fate of the bison. So did the new "acting" superintendent, Captain George S. Anderson, who arrived on February 14 (each superintendent typically served a period of years, then moved on to a new assignment, as was normal in the armed services, then and now). Probably the best known of Yellowstone's Army superintendents, Anderson took to his new assignment with extraordinary vigor.[24]

Burgess went right to work, as Billy reported in the December 17, 1891 *Forest and Stream*. His report made it clear why a "more than natural loss" of bison was to be expected:

> He reports the largest of the bands to number about 100, the next in size about 75, while the smallest has about 20 in all; he thinks there are not less than 350. He did not succeed

in locating the buffalo that are known to range on the east
side of the Yellowstone, where they have often been seen in
summer by members of the Geological Survey, and in winter
by Scout Wilson. All the buffalo are well toward the center
of the reservation, where they can be protected from poachers and specimen hunters. This is important, as $1,000 spot
cash has been offered by Eastern parties for three specimens
(head and hides) three years old or over—quite an induce-
ment for anyone to kill the animals wanted if they could get
them out of the Park. There is little danger of our buffalo
getting outside the reservation lines this winter. Soldiers are
stationed at the Lower Geyser Basin, Norris and Soda Butte;
then there are the watchmen at the hotels; and frequent
snowshoe scouting parties will be sent out from Fort Yellowstone at the Mammoth Hot Springs. If all are vigilant no one
can get near the buffalo without being seen.[25]

That statement proved sadly optimistic. The $1,000 standing
reward for a few heads and hides was a dizzying sum at that date
and an indirect measure of how scarce the animal had become.
Further, the thousand dollars could be had by committing a crime
that had no serious consequences. Billy continued, undercutting
his own optimism in the same article by getting at the real problem: the sheer size of the place. And now the park, in a way, was
bigger. In March, 1891, President Benjamin Harrison had created
the Yellowstone Park Timber Land Reserve, attaching 1.2 million
acres to the existing boundaries of the park and so creating what
was essentially the first national forest:

There has been some hunting in the Park this summer
and fall. The limited number of men at the disposal of the
acting superintendent who can be used as scouts prevents
his men covering as much country as he would like, [be-
cause] since the new Forest Reserve has been placed under

his control he has a section of country 69 miles north and south by 72 miles east and west, almost 5,000 square miles to look after, to keep down the fires and protect the game. This whole section, with hundreds of square miles about it, is without settlements, and is a rough, mountainous and timbered country. The parties who are doing the poaching are well known to the officers, and like the pitcher that goes to[o] often to the well, will get taken in someday.[26]

In this instance, that last line was not overoptimistic. The soldiers and scouts often did know who the poachers were and when a new one arrived, could spot him for the poacher he was rapidly, sometimes instantly. So few people visited during the cold months—in Yellowstone, "winter" even today usually lasts much longer than its official start and end dates—that when a stranger showed up asking about "these here buffalo," he aroused immediate suspicion, as in the following incident that Billy wrote up for the June 9, 1892 *Forest and Stream*. Billy was traveling with one of the privates from Fort Yellowstone, and in this case, they were the ones who got suspicious and called on higher authorities, presumably over the park telephone network:

I was out for twenty days in March and April on a buffalo hunt on snowshoes in the Alum Creek country. I was armed with a Kodak, a very good weapon for securing a large number of buffalo and other gamepictures…. The last night we were camped out we found the camp of a man who came in from Henry's Lake, he said, to see the buffalo; he had no arms in sight, and claimed not to know the country. It is supposed that his object was to kill specimens, that he had a rifle and provisions cached not far from the buffalo range. He was obliged to leave the Park without securing a buffalo head. Lieut. Sands, to whom the man was reported, took such measures that he could not return without being captured. The soldiers stationed at the Lower Geyser Basin had one man with him while he was in the Park. It is now well known that he was not only well acquainted with the Park, but has been on the reservation after buffalo before.[27]

Why were Billy and the soldier—a Private Dare, a fine name for someone doing his type of work—suspicious of this person? Billy had reported earlier that the "spring" had been cold and stormy, with snow every day for twenty days at one point. That was good poaching weather; the snow exhausted the already-worn-down animals and muffled rifle fire. Into the middle of this Little Antarctica (Alum Creek was close to a theoretical middle point in the park) strolled a stranger with a vaguely expressed interest in looking at buffalo. Billy and Private Dare got the right guy.

Through the early 1890s, however, the poaching, with bison usually the specific target, found a place in Billy's articles for *Forest and Stream*, until every story had paragraphs like this one, from his next appearance in the publication, on July 28, 1892. The poachers often were not terribly subtle:[28] "Charles Pendelton, who was ordered to keep out of the Park for catching young buffalo, was arrested on Slough Creek. He is held in the guard house at Fort Yellowstone by the commanding officer, who is awaiting instructions from Washington. Pendelton had permission to travel the wagon road between Gardiner and Cooke City, but not to leave it. He was arrested three or four miles from the road." The soldiers even sometimes had fun, as they did during an incident Billy reported on July 2, 1891: "About six weeks ago the Government scout and soldiers stationed at Soda Butte arrested T. S. Vandyke, a hunter and trapper who for years has been furnishing Cooke City with game, [when] he was found asleep in his camp on Lama[r] River—east fork of the Yellowstone. In his camp was found two beaver traps and other outfit. The party making the arrest removed his arms, field glass and Kodak. With the camera they took several shots at him while [he was] yet asleep,"[29] that last being the classic fraternity house stunt (one cannot help wondering whether they cradled an empty whiskey bottle in his arms before taking the photographs).

It sometimes seems almost cute, this ceaseless cat-and-mouse game. The poacher went into the guardhouse. The only real punishment happened there, because he got the worst of the leftover food, and the officers—this was a favorite trick of Superintendent Anderson—would take their time in asking Washington for instructions. The instructions were always to let the criminal go free, because he was technically not quite a real criminal, as there was no statute on the books to legally hold him. And back he would come, in search of more heads and hides. It might seem cute—but by this point, things were very serious, because these poachers were flirting with the erasure of the last wild herd of one of the most magnificent animals in North America.

And yet, even as late as the winter of 1893, Billy was not unduly worried about the park herd. He had great faith in the soldiers and scouts with whom he was working, all dedicated to the protection of the park in a way that he felt the public should know about. On February 16 of that year, he reported on an ambitious expedition that concluded near the end of January: "A few days ago a snowshoe scouting party returned to Fort Yellowstone from a six days' trip looking up the buffalo in Hayden Valley. The party consisted of Elmer Lindsley, Second Lieutenant Sixth Cavalry; Scout Felix Burges[s], and Privates Crisman and Morrison of I Troop, Sixth Cavalry." They made a thorough survey of Hayden Valley, and Billy was satisfied with the results:

> There is no doubt of there being at least 400 buffalo in the Park, even allowing for all those reported to have been killed along the borders. The buffalo in the Park at this time are well toward the center, and with the men stationed at Pole Cat Creek[30] to the south, Riverside on the west, Soda Butte on the north, impassable mountains on the east, and

scouting parties out very often along the border, I believe
they are as well protected as possible. All the officers and
men stationed in the Park take great interest in preserving
these buffalo. Very few outside of the mountains know of
the trouble, work, and exposure necessary to keep track of
the game in the Park and [to] watch the poachers.[31]

Billy's problem remained: the bison census was still not complete, and gathering information remained difficult. "Besides the
buffalo mentioned above there is a large band that is known to
winter in the country east of the Yellowstone River and Grand Cañon," he noted. "These have not been seen as yet this season. No
snowshoe parties have been in there."

If Billy Hofer wanted a truly complete and reliable census of the
park bison, he would have to strap on his skis and do much of the
counting work himself. Oddly, the worst poacher of all was about
to give him that opportunity.

CHAPTER NINE

Making a Living and Making History

Sometime during the late winter of 1894, Ed Howell emerged from his lair, harnessed himself to a ten-foot-long toboggan loaded with supplies, strapped on his 12-foot-long skis, and left Cooke City, Montana, headed into Yellowstone National Park. He slipped past the soldiers at Soda Butte who were supposed to guard the main corridor of travel in the northeast quadrant of the park and in whom Billy had placed too much faith. The park was simply too big for all its natural entrances to be sealed and protected by a few guys in a few shacks.

In a feat of endurance that might have earned him a place on the U.S. Olympic ski team if he had lived in another century, and not been a probable sociopath, Howell skied out of the Lamar River valley, up and over Specimen Ridge—so named for its petrified forest, another of Yellowstone's many, many surprises—and south to his camp on Astringent Creek, a tributary of Pelican Creek that flows deep in the backcountry north of Yellowstone Lake. When he reached the camp he had occupied since September (he had gone to Cooke City to resupply), he had skied fifty or sixty miles with that toboggan lashed behind him, his only companion being a mongrel dog. Billy, in his last report on the bison from the previous year, confessed that he could not give an exact census of the animals because no one had skied out to count the herd east of the Yellowstone River. Howell had, sadly, found them—and he was, ominously, not just there to count.

But this was to be one of those years when personalities and events converged in Yellowstone in a way that seemed miraculous, and that would change the way Yellowstone and eventually every park was run. No wonder they called it Wonderland.

Howell had settled back into the improvised teepee that he had called home since September when a quite different party skied across the obvious trail he left. They were led by Felix Burgess, the canny veteran scout who replaced Ed Wilson. Behind him followed a soldier from Fort Yellowstone, Private Troike, along just to help and not even armed, and a third man: Frank Jay Haynes, the official Northern Pacific photographer who managed to complete the circuit of the park during the fierce winter of 1887 and who had somehow chosen this month for a return trip. Haynes remains today the park's most famous photographer, Yellowstone's rough equivalent of Yosemite's Ansel Adams. It helped that he exhibited such terrific timing.

The little team followed the snowy trail until they encountered a monstrous display, trees with six giant bundles slung from their branches. They were the heads of bison, strung up to keep scavengers from stripping them of flesh and intended for sale to taxidermists. Then they heard it: rifle fire, six shots, and nearby. Imagine the three men there on a landscape smothered in snow, the nearest humans (other than for the rifleman) probably some soldiers at the Lake Soldier Station, far to the southwest. Imagine the shots, each crack followed by that distinctive rolling echo for which the Yellowstone backcountry is known.

Each man, as far as we know, kept his thoughts to himself as Burgess and Troike followed a fresh trail that led in the direction of the rifle fire (for all his talent, Haynes was not a combat photographer). They saw him in a wide clearing: Howell, who was skinning one of the five bison he had killed, having missed with only one of his shots. The odds looked bad. Burgess was carrying the only weapon they possessed above the level of a knife, namely a single .38 revolver, the U.S. Army standard-issue sidearm of that era. Military sidearms were mostly a kind of fashion-accessory for the officers' class—and Burgess, by the way, was technically a civilian employee. Howell, they knew, would be armed with the kind of siege-cannon that men used to kill bison.

Burgess guessed that Howell was at least four hundred yards away. It looked grim: except in the movies, any .38 revolver in any era is useful at a range of only about twenty feet. But Burgess, who had just missed catching Howell earlier in the year, was grimly determined to succeed this time, and he had an odd advantage. The wind would be blowing in his face with a Yellowstone-in-winter fury, which would likely carry off any sound he made and prevent Howell's dog from catching his scent. Burgess quickly crossed the four hundred yards, at one point jumping a ditch; his mental state could be guessed at from his later inability to remember, when asked, how he got across.

It all worked out as planned ("I expect probably I was pretty lucky," Burgess said later).[1] Howell never noticed anything amiss; he was butchering one of his kills, his hat pulled down over his face, the dog asleep under the fading warmth of a bison's rear leg. The rifle lay only fifteen feet away. Burgess got between it and Howell before sticking the .38 into what was probably the most astonished face in the Rockies. Howell came quietly, although he wanted to execute the dog for failing to warn him. Burgess stopped him, and the dog survived to appear in Haynes's famous photograph of Howell on his way to the guardhouse. The soldiers would ultimately force Howell to ski the entire distance of around sixty miles back to Mammoth.

That evening, the telephone rang at the fort, and wheels began to turn....

Let us now step back in time two days, to the afternoon of Saturday, March 10, when two other key people in this developing drama met for the first time. Billy Hofer, who was now living in Gardiner—he was not home often—hustled the couple of miles up the railroad track to meet the train at Cinnabar station. It carried Emerson Hough, at that time a modestly successful outdoor journalist who later became famous as an author of Wild West novels. His 1922 bestseller *The Covered Wagon*, produced at the very end of his life, earned a huge sum for his heirs when he became part of the very first generation of writers to tap a new vein: he sold the film rights. Hough had been sent by George Bird Grinnell and *Forest and Stream* on what at first was an important but not urgent mission: he was to ski through the park with Billy, try to get an accurate count of park bison, and report on conditions in general. Grinnell, as we will see, had political motives for sending him. Hough's description of his journey ultimately became a fourteen-part series in *Forest and Stream*. He was not expecting a scoop, and he was certainly not expecting to make history. Billy may, even at this early point, have had higher ambitions, but they would have to await developments.[2]

Either way, because Hough described his tour of the park at such length, and with Billy as the star, his account serves today as an exceptionally revealing record of what day-to-day life was like on the "job" for Billy. We need to slow down in this chapter and look at parts of the trip in detail, because Hough did us a great favor by writing this. Billy was in his prime. He was not yet Uncle Billy (no one called him that; he was still too young), but he knew the park and the surrounding terrain better than anyone alive, and his wilderness travel skills were just as unparalleled. Hough caught Billy at his best and saved that person for us. We need to look closely at what he saved.

From the start, Hough was deeply impressed with both Billy and nearly everyone else charged with caring for and protecting the national park. He and Billy hitched a ride on an army ambulance loaded with food and bound for the commissary at Fort Yellowstone. And we must now recall what I said earlier about how Yellowstone saw more snow in the past. Over the next several days, Billy would teach Hough enough about skis for him to at least survive on them and used the Mammoth area exclusively as his schoolroom. Again, among the lessons was a ski-run from the fort to the Boiling River, on the Gardner, a drop from 6200 to 5600 feet. The soldiers at the Fort were taking snow measurements by 1894, and compared to the average depths for the years 1971-2000, their measurements were 200% of "normal." The entire winter had seen comparable depths.[3]

Hough's simple description of his trip from Gardiner to Mammoth made for yet more jaw-dropping sights, for the modern reader. The route he followed in that ambulance for the most part stuck to the route of today's road: it left Gardiner, at 5300 feet, crossed a short stretch of flat bench, then met the Gardner River and soon began a sharp climb that ended at park headquarters.[4] Throughout the climb, the ambulance wheels were "crunching through snow in places apparently four feet deep." The Boiling River itself was a spot in the valley where thermal water flowed down from Mammoth Hot Springs and into the Gardner. Today, it is known the world over as one of the park's only (survivable) natural hot tubs. Hough found it enchanting mainly because it was the only break in the otherwise snowbound valley, and he was delighted to see a bluebird and some mallards there. Above it, however, the ambulance faced a "bruising pull through the deep snow of the last hill." At the top, as we might expect, Mammoth Hot Springs and the surrounding terrain were "all white and shivery looking," the springs themselves steaming madly in the frigid air. After he had toured the area, he commented directly on the weather and the snow: "Let no one suppose that March means spring in the Park. The snow envelops everything there till June. While we lay at the Post it snowed almost every day. A drift 12ft. high lay along the walk in front of the officers' quarters. Around the great springs of the Minerva Terrace the white garment of winter was apparently 6 to 10ft. high, and in drifts we could only guess how deep."[5]

Today, that last hill is still there, although the car engine usually takes care of any bruising pull. In a normal March, the cars raise dust. At the base of the final hill is a hairpin turn with the Mammoth campground on one side and on the other a little village where National Park Service employees live. Their children formerly went to school here but now travel to Gardiner. In a normal March, the kids ride their bikes and skateboards and need only watch out for occasional sidewalk-ice. To function here, skis would need wheels.

Hough, who had honestly expected to be camping every night, was happy to find himself welcomed as a guest in Superintendent Anderson's home at the fort, where he stayed from March 10 to 14. Anderson of course set out to charm this representative of one of the nation's premier conservation journals, but there was no need; they hit it off immediately, both of them lifelong outdoorsmen and utterly committed conservationists. Hough would benefit from the warm place to rest. He was young, healthy, adequately tough, and comfortable in the woods, but he knew nothing of skis. Billy Hofer, shifting into another of his many jobs—that of ski instructor—went to work on him right away.

They started with the basics, and Hough had to explain to his readers the simplest matters of nomenclature and technology. He italicized "*ski*" and at one point even explained how to pronounce it because the word was still a new borrowing from the Norwegian language, little known outside the mountains. "Billy and I had brought in both the Canadian web shoes and the Norwegian *skis*, also a toboggan," Hough began. By "Canadian web shoes," he meant what we call snowshoes. "We thought at first of using the web shoes and pulling the toboggan, but Billy later decided very wisely that it was better to stick to the *skis*, almost universally used in the Rockies, and to leave the toboggan behind, carrying everything on our backs in packs." The problem with their toboggan was its flat bottom: pulling it on skis was like pulling a tree trunk (Ed Howell's toboggan had ski-runners). "It is next to impossible to pull any weight behind the *ski*, and if one wears webs, and so gets traction power, he can not take the long runs down hill by which so much of the time is made in *ski* running." The skis regularly made too much time, as Hough would discover soon and repeatedly; like all beginners, his challenge was not making them go, but making them stop.

Billy had been doing this sort of thing since the mid-1870s— making him, incidentally, among the most experienced North American skiers of his generation—and he had refined the gear he had carried during his 1887 circuit of the park:

> For clothing, Billy's advice was followed implicitly. We wore heavy wool underwear, wool trousers, canvas overalls and canvas leggings. The underwear was supplemented by a lighter wool undershirt, over which a blue flannel shirt was worn. A canvas vest came on top of that, but no coat or overcoat was worn. Of course the latter would have been an impossibility, and the coat was replaced by a light canvas "jumper."
>
> "You've got to have canvas to break off the wind," said Billy, "and to shed the snow, and you've got to have plenty of wool underneath to keep you warm. You'll find that you won't want much on while you're traveling, but when you stop you get cold mighty quick."

They were travelling so lightly that every item counted:

> By Billy's wise advice, we wore wide felt hats of the Western type. These were better than caps, as they kept the snow from getting down the neck. In extremely cold weather we tied up the ears with a large silk handkerchief.
>
> Of course we wore belts, for a belt is warm as a coat. We

carried no weapons except a straight-bladed butcher knife apiece, for we were not hunting and needed to trim down every ounce possible in order to succeed in our mission. On our hands we wore soft castor gloves [that is, gloves made of goat skin], unless the weather was very sharp, when we slipped on over the gloves heavy calf mittens, fleece lined. In travel, the gloves, mittens and handkerchief, with maybe a strip of burlaps for strings, would be often tucked into the belt when not in use elsewhere, and Billy always wore his tin cup at his belt. When Billy got into full regalia, big camera and all, he made a wild sight, and I often teased him to stop and let me photograph him, though he always objected, and I fairly had to do that by stealth.

Hough finished with a few seemingly minor items that were actually the most crucial of all:

The feet are the main thing to be cared for in snowshoeing, for they are ground deep in the snow all day long, and in a climate where the thermometer sometimes drops to 45° below zero it is not hard to freeze the feet. The snowshoer keeps his feet carefully clean, washing them in cold water sometimes. He may wear wool socks, common broad shoes, and overshoes, surmounting the whole with canvas leggins—Billy always preferred the buckled leggins, as easier to handle when full of ice and snow—or he may use the heavy "German sock" (a felted wool sock nearly half an inch thick), which is drawn on over the light sock, and then surmounted by...Arctic overshoes. If the German sock is warm, no leggins are required, the trousers being tucked into the sock, which is drawn tight about the calf of the leg by a string....

Two pairs of colored glasses were taken along by each man, the bows being carefully wound with silk to prevent freezing the face where the steel touched. Without these glasses the glare of the snow would soon render one snow-blind.

A last item in our equipment was a wide canvas patch cemented on the front of our overshoes, where the toe strap of the *ski* passed over, used to prevent the chafing of the strap on the shoe, which is quite severe.[6]

By "leggins," Hough meant not cowboy chaps, but what we would call gaiters. The modern ski boot was not even yet science fiction, and during the trip to follow, even Billy had to stop regularly to let his feet heal.

Hough next explained to his readers how Billy went about training a new skier. Modern ski instructors would disapprove of his techniques, but he was not trying to set Hough on a path to expertise. He was trying to get a physically fit journalist competent enough to go up into the wintertime park and tell its story and not much more. Hough had the normal experience of every beginning Nordic skier to this day: he fell and fell and fell and fell until he despaired. Billy had been through this sort of thing before and kept his composure; he even photographed Hough after an elaborately catastrophic fall, then sent the photo to Grinnell, who ran it with the caption "E. Hough in a Heap." Billy taught him a few simple tricks that at least kept him upright. Hough had only just mastered sidestepping up a hill—skiers then called it "corduroying," because it made the trail (and it still does) look like a corduroy road—when Billy picked up the pace. Hough continued:

> "Come," said Billy, "and I will have some fun with you."
> He did, he did, and let no man say to the contrary. He took me through the heavy pines up to the top of a steep rise above the terrace, and politely requested me to follow my leader, saying which, he let go and slid off down the hill like a bird, calling back to me to "keep my feet together and

put on brakes with the pole." This I did as nearly as I could, and in a moment, with an ease and precision which pleased us both, I also was at the foot of the hill, but upside down, with the *skis* on top.

"We'll try another one." said Billy, who wasn't near as much discouraged as I was. "There's a pretty swift little pitch over here a way, and you can ride your pole down there."

"Riding the pole" I learned to be sitting astride of it, with the rear end of the pole dropping deep in the snow behind and thus serving as a brake. I was rejoiced to see by this means I could regulate the speed a little bit, so that I didn't feel so much as if I was going to get off the earth. Billy was pleased to be flattering when he saw that I was on top of the *skis* at the bottom of the hill, instead of their being on top of me.

"Now we'll take one steeper yet," said he. "I'll show you the way to do where it's too steep to stand up. Come ahead."

Billy stopped at the head of a sharp little pitch, which was so steep that we couldn't see to the bottom of it. All we could see was a rounded curve of white dropping down, apparently off into the blue substance which the poets call æther. Here Billy unbuckled the straps of his shoes, took the shoes off, put them together, pointed them down hill, and sat down on the middle of the two, on top of the shoe-straps. Then he gave a push or so with his hands, started, gathered speed, and whish! he was over into the unknown, apparently sliding on the seat of his overalls.

Hough tried to do the same, and after sliding out of control, flying through the air, and falling to earth, he surveyed the damage:

The dragon-headed *skis* and the eagle-eyed newspaper

man had gone clear over a 30ft. bank of snow, and buried themselves in the soft drift at its base. I had taken my first *ski*-jump, and taken it sitting down, at the take-off and the landing.

"It was steeper than I thought," said Billy, when he could undouble himself from laughing, "and the fact is, I did just what you did. I had to hurry to get out of the drift, or you'd have lit right on top of me.

"Now you've seen the gaits," continued he, "and you see how it's done. The rest you'll have to learn from practice. We'll go home now, for you don't want to get too tired at first."[7]

And that, pretty much, was that. Billy made up their packs, which were substantially similar to his 1887 packs, with one omission and one terrible addition: they left the revolver, because Anderson had arranged military escorts for much of the trip, and the Smithsonian Institution had provided a camera and equipment that was cutting-edge high tech for the era and that weighed an appalling 25.5 pounds.

Billy joined Hough at Capt. Anderson's house on the evening of the 12th, where, at 9:30 pm, Anderson answered the phone. Felix Burgess was at the other end, where he had Ed Howell in custody at the Lake Hotel. The arrest had happened that afternoon. The delighted Anderson could hardly sit still, but all three knew what would follow. At least eleven of the park bison herd were dead—counting the six hanging in the tree with the five newly shot—and the culprit would be turned loose once the Secretary of the Interior got word. Yet here, in this small disaster, lay a great opportunity. The crime and criminal both were so vile, and the lack of recourse so asinine, that this incident at last provided a lever that could be used to change the law.

Hough's series ran months after his journey through the park, not finishing until the following summer, so as he wrote, much later, he knew what the outcome would be, and we can hardly blame him for wanting to take credit: "I learned the news at once, and at once put it on the wire for FOREST AND STREAM, which had the information within twelve hours of the capture, which latter had occurred 2,000 miles away in the roughest part of the Rocky Mountains, and four days' journey from the nearest telegraph station, by the only possible means of travel. The next day FOREST AND STREAM was represented in Washington."[8]

The story had gone out through the military telegraph at Fort Yellowstone, available to the press for a fee. *Forest and Stream* announced the capture in its March 24 edition, on the front page, as the first item in the journal, but Grinnell made telephone calls of his own once he got the news. The conservation faction among wealthy East Coast outdoorsmen was by now well-organized, especially as the Boone and Crockett Club. They were more outraged than anyone, and they were in a position to get things done.

In the Beinecke Library at Yale University today, however, there exists a handwritten letter from Billy Hofer to Grinnell, written in 1918, to judge from its references to a Hough article that had run in *Forest and Stream* that year. It contains a revelation. "I see you give Hough credit" for what followed after Grinnell got the news, Billy wrote to his old friend. "Hough and I were at Andersons when the news of the capture of the buffalo hunter came in[.] Hough did not know what to do—we were to start next morning—I told him you had requested me to wire (press rates) any important news to the Forest & Stream and for him to go too[.] [A]t that Capt Anderson would see that his message got off next day." Therefore, because the truly crucial factor was Grinnell and his friends' instantaneous reaction to the news—happening long before Hough's series—it was really Billy Hofer who "lit the fuse" and thus deserved credit for the entire affair. He and Anderson both saw the outright world-historical importance of what had happened, but Billy knew immediately how to use it. The credit for that use has always gone elsewhere, but it was Billy who made the crucial connection regarding what was happening and what to do about it.[9]

Hough was himself generous about credit. In a retrospective article published in the *Saturday Evening Post* in 1920, he said that the most important news they reported was not the arrest, but the results of the bison census they conducted. "Here then we had something of a story, with some rather startling facts, gained at first hand at cost of considerable effort. We had not gone in so much for a story as for an adventure, but we had a story none the less—I do not doubt, the best one I ever did, how much or little that may measure, though it should be accredited rather to Hofer than to myself."[10] If the census was the most crucial piece of news, then Billy deserved not most, but all the credit.

However, both the story and its credit lay far in the future. For now, the two had some skiing to do. On the morning of the fourteenth, they left Fort Yellowstone, their goal the Norris Geyser Basin. Here, Hough's articles allow us to see a side of both Billy and the wintertime park that rarely appear in his own writing. It helped that Hough was effectively an outsider; he noticed phenomena that Billy took for granted. The pair faced their first challenge at almost the moment they left the fort, where they started climbing. They would have to ascend about a thousand feet to clear the Golden Gate, reach Swan Lake Flat, then head south to Norris. The physical condition of the snow would regularly be a problem throughout their circuit of the park, as Hough discovered immediately: "The worst of it was the snow stuck to our shoes and made it hard going even on the places where we didn't want to slip back any. We paused at the end of the first half hour or so and scraped off our shoes."[11] The scraping, then as now, solved the problem for a few strokes. Billy asked the soldiers traveling with them to ski ahead to Swan Lake Flat and get a fire going. When the pair at last caught up with the soldiers, Billy performed a chore he would perform many times daily while traveling and which was an inescapable part of skiing during this era. Normally, he also had to build the fire himself (Hough came to believe he could get a fire going under any conceivable circumstances):

> At last Billy and I made the last rise—I'm sure I don't know how—and in a moment more we were beside our little fire, melting snow to make tea. I drank about a quart of strong tea—and nearly met a Waterloo by doing it, for it made me sick. We ate also a bite of lunch, and fixed up our shoes, heating them scorching hot and then rubbing them quickly with wax. Billy showed me how, enjoining me by no means ever to allow a drop of water to fall on either surface of the *skis*, as it would freeze and cause the snow to stick to it. The theory of the *ski* is to slip over and through the snow without dragging any along. It is quite an art to learn all the tricks of *ski* work, and keeping the *skis* in order is one of the most important ones.

At the same time, the day revealed a fact about Billy that has never gotten much attention: he did not know everything, and like anyone, he was capable of drastic errors: "And stop eating that snow," he barked at Hough in a moment of rare impatience. "Whatever you do, and no matter how thirsty you get, you must not eat snow. If you get heated up and take one drink of cold water, that knocks you out worse than four hours of work. It weakens you right away. You must not drink between meals, and you mustn't eat snow." Unless the skier was actually hypothermic or at risk of getting there soon, Billy was wrong. Eating snow is harmless. It is today the fifth food group for the Yellowstone skier.

Furthermore, the tea did not make Hough sick. If anything, the caffeine probably helped. He likely had hypobaropathy—altitude sickness, that is. His home in Chicago was at six hundred feet above sea level. Swan Lake Flat was above seven thousand. The mere four days he had been in the park was nowhere near adequate for his body to acclimate. The two kept skiing, but it soon was clear that Hough would never make Norris in one day, so Billy called an emergency halt at the nearest backcountry patrol cabin, the Crystal Springs shack, as soon as they could get there. It was still miles ahead, however, and Hough grew more and more ill. Billy nursed him along in a manner that he must have had a great deal of practice at, over the years:

> If Billy had not stayed back with me, it is very probable I should never have gotten into camp that night or any other night. That he did so was only what he would in mountain honor consider himself bound to do, but none the less the fact that he did has always left a soft spot in my heart for Billy, and a feeling that if he were in a tight place I should like to stay with him in turn. Certainly he helped me through a tight enough place—about as bad an afternoon as I care to put in....
>
> Billy was anxious, I know, for the day was waning, and it had come on to snow most dismally. Worse still, the snow began to stick to the shoes when we entered the dense forest, and it was hard plugging for a man even at his best. We worried along over one little hill after another, not daring to stop long enough to build a fire and wax our shoes. Once in a while we would turn from the trail, tramp a hole down in the snow— which was 8ft. deep on the level here—and sit for a moment resting, with our packs leaning on the snow. Then we would cut a pine bough and rub the *skis* hard with the resinous tips and needles. This would help the shoes for a way, when perhaps we would cut off another bough, throw it on the snow and drag the *skis* across that to cut off the adhering snow, and "slick" the shoes a little. Billy would not let me sit down long at a time, but kept me moving; and at length toward evening I began to get stronger.
>
> "It's only three-quarters of a mile further now," said Billy finally. "Can you make it?"

"Betcherlife, Billy," I said, making an awful bluff.

"Come on, then," he said, and so set out at a better pace. But it transpired that he had feared I could not go even that distance, for it was not a quarter of a mile further before he turned out to the left from the trail, into a deep thicket of pines that fringed a little stream.

"Brace up, old man," said he, "we're home now."

Hough collapsed on the floor of the Crystal Springs patrol cabin, now stuffed absolutely full of soldiers, and drifted into an apathetic sleep. As is normal with altitude sickness, he was fine in the morning.

The pair arrived at Norris Geyser Basin the next day. Their feet already blistered and fighting sticky snow, they decided to spend the night at the Army patrol cabin there, and so had the dubious privilege of meeting Ed Howell as Felix Burgess escorted him through on his way to the hoosegow at Fort Yellowstone. Granted an afternoon off the trail, Billy slid easily into another of his many jobs, and showed Hough the entire Norris basin, identifying and explaining every major spring and geyser.

Here was an unusually forceful demonstration of what made him different from nearly any other guide: he had worked for so many scientists that, given his voracious curiosity, they had nearly made him one himself. He had the single essential quality that would, for instance, have enabled him to likely sail through one of the new Ph.D. programs in his hometown at Yale, had he been born wealthy: he liked science because it was fun. This quality was infectious, as Hough discovered (we saw it before, but it bears repeating):

> "[T]hose to whom the geysers are an old story in summer became enthusiastic over them in this winter aspect, and even Billy was eager to go over the entire basin again. To Billy, of course, much of our pleasure was due here, for

he knows every geyser thoroughly, and is a most interesting and thorough and enthusiastic guide. If I had a friend wishing to make the Park trip, I should by all means advise him to get Billy to go along, for he knows the Park inch by inch, and even its scientific features and scientific history are not strange in the least to him, since he has been so much associated there with parties of scientists of all sorts. Billy could talk of rhyolite and algae and silicates in a way to make your head swim."[12]

They arose before dawn the next day. They would do so often in the next few days, trying to catch the snow at its coldest, iciest, and least sticky. This time, they failed, and the relatively short, twelve-mile trip to the Grand Canyon of the Yellowstone turned into one of the more punishing of the entire journey. They were pleased to move into one of the hotels at Canyon, and they prepared for the real business at hand: counting the animals, especially the bison, of which Billy, Hough, Grinnell, and plenty of others wanted a precise census.

That may strike us today as impossibly ambitious, but while the bison were clustered into geographically distinct and not terribly large groups, the general location of the groups was known to park experts like Billy (if not to their entire satisfaction), and they soon would have some impressive reinforcements. The apparently unfreeze-able F. Jay Haynes was still at the Lake, but intended to ski north and join in the effort, adding his own small military escort to help. They arrived that evening.

Billy, fighting an injury to his ankle that may have hurt worse than Hough realized, called another halt and spent a day reading a novel. When not touring the geyser basin, he had done the same at Norris, and anyone who had seen him, Hough remarked, would have "thought he was plenty lazy. That is correct. All mountain men are lazy when at home. It is the delving lowlander who gets out before breakfast to plow corn. But on the trail I found Billy an energetic and tireless commander-in-chief, always alert, but alert for all and not for himself alone."[13] Interacting with the man daily under often trying circumstances, Hough had noticed a quality that is today still visible in his *Forest and Stream* series, but only with careful study, because of Billy's easy-going style. He was in fact in charge of everything. The soldiers were of course following Superintendent Anderson's orders and those of his handful of junior officers, but on the actual trail, Billy called the shots, as he should have because he had the most experience in both skiing and Yellowstone.

With their leader reading a romance novel with his foot in the air, the whole combined effort fell into a state of temporary collapse. Hough and some of the soldiers built a ski run and held a little Winter Olympiad thirty years before the first real one. Haynes tried to teach Hough how to use a camera. Then, on March 21, with a palpable feeling of quickening, the combined party skied south five miles to Hayden Valley: "Here we were no doubt to determine the success or failure of an important part of our work. Somewhere, behind some of those long tongues of timber which pierced the five miles square or more of open whiteness, there were without doubt numbers of the greatest and the rarest game of the American continent, which we had come so far to see at home on the winter range, and to enable others to see, if we might be so fortunate."[14] Hough meant that they were going to try to photograph the bison while counting their numbers, but they did not then know that they would "enable others to see" in more ways than they thought.

First, Billy had to enable them to stay alive, because they intended to spend the night outdoors in the valley. The party had split up, and he had given the others instructions to fulfill. The soldiers likely did the heavy work. Hough wrote:

> We found that the others had dug a hole in the snow
> down to the ground, the level of the snow being about even

with one's face as he stood on the ground. The hole was about 12 feet across. Around the edge of this, following Billy's general advice given earlier, they had stepped a number of poles, cut from young pines, about 18 or 20ft. long, there meeting at the top lodge-pole fashion. On the inside of these poles was stretched in a semicircle the light [canvas] lodge-lining which Billy had brought all this way for this express purpose. This lining was about 5ft. high. Above its height there was absolutely no covering at all, as the lodge poles were not numerous enough to make any covering or wind break. A fire was built in the center of this "tepee," if such we could call our extremely well ventilated winter house, and the boys had cut a plenty of wood. A stairway, made by treading short logs into the snow, enabled one to get downstairs into the hole in the snow, which constituted the salon, dining room and sleeping apartments of the edifice. Billy looked at it critically and said it would do as long as it didn't rain.[15]

The temperature had dipped below zero that morning, so we might guess that he was joking. Indeed, the entire trip was not without its moments of humor, as when Billy had to cross Alum Creek twice, first to transport the leviathan camera, then to retrieve his skis. During that era, in the winter, travelers—incredibly—forded creeks in bare feet. Haynes was already across and geared up when Billy reached midstream: "Mr. Haynes called to him to hold still while he got a picture of him. Billy posed patiently, out in the ice water, and Mr. Haynes made a careful shot. The result is a very interesting picture, showing Billy in the creek, with others just putting on their shoes."[16] It is another famous image of this crucial winter, although Hough did not preserve Billy's comments. We might again guess at what happened: the comments were unprintable.

The combined parties spent the day in a mad dash after both the elk and bison that wintered in the valley. They worked late, and in the deep twilight, the parties broke up, Billy and Hough intending to spend the night in Billy's teepee. There followed an ordeal that came close to unsettling Hough, although with the perspective of time, he was able to write a portrait of what winter camping was like in the age before equipment from The North Face and Patagonia even existed. As it developed, the teepee that the soldiers had built that morning was only an approximation of what Billy wanted, a kind of crude rough draft that he now spent hours polishing (although he did not admit to it, he likely recruited the soldiers in order to hand part of the grunt-work to someone else; they had moved an immense quantity of snow and lumber):

> "We can't sleep in this place the way it's fixed now," said Billy, after the others had gone. "We've got to shorten those poles, so the lodge lining will lean over us a little more and throw some of the heat down." So saying, he went to work with the axe and proposed to make a more woodsmanlike tepee than our friends had done. He cut about 4ft. off the end of each pole and rearranged them all at the top. This left them closer together at the top and not so high above us, with a much less acute angle at the top. Then we cut pine boughs and filled in all around between the snow wall of the lodge poles and put chunks of snow back of that, so that the wind would not suck down the wall behind us. After that we tied the light lodge lining around inside, and the tepee now being smaller, the lining met at the door, so that we had a fair wall around us, though no roof to speak of. The lining pitched forward pretty well, making a circular "lean-to" wall, which would throw the heat of our fire in and down. We got in a lot of wood, and of course built our fire in the center of the tepee, of necessity not a very big fire. Under the lining we laid down the side logs of our beds, of which we made two. Between the logs we piled in pine

boughs for bedding, as many as we could find out in the snow, for we had now been working an hour and a half, and it was about as dark as it ever would be that night.[17]

They ate a little and tried to sleep. Hough was haunted all night. "How shall I describe it—this feeling that there was a Spirit of Cold about on every hand, eager to destroy? One could feel it tapping, tapping, for weak places in one's covering and in one's vitality." But he also remembered Billy feeding the fire, even disappearing outside in the middle of the night to find more wood. Did Billy keep him alive? It is likely; Hough believed he had. When the soldiers arrived the next morning, they were surprised to find the pair unharmed. The thermometer at Canyon had hit 21 degrees below zero.[18]

There followed another day of frenzied chasing after the bison herd—stressful to the animals, but at that point in history, a census was a tough-love necessity. Hough and Billy spent the night at the patrol cabin the Army had built on upper Alum Creek, in Hayden Valley. After the night in the teepee, Hough found it a great relief. In the morning, March 23, they left for their next destination: they intended to cross the Continental Divide and reach the even more "luxurious" accommodations at the Fountain Hotel, in the Lower Geyser Basin. They would travel from the Alum Creek shack roughly southwest to cross the Divide and intersect the Firehole River, at which point they would turn toward the hotel. The route followed, if roughly, the modern Mary Mountain hiking trail, and they were doing double duty: they were chasing rumors of more bison in the thermal area at Mary Mountain, probably the one named Highland Hot Springs.

Both Billy and Hough had a soldier with him, and Billy went first because he was by far the superior tracker. He located the Mary Mountain herd, and Hough arrived at a final and reliable count of eighty-five bison in the whole of Hayden Valley. Haynes and his party had counted the bison Ed Howell left alive in Pelican

Valley, so they were approaching a final count, and would continue
to chase rumors down to the level of individual animals. Billy had
been both incorrect and correct about the number of bison. There
were far fewer than he thought, but at the same time, he was right
that a full count required an animal-by-animal census on skis, pref-
erably done by one T.E. Hofer. Obviously anticipating objections
to his claim, Hough defended his numbers as he wrote them:

> We were now well settled in the conviction that the
> number of buffalo left alive in the Park was not one-half or
> one-third that [other people] generally supposed, and from
> what we had seen we feared that the killing had been heavier
> than anyone had dreamed. I would state here that I think
> our view of the case was conservative and fairly accurate.
> One knowing the country less thoroughly than Billy might
> have supposed that the buffalo seen this day and the day be-
> fore were two distinct herds. Believing this, his report would
> declare the number seen and actually counted to be just
> twice what it really was. Let us wait till some one has seen
> in one day and in one herd 200 buffalo in the Park before
> we ever again believe there are so many as that left. I do not
> believe there are 150.[19]

There followed another mad dash. Then as now, mad dashes
were a part of winter travel because the traveler so often had to outrun bad conditions or a turn in the weather, and was so often fighting the clock in the abbreviated little hiccup that is a "day" during
northern winters. They got to experience all the extremes of cross-
country skiing: the exhausting climb up, the terrifying, exhilarating
run down—this time up and down the Continental Divide—and
finally a long, flat slog over level ground that delayed their arrival
at the hotel until well after dark.

The pair had adopted, from the start, a pattern of travel that made
sense and might even have been adopted without much thought:

sprint-rest-work, sprint-rest-work. It was past time to rest, especially because, although he remained the fastest skier in any group
that coalesced, Billy's heel was now hurting so badly that he had sat
on a stump, examining his bad foot bare in the evening air, while
the others went on toward the Lower Geyser Basin and left him to
catch up afterward.[20] (Hough later blamed the Smithsonian and
took charge of the camera that Billy had hauled all this way; to add
insult to literal injury, the museum lost the photographs—without
Haynes, Grinnell would have been nearly without photographs of
the expedition). Hough rested at the hotel, then did what for him
was actually work: he toured the geyser basin, producing the kind
of florid description that he actually apologized for, but that kept
his audience reading and that the geysers deserved anyway.

There was a hint of spring in the air, however, if virtually un-
noticeable to the modern reader (during this week, one of the soldiers on the west boundary of the park, a Private Mathews, froze
to death).[21] As they toured the Firehole River geyser basins, they
found the trails covered with the kind of snow that nearly always
appears as the sun gets higher in the sky and the skiing assumes
its spring aspect: the surface became a pasty nightmare. The most
expert waxing job Billy could provide could not stop it from sticking and turning their skis to rocks.[22] They left the Fountain Hotel
at midnight, intending to make Fort Yellowstone in two final mad
dashes. They succeeded, if we can ignore Hough's near-fatal slip on
the log bridge over the Gibbon (where, recall, Snowshoe Pete himself had gone swimming in winter 1887). Hough managed to crawl
across the bridge without losing his skis or his life and found Billy
calmly waxing his own skis not far ahead, unaware that anything
was amiss.[23] It was Billy's one serious miscalculation of the trip: he
had confidence in his skills as a ski instructor and thought Hough
fit to keep up with the best. His normally near-infallible ability to
assess actual danger in the outdoors had for once failed him.

They arrived without incident at headquarters, where Captain
Anderson again put Hough up and was pleased to report that Ed

Howell remained in the frigid little Fort Yellowstone calaboose. He would have a longer stay there than the average tenant. In the reminiscence he wrote for the *Saturday Evening Post* in 1920, Hough recalled an orderly bringing Anderson his morning mail, which included an officious looking package from the Department of the Interior, containing, they knew, the order to turn Howell loose. "I know what's in it," said Captain Anderson, "but I can't see it if I don't open the envelope. I won't open it for about a week."[24] In reading this, it is hard not to laugh out loud today.

Hough had one more task to perform; Grinnell also wanted to publicize the size of the elk herd. As we have seen, the herd had grown prodigiously. Although Billy had already provided the most accurate counts he could, in the pages of *Forest and Stream*, Grinnell had journalistic plans for them. For their own good, he intended to use them as a grand political "MacGuffin."

So on March 30, Billy and Hough once again left the fort, their trip shorter this time in part because the always helpful Captain Anderson arranged a wagon ride as far as the wagon could go, in the early spring conditions. It went about as far as Sheepeater Canyon, where today the steel span that locals call the "high bridge" provides a little terror for the motorist afraid of heights. The pair struggled up the hills on the east side, slowed by the spring snow, then crossed the Blacktail Deer Plateau to reach Yancey's, where Billy had counted elk in vast numbers just sitting at the primitive inn.

Uncle John Yancey was still alive and still running his peculiar little hostel. ("My impression," Hough wrote with tongue in cheek, "is that he was there before the Cañon was finished.")[25] Yancey would live for nearly another decade and would have to leave the scene before Billy could quite become the park's new Uncle. They also found Tazewell Woody, the grizzled mountain man whom Billy had met during his very first tour of the park.[26] It was Woody who made what may at first have seemed a rash promise, to Hough: "Learning of our purpose, Woody quietly told us that he could take us to a point within two miles where we could see over 1,000 elk at one sight."

After a day spent resting, he fulfilled his promise, taking the group to a nearby promontory, where, standing on the south side of the Yellowstone River canyon and surveying the north, the African savannah again appeared in the early spring Rockies. Woody, like an honest frontiersman—they had a well-earned reputation for just making things up, when they talked to outsiders—had understated his case and let the animals make it for him. Hough was first mesmerized and then something more—delighted, yes, but stunned:

> Below us we saw some dark figures outlined against the snow. They moved and we looked more closely. A dozen elk came out from behind the point of timber in which they stood, and looked curiously up at us on our lofty perch, but they did not take alarm. Then beyond the river, on the bare ground, we saw another group, and another, and another, and then dozens of others. In singles, in pairs, in groups, in small bands, the elk were feeding in hundreds and hundreds, scattered all over a strip of country five miles across. The whole further bank of the Yellowstone, here laid open before us as though by special plan, was alive with elk. In all my life I had never seen so much game at one sight.
>
> For the first time in the Park I felt an absolute thrill of amazement and delight at seeing the great animals in such numbers, in such content, in such apparent security and freedom from suspicion. There are few hunters who have seen enough of the more fertile game countries of the now barren West to remember any such sight as this. There is no other part of America where such a sight will ever be seen again. Here, protected by the Park, these noble animals had chosen out a ground where nature had provided opportunity to feed throughout the winter.... We had found the elk

just where we thought to find them, and in numbers which
set at rest all theorizing as to where or what was the winter
range of the elk of these mountains of the Park. Here was
their range, below us, before us, around, on every side of
us, and the elk were there, there not only in hundreds, but
absolutely in thousands.[27]

Actually, the elk would have preferred to leave for lower ground,
probably down the Yellowstone River valley and into Montana—
as noted, you will not see them in such numbers today, not in
that spot—but they knew, or sensed, enough to know that guns
awaited them if they crossed that strange, imaginary legal barrier
to the north. Billy and Hough skied up and down the Yellowstone
and ventured up the Lamar, counting elk until the exercise lost all
meaning. Hough's own report merely served as corroboration and
support for the counts Billy had been providing *Forest and Stream*
readers for years. Given that those readers were nearly all hunters,
we can easily imagine their reaction. It must have lit their imaginations like a powerful psychoactive drug.

Hough's assignment was complete. The party had planned to
leave for the fort on April 2. Billy now showed greatness as an
educator: he understood that for an advanced student to learn, that
person had to be allowed to make stupid mistakes and learn from
them, and he was not just teaching Hough to ski. Those lessons
were done. He was trying to teach him Yellowstone:

Billy set this date conditionally, as there were threats of
a storm which might stop us. When the morning came,
Billy did not want to start, for he could see by looking at the
tops of the peaks about us that it was storming up above,
even though in sheltered Pleasant Valley it all seemed quiet
and peaceful. It looked like a bad snow, Billy said, and he
advised holding up for the day. We would much better have
taken this advice, as indeed most of Billy's advice on such

matters, but I was getting uneasy about being so long in the Park, and besides was afraid Capt. Anderson would send out a team to the Gardiner [River] hill to meet us, in which case I thought we ought to be there. I therefore insisted on a start, and that we did, though Billy was none too willing.

For some reasons I am glad we did start, because I got a chance at the one remaining mountain experience which we needed to complete the eventfulness of our journey. I had heard of the storms of this region, whose violence and intensity were such that the traveler was entirely bewildered and forced to stop where he was, unable to tell the points of the compass or to see any landmark. Of course, I had read all about Dakota blizzards and I had been in a blizzard on the Western plains hard enough to "drift" all the range cattle for fifty miles, but I could not say that I had ever seen a blizzard quite bad enough to warrant the timidity which all these mountain men seemed to feel about the storms up in the Park. Billy seemed to think that being caught in a storm was about the only real danger there was in this winter voyaging, but that one thing would always make him serious. He was serious as we said good-bye at Yancey's and started up the first hill. At that time there were a few flakes of snow falling.

When we topped the first pitch and reached the ledge, from which we could almost toss a stone down on the cabin roof below, our few flakes of snow had become a few thousand and we saw that the storm was coming. We pressed on for a quarter of a mile, perhaps, and the storm thickened so fast that we could hardly see.

"Have you got enough of it," Billy asked, "or do you want to go ahead?"

"Go on ahead," I said, "it can't snow this way very long." Billy grunted and went on. I could not see him 30ft. ahead of me. The trail of his *skis* filled almost as fast as he passed. We made the top of still another little hill. It seemed only to reach another level of the storm. Raising my head, I tried to look ahead, half-blinded, but all of which I could become conscious was an advancing wall of thick, smothering white. There was no landscape. I could not see a tree. The trail had no sides, no end. There was no distance, no direction. Everything was swallowed up in an eddying, whirling, impenetrable mask of snow. There was no atmosphere. It had all turned to snow.

"Have you got enough?" Billy asked again, calmly.

"No!" I said, idiotically proud and ashamed to go back. "Go ahead. We'll hole up over the next hill and wait till it blows over."

Billy was dead game, and once more turned forward.

I suppose we went to the foot of the next hill. I lost him in the snow, and could only keep the trail by looking close down at my feet. The snow was damp, and came down in sheets rather than in flakes. I never knew before how snow could fall. We were all wet through in a few moments. We could see nothing and hear nothing. At every breath I was learning how a fellow could get lost in the mountains, how in a storm like this, which might last for days, he would lose all sense of direction and wander he knew not whither; how he would become wet through; how he would chill in the cold following the snow; how he would try to build a shelter and perhaps fail, perhaps succeed; how at last he would sit down by his little fire, perhaps, and give up, and be buried by the snow and perhaps never seen again, even though close to the trail.[28]

It was Billy who finally turned them around, but Hough had learned his lesson. They made an uneventful trip to headquarters the next day. Hough rested, and like anyone who experiences Yellowstone the way he had, he fantasized about staying forever. Instead, he boarded the train, returned to Chicago, and started hammering hard on his typewriter.

The wheels were in motion. Hough would soon give George Bird Grinnell what may have been the best long feature series *Forest and Stream* ever published. Much more important, as we will see, history was changing.

Members of the epic 1894 Yellowstone ski trip cross Alum Creek. Forest and Stream *writer Emerson Hough is seated, far left, U.S. Army Sergeant Morrison is standing, Bobbie Burns is seated next, and Billy Hofer is fording the creek. The photograph is by noted Yellowstone photographer F. Jay Haynes. This is the photograph for which Haynes made Billy stand still in the cold water and wait for Haynes to compose the photograph. See page 205.* MONTANA HISTORICAL SOCIETY RESEARCH CENTER, PHOTOGRAPHIC ARCHIVES, HAYNES FOUNDATION COLLECTION.

CHAPTER TEN

An Influential Man

That moment at Captain Anderson's house at park headquarters, that moment when Felix Burgess called in to say that Ed Howell was on his way to the "cooler" (pretty much literally), was a pivotal event in the history of environmental politics. We can hardly fault Hough for at first missing its significance. After Billy told him to send the news to Grinnell immediately, as fast as the Army telegraphers could deliver it, events moved with dizzying speed. Indeed, given the previous environmental history of the West, dominated as it was by rapid and nearly nonstop destruction, the speed of events is surprising merely to look back on today, over a century later. The very legal status and significance of the park changed almost before Billy and Hough had finished skiing through it. Senator Vest for years had been advocating stringent penalties against poachers. That year, however, it was Congressman John F. Lacey of Iowa who sponsored the act that would provide for such penalties, and so the law that came of it has been known ever since as the Lacey Act. Its formal name was the National Park Protective Act, and it placed Yellowstone National Park under the jurisdiction of the United States Judicial District of Wyoming. The park would now be subject to federal law, Interior Department regulation, and the laws of Wyoming. Harming any animal above the level of a mosquito would be illegal—fish, then as now, were the major exception—and the punishment was no longer a joke. Instead of a brief spell in Fort Yellowstone's clink, the poacher would now face a fine of $1000, two years in a for-real penitentiary, or both.

When Burgess captured Howell, the bill was in subcommittee. The news put it on the fastest of tracks. Richard Bartlett summarized what followed: "In presenting its recommendations to the House favoring passage, the subcommittee noted that 'a few days ago poachers entered the park and commenced the slaughter of these animals....Prompt action is necessary or the last remaining herd of buffalo will be destroyed....'" This account had been a bit garbled, but the congressmen heard about Burgess and Howell. "Thus was the Lacey Act brought before the House," wrote historian Bartlett, "and guided through [it] under the watchful eyes of Congressmen Lacey and [David B.] Henderson; through the Senate the bill was shepherded by Senator Vest. Differences were ironed out in conference committee and the bill became law May 7, 1894."[1]

In future years, the Army would decide it had no choice, and would round up the remaining bison and breed them to keep them from vanishing entirely. The very first efforts along this line actually occurred not long after Hough's visit, with Billy again in charge. Here was yet another of his dozens of jobs, that of a game warden, engaged in a kind of practical wildlife management. The initial plan involved a feedlot in the same area where Hough and Billy had found the largest concentration of the animals a year and a half earlier, as Aubrey Haines explained: "The enclosure was constructed by Hofer on Alum Creek in the fall of 1895. A stout fence of poles encompassing a considerable area was arranged to follow the higher, windswept ground, and openings were left on the east and west sides for a buffalo trail that passed directly across the area. A stack of wild hay inside the fence was the bait that was expected to attract any buffalo visiting Hayden Valley, and it was arranged for soldiers to watch the enclosure and shut the herd up when the time came."

Of course, not even Billy could manage such unmanageable animals. Nor could he control the weather. "The plan was a total failure. A few buffalo visited the enclosure early in the winter, but it [probably a gate on the fence] was left open in the hope that others would be attracted there. The snowfall was light that year, however, and the animals soon scattered beyond reach."[2]

Surprisingly, as recently as the late 1990s, this corral was still partly intact. Haines examined it in the 1930s, and Lake District ranger John Lounsbury in turn rediscovered it in the 1990s, when a team from the National Park Service rode horses to the remote location and were able to document the entire structure. They found, riding its perimeter with GPS units, that each of its four sides measured at least a half-mile. Billy had not done all the physical labor himself; he hired youngsters from local ranches, kids who knew this sort of work, using money provided by the Smithsonian (so perhaps lugging their camera all that way, during the 1894 ski, had an indirect payoff). Billy chose a classic Western buck-and-rail fence design, made of local lodgepole; the stumps, with axe marks still visible, today stand nearby, with the baling wire that held posts and rails together littering the ground. Billy built the structure to last, but he was up against insuperable challenges. "Bison go where they want," Lounsbury commented, explaining that even during 1895-1896, a winter of light snowfall, enough snow still covered the ground that it drifted over some of the fence rails and froze. Any bison remaining in the enclosure simply walked over the fence and wandered away.[3]

In the end, the Army decided that the effort to save the bison would require a substantial ranching operation in the Lamar River valley. Still, the bison we see in Yellowstone today are descendants of that last wild herd that Billy, Haynes, Hough, and the rest of their combined teams had counted in March 1894.

Those hordes of elk that Billy had been reporting for years—

and which, to speak anachronistically, had so thoroughly blown Hough's mind—served a different but related purpose. Grinnell trumpeted the high number of elk because it served yet another of his causes: that of finally killing all efforts to build railroads through the park.

As we have seen, one of Billy's first jobs had been to assist in a survey of prospective Northern Pacific routes through the park, a project that was soon abandoned. However, the railroad men and their allies had never given up. In 1894, the major effort was known as the "segregation scheme," one of many such schemes through the years.[4] The idea this time was to remove the "Montana strip" from the park by privatizing it. Look at a map of Yellowstone. Although the precise lines have been altered through the years, today as then, a significant section of parkland lies suspended in a long, Montana rectangle between the northern boundary of the park and the state of Wyoming. The scheme involved levering this section off and using it to construct a railroad from Livingston, Montana, to the gold mining camp at Cooke City. Anyone at all familiar with the terrain, however, could see instantly that the Montana strip was hopelessly rough—full of mountains and canyons—for such a purpose. A railroad would instead have to follow approximately the route Billy and Hough had skied to reach Yancey's, which is also approximately the route of the modern road. That route veered well into Wyoming.

Even the arrival of the automobile could not kill dreams of rails through Yellowstone. They are not even dead yet. During the 1970s, the National Park Service seriously studied the idea of a monorail to replace the Grand Loop Road, and my contacts among the old timers in the park tell me that, while the plan was shelved long ago, it is still on that shelf, and some park managers still quietly consider it a fallback option if repairing the roads becomes prohibitively expensive. But the Cooke City segregation scheme of 1894 did die. Grinnell and his friends killed it, and they used that elk herd as their lever. A Cooke City railroad would have had to be routed right through the elk, destroying their habitat, killing quantities outright, and turning the survivors into refugees. Too many influential and wealthy sportsmen now knew about that herd to allow it to be destroyed, especially for so marginal a purpose. To be honest, they wanted to shoot a few (or many) themselves. And the Lacey Act came into play here too, as Haines perceptively noted: "The legislation enacted with such ease did cure a congenital defect that had troubled our first national park from its birth, but it did more than that. It meant ultimate defeat for the... segregationists who had been attempting to turn the Park to their own advantage, a result that did not stem from any provision of the Lacey Act but only from its existence. With passage of that legislation, opponents of the Park lost the leverage that had been their only hope: the ability to deny what was so desperately needed."[5] The act had, figuratively speaking, broken a years-long filibuster, providing both a protection and a sense of permanence for Yellowstone National Park that had not yet entirely taken hold.[6]

But who, exactly, were "Grinnell and his friends"? The question is especially important because so many were Billy's friends, too, or at the very least his employers. Digging into his life, one is continuously surprised at the range of people he knew, so many of them wealthy, powerful, famous, and accomplished. One of them still stands out more than any other, because he remains a household name: Theodore Roosevelt.

When Billy Hofer first met him, Roosevelt was still only a modestly well-known politician, although he had been born with the bluest of blood, a member of the old East Coast aristocracy. He had been crucial, with Grinnell, in helping to turn conservation as a political movement from a hole-and-corner affair into a force to be reckoned with, capable of, say, pushing the Lacey Act through Congress with such extraordinary speed. It helped that the movement was now organized. In 1887, Roosevelt helped Grinnell found the Boone and Crockett Club, among the world's first organizations devoted to environmental activism, and he was president of the organization when Ed Howell opened fire on the Yellowstone bison in 1894. Billy had already worked for Roosevelt in Yellowstone, the beginning of a long association he developed with a family that was then entering its period of greatest influence over the nation and the world. Here is the story.

Roosevelt first employed him in September, 1891, on a hunt south of the park that the future president described in one of his early hunting books, *The Wilderness Hunter*, published in 1893. The trip took them to a place Billy had known long and well, and to which he kept returning: the Two-Ocean Pass region south of the park. Roosevelt found the affair glorious: "This was one of the pleasantest hunts I ever made. As always in the mountains, save where the country is so rough and so densely wooded that one must go afoot, we had a pack-train; and we took a more complete outfit than we had ever before taken on such a hunt, and so travelled in much comfort."[7]

In fact, in Roosevelt's account, it began to resemble one of his later African safaris. "On this trip we had with us two hunters, Tazewell Woody and Elwood Hofer, a packer who acted as cook, and a boy to herd the horses. Of the latter, there were twenty: six saddle-animals and fourteen for the packs—two or three being spare horses, to be used later in carrying the elk antlers, sheep-horns, and other trophies. Like most hunters' pack-animals, they were either half-broken, or else broken down; tough, unkempt, jaded-looking beasts of every color—sorrel, buckskin, pinto, white, bay, roan. After the day's work was over, they were turned loose to shift for themselves; and about once a week they strayed, and all hands had to spend the better part of the day hunting for them."[8] The horses were needed to haul the party's considerable baggage.

From our point of view today, the trip was most useful in showing us that Billy, even at this relatively late date, was not always the star. The problem here was that he was effectively outranked, because Tazewell Woody was along (Roosevelt alone, it seemed, could spell his first name correctly). Woody was just the sort of frontiersman whom Roosevelt loved, and everyone else fell beneath Woody's shadow. As Roosevelt explained: "The train travelled in Indian file. At the head, to pick the path, rode tall, silent old Woody, a true type of the fast vanishing race of game hunters and Indian fighters, a man who had been one of the California forty-niners, and who ever since had lived the restless, reckless life of the wilderness. Then came [Monroe] Ferguson"—Roosevelt's partner in his ranching business—"and myself; then the pack-animals, strung out in line; while from the rear rose the varied oaths of our three companions, whose miserable duty it was to urge forward the beasts of burden."[9]

How miserable was it? Considerably miserable. Billy's major responsibility was probably in serving as a kind of foreman over the packer and the "boy" who were also along. The horses were actually a nightmare, as TR made clear: "It is heart-breaking work to drive a pack-train through thick timber and over mountains, where there is either a dim trail or none. The animals have a perverse faculty for choosing the wrong turn at critical moments; and they are continually scraping under branches and squeezing between tree-trunks, to the jeopardy or destruction of their burdens. After having been laboriously driven up a very steep incline, at the cost of severe exertion both to them and to the men, the foolish creatures turn and run down to the bottom, so that all the work has to be done over again."[10]

No wonder that Billy was cursing. Roosevelt got his trophies with Woody showing him the way and Billy following behind in the dust and mud. Roosevelt ended his trip by killing "three great bulls"—bull elk, they were, and enormous ones. He was pleased indeed. Modern environmentalists always have trouble with Roosevelt on this point…but as Billy had shown, there were plenty of elk, he was not slaughtering indiscriminately, and he was doing everything in his power to ensure that even if he killed a few, there would be even more next year. For his era, these actions made him a wild-eyed environmental militant.

Then, surely to Billy's relief, the party broke up and dumped most of the horse herd: "a day later Hofer and I, with two pack-ponies," wrote Roosevelt, "made a rapid push for the Upper Geyser Basin." Surely they killed the elk below the south boundary of the park and not inside the sacred lines…but the boundary was not always marked, they had wandered broadly, and one wonders whether they knew it or not (the irony, if they had unwittingly killed the animals in the park, would have been acute). "We travelled fast. The first day was gray and overcast, a cold wind blowing strongly in our faces.…At dusk we halted and went into camp, by some small pools on the summit of the pass north of Red Mountain." The quickest route from Two Ocean Plateau to the Upper Geyser Basin would have led them over Paycheck Pass, north of the Red Mountains; here surely was their campsite, even though Roosevelt had used the old name for the tallest mountain in this small range, Mount Sheridan.[11]

The elk were bugling all around, deep in the "autumn" rut; that sound was the hauntingly distinctive warning that the Yellowstone winter had essentially arrived, as Roosevelt noted: "We pitched our cozy tent, dragged great stumps for the fire, cut evergreen boughs for our beds, watered the horses, tethered them to improvised picket-pins in a grassy glade, and then set about getting supper ready. The wind had gone down, and snow was falling thick in large, soft flakes; we were evidently at the beginning of a heavy snowstorm. All night we slept soundly in our snug tent." But now the trip started to go sour for Roosevelt: "When we arose at dawn there was a foot and a half of snow on the ground, and the flakes were falling as fast as ever. There is no more tedious work than striking camp in bad weather; and it was over two hours from the time we rose to the time we started. It is sheer misery to untangle picket-lines and to pack animals when the ropes are frozen; and by the time we had loaded the two shivering, wincing pack-ponies, and had bridled and saddled our own riding-animals, our hands and feet were numb and stiff with cold, though we were really hampered by our warm clothing."

Then it got really sour: "My horse was a wild, nervous roan," wrote TR, "and as I swung carelessly into the saddle, he suddenly began to buck before I got my right leg over, and threw me off. My thumb was put out of joint. I pulled it in again, and speedily caught my horse in the dead timber. Then I treated him as what the cowboys call a 'mean horse,' and mounted him carefully, so as not to let him either buck or go over backward. However, his preliminary success had inspirited him, and a dozen times that day he began to buck, usually choosing a down grade, where the snow was deep, and there was much fallen timber."

As we have seen, Billy's life is actually well-documented, the documents simply being badly scattered. As we will see, Roosevelt and Billy became friends, but here, the documents largely fail us. Virtually no communications between the two have survived from the early 1890s, and Yellowstone was only a small part of an absurdly full life for Roosevelt. What follows is speculation, but I believe that their friendship was born that night and morning, when Billy had Roosevelt to himself, beneath the stately red-and-white flanks of Mount Sheridan, and Roosevelt learned that this was no mere hireling. For Billy, watching a wealthy Easterner as he had his thumb nearly ripped out, who then calmly performed an anesthetic-free emergency reduction procedure on himself, then rode one of those tumultuous horses through the snow all the way to Old Faithful—a ride requiring that they cross the Continental Divide at least once and, given their direction of travel, probably again and again—it cannot help but have impressed Hofer.

At least the ordeal was nearly finished, as much as Roosevelt had enjoyed himself: "All day long we pushed steadily through the cold, blinding snowstorm.... At nightfall, chilled through, we reached the Upper Geyser Basin. Here I met a party of railroad surveyors and engineers, coming in from their summer's field-work." And here were those railroads and their officials, *again*, this time at least offering some help in a pinch: "One of them lent me a saddle-horse and a pack-pony, and we went on together, breaking our way through the snow-choked roads to the Mammoth Hot Springs, while Hofer took my own horses back to Ferguson."[12]

Billy's own memory of the trip made it appear he simply wanted this job done and to be rid of his employer, future president or no. The autobiography that he sent to Horace Albright skipped nearly the entire trip, noting only that "Another trip was with Theo. Roosevelt and his ranch partner Mr. Ferguson. On that trip Mr. Roosevelt on his way home met a Burlington route survey party at the Upper Geyser Basin. We had been travelling in two feet of snow most of the day"—on horseback, not by ski, which made a world of difference to Billy. "I had to take Mr. Roosevelt into Mammoth Hot Springs. The engineer in charge took Mr. Roosevelt to the Mammoth Hot Springs while I returned to camp for my outfit."[13] At least a seed of friendship, we can conclude, had been planted between the two men. Later in *The Wilderness Hunter*, Roosevelt called Billy "an old mountain-man," "trustworthy," and a "friend."[14]

Two years later, Billy took on perhaps the strangest job of an unusual career, working directly for the Boone and Crockett Club at the World's Columbian Exposition in Chicago in 1893. Either Roosevelt or Grinnell, and possibly both, would have thought of him for the odd task they had in mind.

The World's Columbian Exposition—then and now, usually just called the Chicago World's Fair—was a vast showcase of American science and industry, not built to last, but consuming nearly seven hundred acres and serving over twenty-seven million visitors during its six-month run. Imagine a Disneyland of the Gilded Age, but much larger and with far more visitors than little Disneyland. In the middle of one of the many water features, the designers built a "Wooded Island," and Boone and Crockett prevailed upon them to include a "Hunter's Cabin." A contemporary reporter explained that "He who is so disposed may wander over the bridge connecting, toward the south, with a smaller island, and there for a moment linger over the picturesque reproduction of an American hunter's camp," serving as "the headquarters of the Boone and Crockett club.... The structure is built of rough logs, and within, over the rude fireplace, is the skull of a grizzly bear.... The camp is under charge of Elwood Hofer."[15]

Historian Michael Steiner credited Roosevelt himself as having ordered the Hunter's Cabin; a colorful Billy could be seen there telling tales of the vanished frontier, "Wearing fringed buckskins and sporting long hair and a wide-brimmed felt hat."[16] The situation was truly bizarre. Billy Hofer, one of the most skillful wilderness guides of his time, traveled east to the great city of Chicago in a railroad car. Once there, Billy, a genuine, living mountain man, played a fake mountain man in a fake mountain camp in the middle of the sweltering Chicago fair, and vanishingly few of the fairgoers had any idea that they were actually looking at the real thing.

The Exposition made it clear that the world was changing, and as we will see, Billy was not changing to keep pace. Indeed, he refused to—and yet, in a small way, he was helping to smooth the destruction of the wilderness he loved. Living the life he did, he had to take employment where he could get it, and he would never have said no to Roosevelt and Grinnell, even though the fair represented another step toward what he abhorred, the industrialization of the continent. As Steiner noted, "Hidden on a tiny island and overshadowed by shining emporiums of the industrial future, the rustic Hunter's Cabin was an obscure attraction at the Exposition. Like other nostalgic features, this sliver of simulated wilderness paled before the wonders of the White City. Hofer's 'Old Geezer' tales of an earthier past were lost in the technological din of the nearby Mines, Electricity, Transportation, and Machinery Buildings where, in the awestruck words of a guidebook, 'The whir of wheels and the clamor of engines is almost deafening, and yet in the midst of all the noise and confusion, each machine works hour by hour as if with brains of steel too strong to be dazed or troubled.'"[17]

Nevertheless, the Boone and Crockett members who attended were pleased with the display. In a book they co-edited in 1901, *American Big-Game Hunting: The Book of the Boone and Crockett Club*, Roosevelt and Grinnell explained its genesis. "At its last annual meeting," which took place the previous January, "the Club determined to have an exhibit at Chicago. It was felt that it would be a pity if at the World's Fair there was no representation of so typical and peculiar a phase of American national development as life on the frontier." The book gave the only full description of the cabin where Billy spent much of his strange summer of 1893. It must have made him miss his more modern home in Gardiner: "There was a rough table and settles, with bunks in one corner, and a big open stone fireplace. Pegs and deer antlers were driven into the wall to support shaps"—an eccentric spelling for "chaps"—"buck skin shirts, broad hats, stocksaddles, and the like. Rifles stood in the corners, or were supported by pegs above the fireplace." The paraphernalia had been donated by Boone and Crockett members, "and, as a matter of fact, the various rifles, stock-saddles, and indeed the shaps and buck skin shirts, too, had all seen active service." Antlers and hides hung or lay everywhere, and outside they parked a covered wagon, "a white-capped prairie-schooner, a veteran of long service in cow-camps and on hunting expeditions."[18]

This "simple" cabin set them back $2,500, and on the night after it opened, June 15, it closed its doors briefly and served another purpose, as a temporary clubhouse, where the sponsors, according to several reports, dropped the pretense of rugged simplicity and chugged champagne instead.[19] But that probably did not include Billy; another quality that set him apart from the average frontiersman was that he was not much of a drinker. He and Emerson Hough carried between them a single bottle of brandy throughout their grueling 1894 ski, and there was brandy left in the bottle when they were done. He seems to have been hired to run the Hunter's Cabin for his charisma and probably to provide a little light propaganda for the preservationist cause, here in the middle of its stark opposite. One of his major tasks in life was simply to read his audience and pour on the appropriate charm, which could happen in a fake wilderness as easily as a real one.

It was a crucial skill, arguably his one *most* crucial skill. Looking back, we can see it in operation throughout the fair. In a note in *Forest and Stream*, a regular correspondent who had played a role in the show recalled "the ladies sitting about over their coffee among the FOREST AND STREAM representatives, with the mountain hat of Billy Hofer conspicuously in the midst.... Billy was a treasure. I came upon him one day in the forest when he was in the act of offering assistance to a distressed wood nymph"—a young woman, that is, wearing the horribly voluminous and demanding feminine clothing of 1893, which had gone wrong in a manner embarrassing enough that *Forest and Stream* had kindly camouflaged the problem. "He told her that the hunter's cabin could supply the means to meet any emergency and proved it; for she departed radiant and happy, having been offered a choice of elk skin or buckskin 'whangs,'"—the ubiquitous leather strips that served as light rope in the Old West—"or of more prosaic threads for the renovation of her damaged robe, and I observed that she accepted the loan of Billy's hunting knife to sever the whang, or thread, at the conclusion of her task."[20]

So it was not all life-and-death exploits in the savage wilderness, for Billy. Later, when Roosevelt became president, Emerson Hough wrote an article for *Field and Stream*, the relatively young competitor to *Forest and Stream*, and he wanted his new readers to know who Billy was. He explained that Billy had "taken care of some of the wealthiest sportsmen of the East, and some of the best known, among these President Theodore Roosevelt, who loves Billy Hofer very much." Even at second hand, it was natural for a journalist to want to claim acquaintance with so popular a president. "In the fall," Hough continued, "after the hunting season, Billy Hofer sometimes dresses up and comes East. He then carries an engraved visiting card, and I don't know but [that] he will be wearing evening clothes before long."[21]

Billy had developed a habit, common among Yellowstone people to this day, of taking what we can think of as reverse vacations: while the rest of the country was only too happy to escape Chicago or New York for a week in Yellowstone, the Yellowstone resident was (and is today) only too happy to spend a week or two as far as possible from Wonderland. This habit led to an extraordinary little incident that happened to Luther Kelly in New York City.

"Yellowstone" Kelly had actually not spent anything like as much time in Yellowstone as Billy had; a soldier and scout, he had ranged all over the world. The two knew each other for years, however; recall that, during Billy's first trip through the park in 1879, they met at Gibbon Meadows. In 1897, according to Kelly's biographer, Jerry Keenan, they encountered each other under absurdly different circumstances (it is fitting, if accidental, that the last two numerals in the dates, 79 and 97, are mirror images): "One day, while strolling down Broadway, Kelly met another old acquaintance in the person of Thomas Elwood 'Uncle Billy' Hofer…who had just arrived in town from the park. Hofer suggested they pay a visit to Theodore Roosevelt, who was then New York City Police Commissioner." The two old frontiersmen just dropped in, and Roosevelt reacted in a typical Roosevelt manner. He "was delighted to see both men, and after a nice visit about the West, Roosevelt invited them to join him for lunch. Accordingly, at noon, the trio rendezvoused outside Roosevelt's office and walked down to Five Points to 'Beefsteak John's.'"[22]

Indeed, you could never tell where and under what circumstances Billy would pop up. In 1900, Roosevelt, now governor of New York, was on the Republican ticket as William McKinley's candidate for vice president, and Billy found himself embroiled in the presidential election. The Democrats, hopelessly behind, launched the kind of attacks that smacked of desperation (their candidate, William Jennings Bryan, would, that November, be at the wrong end of a landslide). They alleged that Roosevelt's adventures in the West had been overstated, that he was only an Eastern dude playing at being a cowboy—an accusation made regularly about him to this day. Billy was among the old frontiersmen called to TR's defense. During a visit to the city, on August 5, the *Chicago Tribune* caught up with him and liked him so much they splashed him over most of a page, including a portrait in an elegant coat, shirt, and tie that clashed badly with his cowboy hat.[23] "Any man who says that Theodore Roosevelt is a coward is a liar himself," Billy declared, "and I can whip him." So, he said, could Roosevelt himself.

The article was mostly a partisan slam (even though it assured its readers that Billy "can be found during his stay in Chicago at THE TRIBUNE office by any one who wants to verify the statements herein"). The famous incident in which Roosevelt refused to shoot a tethered bear—the affair that led to the creation of the teddy bear—did actually happen, but at a later date, in Mississippi in 1902. The rumors that Roosevelt's political enemies were circulating unconsciously foreshadowed the later incident; in some of these rumors, Roosevelt could only hit a bear precisely if it *was* tethered. Billy lit into their purveyors with a vigor that never appeared in his formal writing, but that sounds today precisely like the letters he wrote to friends. "'I see that they are reviving that old, low-down, absurd lie about Theodore Roosevelt never having shot a bear in his life except one that was in a log trap'"—a kind of corral—"'and which he couldn't hit between the logs until his guide poked the gun through for him,' said Mr. Hofer yesterday. 'Now, I suppose that a good many things are allowable in politics, but I want to say that of all the ridiculous and no-account, low-down lies, that is about the worst.... He wouldn't any more shoot a trapped bear than he would his own son." Behind the verbal gunplay here lies a serious issue for us. Roosevelt, along with the rest of Boone and Crockett, were the leading advocates of "fair chase," the ethic that stated that the hunter had to give the animal a chance, or else he was only engaged in slaughter. It was a relatively new and somewhat radical idea.

Partisan slam or not, the article is filled with interesting biography for both Billy and TR. We learn from it a major reason that people like Billy enjoyed Roosevelt's company: "He can have a good time on a hunt," said Billy, "and no one is any better than he is, and he is no better than any one else. He can make any decent man feel he is his friend and equal, and he can do this without seeming to try and without any trying. It's because he's built right."

The article also cleared up some lingering mysteries about the 1891 Two Ocean Pass expedition. Tazewell Woody was always the head guide, in charge of the party, and Billy only joined them at the Upper Geyser Basin. The weather was normal for that date, wet and cold and sunny by unpredictable degrees. Roosevelt's shooting was hampered only by his eyesight, and he carried multiple pairs of his distinctive pince-nez glasses with him "for fear he might get left without eyes." Nevertheless, Tazewell Woody had been out hunting with Roosevelt before, "and Woody told me," said Billy, "and I reckon one guide would pretty near tell the truth to another about an Eastern outfit—that Roosevelt was the best shot on big game he ever had out, and rarely missed a decent shot." Woody made similar statements to both Emerson Hough and to Roosevelt himself,[24] and modern writers who like to sneer at Roosevelt as a poseur need to hear about it.

During the Two Ocean Pass hunt, TR's man Monroe Ferguson had all the shooting luck at first, until, to Roosevelt's delight, he broke his expensive English express rifle. After that, Roosevelt got all the game. Then came the long trip back to the Upper Geyser Basin, and Billy told the *Tribune* the story of Roosevelt's struggle with his horse in the snow. The animal was on loan from Woody. We learned the full story of the dislocated thumb. The sound of a rain slicker rattling, said Billy, was enough to set the horse off:

He would jump if he heard a slicker scrape against a tree,

and sometimes for a whole day at a time he'd get spells of
being ugly. Roosevelt was riding in a sort of slicker, and
had dismounted for a time, and was leading his horse along
the side hill. He started to get on again, while this slicker
was sort of wet.... It was his slippery slicker and saddle that
made the trouble, I reckon, but someway, he never got into
the saddle at all, but went clean on across it on the down
hill side. He landed on his hand, and put his thumb out
of joint. I didn't know he was hurt at first. He came up,
pulling at his thumb, and by that time he had about got
it pulled back into place. I told him he was hurt, that his
thumb was out of joint, but he said he wasn't hurt, that it
wasn't anything to mention. His thumb was all swelled up
pretty soon, but I didn't hear him mention it again. I did
hear him mention that horse several times, though, and he
said it as though he meant it.[25]

Billy's political allegiance—and that of the *Tribune*—could
hardly have been clearer, but he hit the point hard once more at
the end: "As for these fellows who sneer at him for [being] an Eastern dude who tried to get a little story from hunting out in the
West, they don't know what they are talking about, and they are
either ignorant or malicious liars, and that goes.... He's a straight-
up rider and a straight-up man, and he'll carry the Western vote
from St. Paul to Seattle, and I shouldn't wonder if a few votes east
of there."[26]

The *Indianapolis Journal* picked up the story on August 20 and
gave an amusing taste of what political journalism was like during
this era (and Billy's dealings with Roosevelt did have the habit of
turning amusing, no matter what the circumstances). Billy again told
the story of the Two Ocean Pass hunt. But here, the snowstorm at
the end of the trip, which, in Roosevelt's description, was merely an
annoyance, turned into a brutal struggle for survival. "Man and boy,
I have been out in the weather all my life and am about as tough as

they make 'em," said Billy, "but that was about the worst storm that ever caught me on an open range and no shelter for eighty miles. We were traveling light, too. We didn't have nothing but our blankets and some cold pork and biscuits in our grub bags, and didn't have no chance to make coffee. I thought Roosevelt would be pretty much used up. I could have cried like a girl myself, but he never let on that he was hungry or cold, or but what he was as comfortable as if he had been in the capital at Albany."

Billy's grammar had degraded, it would seem, surely altered by the newspaper to match the reporter's guess at what he or his readers thought a crusty mountain man should sound like. Billy again told the story of Roosevelt's horse tossing him and dislocating his thumb; that thumb gained a certain improbable fame the more often reporters made Billy tell the story. The fall "throwed his thumb out of joint." Billy suggested they switch horses. "'No, Billy, by Godfrey,' says he, pulling his thumb back into joint and showing his teeth as big as gravestones; 'I've started out to teach the critter who is master,' says he, 'and I'm not a man to throw up a good job,' says he."[27] But Billy was a careful and experienced user of the language, by Godfrey; he would never have said "throwed."

Billy had other reasons to travel east, as he did regularly through the later 1890s and past the turn of the century; such travel had become nearly routine once Yellowstone was integrated into the growing national rail network (and again, Billy was at least a participant, if not a creator, in the destruction of what he loved, a West that was mostly empty because travel for everyone, native and immigrant alike, was so long and difficult). As we shall see, he augmented his income for years catching Yellowstone animals in small numbers for eastern zoos. It led to a small visit that Hough recorded in 1903, Billy again just dropping in: "To-day Billy Hofer… dawned in Chicago without any previous warning. Billy is on his way with a couple of mountain lions, some deer, etc., for the Cleveland Sportsmen's Show, where he expects to remain for a week or so. Early in April he will start back for his quarters at

Gardiner, Montana, where he will have business of an interesting nature. It is known that President Roosevelt is to visit the Yellowstone Park early in his coming Western trip, and it goes almost without saying that Billy Hofer will be his guide and companion during his stay at the Park."[28] This was indeed about to happen.

And so Billy "summited a mountain" that he had not originally set out to climb. Ironically, by integrating himself into Yellowstone to such an extent that he fit there like a grizzly bear or a Douglas fir, Billy had also succeeded in integrating himself into the highest levels of national political power. This strange alchemy made him the default-guide for his best-known client of all, who, during the journey soon to come, would be accompanied by a pretty famous friend.

Theodore Roosevelt's 1903 trip to Yellowstone National Park was, like many presidential trips, a mix of vacation and politics.[29] He was accompanied by John Burroughs, the reputable naturalist who was then a bestselling author and a living national icon. In Yellowstone, at least, Roosevelt's major politicking waited until the end, when the president dedicated a masonry arch over what was then still the main gateway to the park, on the road that led south from the railroad depot in Gardiner. The structure is known today, of course, as the Roosevelt Arch. By yet another irony, Uncle John Yancey made the trip to see the dedication, fell ill, and died on May 7. No one called the event such at the time, but Yancey's death represented a symbolic passing of a kind of deferential torch to Billy. He was the park's "Uncle" now.

He would, however, have precious little "guiding" to do for this, his most well-known bit of employment. Burroughs recorded the visit in a short book he wrote later, and their excursion was not exactly a venture into the brutal wilderness.[30] Leaving Gardiner, Roosevelt ditched the press and even his Secret Service detail and the rest of his staff, escaping onto his horse. These were not the sorts of clients Billy would have to hustle to meet at the train, alone. Instead, the park superintendent, Major John Pitcher, came along, with other officers and soldiers appearing as needed. Burroughs and Roosevelt, along with Billy Hofer, stayed in the park from April 8 to 24, and since it was so early in the year, they camped only on the northern range. While they were camping, Burroughs acted—perhaps unintentionally, but firmly—as a tether for Roosevelt. Should the president charge south into the wild white-and-green yonder, the great naturalist could never have kept up.

They stayed at a series of three campsites, the third one being best remembered today because the Roosevelt Lodge was built later in approximately the same area. They were not quite roughing it. Burroughs gave an inventory of their equipment: "we had a mule pack train, and Sibley tents and stoves, with quite a retinue of camp laborers, a lieutenant and an orderly or two, and a guide, Billy Hofer."[31] So most of Billy's ordinary, mundane tasks on the trail—providing food, shelter, transportation, and generally keeping his charges alive—were not really needed. Another major task, that of providing entertainment around the campfire, was nullified by Roosevelt himself, who talked nonstop. Billy must have been asking himself, "Why am I here?"

Sifting through the sparse records of the trip, we find that his role does slowly become clear: he alone really knew the local wildlife. He was, as we have seen, the leading expert on the northern range elk herds. Roosevelt later recalled how, "From a spur of Bison Peak one day, Major Pitcher, the guide Elwood Hofer, John Burroughs and I spent about four hours with the glasses counting and estimating the different herds within sight. After most careful work and cautious reduction of estimates in each case to the minimum the truth would permit, we reckoned three thousand head of elk, all lying or feeding and all in sight at the same time."[32] Billy undoubtedly led them to these elk, and it was a sight that he showed his clients again and again, because it was so memorable.

But it did not require a tremendous show of tremendous beasts to get Roosevelt's blood up. Any kind of new or rare wild animal generally drove TR wild with glee. He was comical that way, although in a highly appealing manner, and if an animal revealed itself to Billy, he could, by disclosing or even merely mentioning it, set Roosevelt off like a stick of dynamite.

Two incidents from the camping trip stood out in Burroughs's book. One took place at their second camp, along the Yellowstone River at Cottonwood Creek. "Very soon," Burroughs recalled, "my attention was attracted by a strange note, or call, in the spruce woods. The President had also noticed it, and, with me, wondered what made it. Was it bird or beast? Billy Hofer said he thought it was an owl, but it in no way suggested an owl, and the sun was shining brightly." No need for further motivation: "'Let's go run that bird down,' said the President to me." Run they did, literally. They came to understand that they had forgotten their binoculars. "So off he went like a boy, and was very soon back with the glasses. We quickly made out that it was indeed an owl,—the pigmy owl, as it turned out,—not much larger than a bluebird. I think the President was as pleased as if we had bagged some big game. He had never seen the bird before."[33] He should have been pleased; that was indeed a rare sighting, for Yellowstone (a good guess would be that it was a northern pygmy owl, *Glaucidium californicum*). And Billy had managed to make that tentative identification from sound alone!

The second incident was downright funny. At the party's final camp, beside the deep canyon the Yellowstone had carved near Tower Fall, they learned of a band of mountain sheep on the opposite canyon wall. They wondered whether the sheep would make the trip down to the river to drink, and wondered how they could survive a trip down what looked to be, in most places, a vertical face. Billy knew of an overlook near Rainy Lake that provided the perfect view, "and sure enough, late in the afternoon the word came to our tents that the sheep were coming down. The President, with coat off and a towel around his neck, was shaving. One side of his face was half shaved and the other side lathered. 'By Jove,' said the President, 'I must see that. The shaving can wait, and the sheep won't.'"

It is a pity that the press was stuck in Gardiner and so we have no photograph, although Roosevelt's face and mannerisms are so well known that it is easy enough to picture the scene: "So on he came, accoutred as he was,—coatless, hatless, but not latherless, nor towelless. Like the rest of us, his only thought was to see those sheep do their 'stunt.' With glasses in hand, we watched them descend those perilous heights, leaping from point to point, finding a foothold where none appeared to our eye, loosening fragments of the crumbling rocks as they came, now poised upon some narrow shelf and preparing for the next leap, zigzagging or plunging straight down till the bottom was reached, and not one accident or misstep amid all that insecure footing. I think the President was the most pleased of us all; he laughed with the delight of it, and quite forgot his need of a hat and coat till I sent for them."[34]

Burroughs's brief narrative is not the only contemporary account of the trip, of course. Billy wrote a short one for *Forest and Stream*, giving the same details, but adding a scene similar to the two above. This sort of thing was happening all the time: "Both the President and Mr. Burroughs were interested in all the small animals and birds. It was a little early for the birds; still they saw a goodly number and heard many sing. The little water wren did his best to entertain the party. Once when the President and Mr. Burroughs were watching a family of woodchucks, they were stampeded by the song of a Townsend's solitaire. Mr. Burroughs made a run over rocks and down-timber to the edge of a cañon and part way down the cañon to hear the full song. The bird did not do its best, having a bit of a cold, I suppose."[35]

It may have been the easiest dollar Billy ever earned, merely riding along and acting as a living Audubon Guide Book, although when they were sheep-watching, he may also have taken on the Secret Service's normal role of keeping the president safe; quite a few people have died falling into that same stretch of canyon while trying to get a better view, humans not being as agile as sheep.[36] When they were through with camping, the party toured most of the other famous locations in the park by horse-drawn sleigh, and skied around the Grand Canyon of the Yellowstone, although even here, Billy's practical knowledge was not needed. Amazingly, or maybe not so amazingly, Roosevelt already knew how to ski.

The party returned to Gardiner. Roosevelt gave his speech dedicating the arch, and the train carried him off from what had merely been a break in a 14,000-mile journey, and carried him mostly out of Billy's life. Some Yellowstone people today tend to believe that Yellowstone was a huge part of TR's existence. It was not. Look at a brief biography of the man; that life was stuffed so full that Yellowstone was just a momentary blip. The illusion that the place was crucial to him comes partly from the place names that his visit scattered around the region, and partly from the way his image has been perpetuated for commercial reasons: businesses around the park today still stock plenty of Roosevelt books and teddy bears and tchotchkes simply because the name sells.

But again, Billy was by this time a well-known appendage to the elite class, much sought after when that class went on vacation. His connection to the extended Roosevelt clan was hardly limited to TR. Another connection, to a different and fruitful branch of the clan, went back to 1899. During that year, in August and September, Warren Delano III, his friend, H.A. deWindt,[37] Warren's brother Frederic, and his son Lyman Delano made a trip to Wyoming and Yellowstone National Park, where they naturally fell under Billy's care. And if that name, "Delano," rings a bell today, it should. Warren was Franklin Delano Roosevelt's uncle. His sister was the future president's mother, to whom FDR was deeply attached.[38]

Happily, Warren Delano recorded the entire journey in a diary that makes for a rough but readable account with a certain period charm.[39] They intended to ride through the entire park and hunt—appropriately but unsurprisingly—in the area of Two Ocean Pass. They left Chicago on August 16, 1899, and arrived in Livingston, Montana on the nineteenth. Billy took the trouble of riding up to meet them, but he was not happy with their plans: "We woke up

early at Livingston & soon were about – getting our 'outfit' and
'war paint.'" Delano wrote. "Hofer came in about 7:30 and gave
a general synopsis of his plans. Is very disgusted at the idea of having to be back here by the 15th, and I finally suggested we might
send 'the cub' (Lyman) out to Cinnabar & express him to Boston.
Hofer thought it a good scheme & said he would personally bring
him out & 'tag' him."[40]

Poor Lyman—the joke here was that he would be treated like a
piece of baggage and mailed home. He had in fact turned sixteen
that summer—which, however, meant that he had to leave in time
to be back in school. The problem was that the party intended to
ride horses all the way through vast Yellowstone National Park,
hunt below the southern boundary, then ride back. Nineteenth
century or twenty-first century, it does not matter: the problem
remains the same. People generally were and are in too much of
a hurry in Yellowstone, and this was a lot of geography to cover.

Delano gave us a detailed picture of how the upper crust camped
in that era and how Billy did his work when dealing with the upper edge of the upper crust. Delano's journal is rare in recording,
in detail, how the "sausage got made" in the outfitting business:
what exact steps had to be taken, and what precisely it cost, to
travel comfortably under the care of a highly experienced guide
at the head of a large party, with a substantial mobile infrastructure—horses, mules, and supplies of all kinds—for Billy to worry
about, too.

When the party reached Mammoth, they dined at the hotel, selected saddles, had the stirrups fitted to their legs, and then picked
out horses from the nearby corral. "After our horses were selected
some hats & 2 waterproofs were secured; and then, after some
trouble, we got hold of the Commandant"—the superintendent,
that is—"to whom I presented my letter & got letters from him
to different [soldier] stations so we shall have no trouble." Letters of introduction were a common appurtenance of travel during
that era and performed roughly the same function as the letters of

recommendation college professors write today for law or medical school applicants. "Then the guns were all sealed and some last advice given."[41] Another period detail: during this era, travelers carrying guns through the park had the firing mechanism sealed by a soldier when they entered the park. When they left, the seal had to be intact or trouble ensued. The real journey at last commenced, and Delano took up the story:

> Then we retd [returned] to the hotel & soon got off. – It was then nearly four o'clock and we were glad to start. – A wagon taking the heavier things to the camp. – We were there before five o'clk and found quite a party. – In addition to our party of four – which have been dubbed "Had," [H.A. deWindt] "Fad," [Frederic A. Delano] "Dad" [Warren Delano] and "Kid" [Lyman Delano]: we have Elwood Hofer – called "Billy" – as chief guide; "Dusty" the cook; "Doc" chief camp tender; "Frank," "Joe" and "John" who are packers and hunters – i.e. they will accompany us on our daily hunts when we reach the hunting grounds.
>
> "Frank" is the only licensed hunter for "Wyoming." – It is not necessary to have more as the hunters merely find game but don't kill it.
>
> Each member of this party often (including ourselves) has a saddle horse in addition to which there are two extra saddle animals.
>
> Then there are 18 pack animals just to carry the tents, bedding, utensils & our own impedimenta. – Lyman & I occupy one 10ft. x 12ft. tent and "Fad" & "Had" have another just like it.[42]

It was quite an outfit and quite a lot of worry for Billy (compare it to the journey with Hough, when the only pack animals were the two skiers). He also now regularly had problems that we would call "managerial"—that is, he had human resource problems, since, then as now, lower-level jobs in Yellowstone meant temporary work for unimpressive wages, the employees often being drifters of questionable or simply unknown character. Note that Delano put quotation marks around almost every name, on the assumption that each was an AKA (the habit got out of hand, so that he turned the name of the State of Wyoming into an alias). That was traditionally a good assumption, in the West, where so many people, in one way or another, were on the lam.

But who were these employees? And how much did such a trip cost? After a month with the gang, and after settling the bill, Delano wrote a summary, including one of the few physical descriptions we have of Billy, extending even to the sound of his voice:

> Elwood Hofer – born near New Haven, Conn. – is a man of about 50 yrs. of age. – He is small & wiry with high-pitched voice – smooth face – gray eyes – frank, pleasant countenance. – He is an ideal guide! – Extremely alert & intelligent, he has improved his opportunities of observation and contact with a notable list of scientific and other intelligent men whom he has met and guided. – He talks well and entertainingly on all topics & was constantly surprising us by his knowledge of things that it did not seem possible could have come within his observation. –
>
> "Doc" Hall was our camp tender – a "side partner" of Hofers. – He is a Kentuckian – educated as a druggist – a drunkard reformed! – Has not drunk for ten years (they say) but shows that he has had a history. – Is a very respectable fellow now, however, and shows, as all do to a surprising extent, an alert knowledge of & interest in all topics of the day! – He does not hunt but has general oversight of the Camp equipage & c., & c. –
>
> Of the other men – we liked our Cook – "Beaman Anisden" – a character! – With evident education, au fond [French for "in essence"], a roving disposition had sent him

west to hustle for himself. – We heard that he had prepared for the Naval Academy at Annapolis. – He has a brother in the "Coast Survey Service." "Frank Futter" was our "Wyoming Guide" – a very nice fellow 6 ft. 2" in height and well built. – "Johnny Ballinger" a Montana product – good hunter – careless & good natured – the youngest of the men – found more game than all the rest put together! – "Joe Cole" we named "The Melancholy Jacques." The name does not quite fit him. He is an ex-sheep-herder, Cow-puncher & hunter. – Had been out with Lord Dunraven and – in fact – "had had" & "had been" everything under the sun! – But he was our least satisfactory man – in fact the only one I should not care to have again – and yet – he was really unobjectionable beyond a natural laziness.[43]

This was a typical team of Yellowstone wranglers, hunters, and camp assistants, for this era; Delano probably would not have bought a used horse from any of them except Billy, but at the same time, they were not dangerous or incompetent. Even Cole was "unobjectionable," despite the reference to the melancholy Jaques, Shakespeare's famously cynical layabout in *As You Like It* (writing from memory, Delano modernized the spelling of "Jaques"). Lord Dunraven was, to give his full name, Windham Thomas Wyndham-Quin, 4th Earl of Dunraven; he visited Yellowstone way back in 1874, giving his name to the pass beneath Mount Washburn, and Delano apparently did not believe Cole had had anything to do with him.

The trip itself was unexceptional, for Billy and his crew, at least: the party rode through the park, saw the usual sights, hunted around the general vicinity of Two Ocean Pass, killed plenty of elk, and returned on schedule. Even if it was business as usual for Billy, deWindt and the Delanos had the time of their lives—also business as usual. What is striking to the modern reader, again, was the weather. On August 21 the party tried to climb Mt. Washburn:

"We got above the snow line but it became so cold & threatening, with high wind, we gave up the last 1000 ft."[44] Today, there is virtually never a "snow line" on Mount Washburn in late August. Indeed, there should be no snow on the mountain anywhere. But they had weather blowing in: "A sharp snow storm set in before we reached camp," and the snow fell throughout the night of August 21, continuing off and on through the next day. Riding from the Canyon to Nez Perce Creek, they fought the weather nearly the whole way.

Delano recalled "Coming down a steep mountain side from which the view was beautiful – helped, too, by a burst of sunlight thro' the clouds which had been heavy thro' the day & poured sharp flurries of snow on us that almost blinded us."[45] They encountered a snowcap on Mount Washburn during the third week of August? They experienced significant snowfall that same week? Again and again, twenty-first century readers who know Yellowstone feel their jaws falling open.

Finally, what did the trip cost?

> The expense of a trip like this depends on the outfit requirements. – We had rather a large one – carrying abundance of tent room & table & chairs for our party. – We had 33 animals including a colt which follows its mother. – "Dick" (the colt) & Lyman became great friends. –
>
> The men provide their own horses & receive 3.00 to 3.50 pr. day, & Guide (Hofer) receives $5. – pr. day. – He furnishes tents, blankets, & c. –
>
> We each took simply a sleeping bag – fleece-lined! –
>
> We had 6 saddle horses (2 spare – in case of need) @ $1.00 pr. day – and 18 pack horses @ 75¢ pr. day. – Frank Futter had 2 extra horses for teaming – at the beginning & end of our trip – wh. makes the complement of 32 horses (exclg. Colt.)–[46]

The trip had lasted the precise length planned, August 19th to September 15th, twenty-eight days, inclusive, making Billy's total guiding fee $140. Given the absurd size of the horse herd, some of the horse rental money likely went to him. They shot so many elk that, for much of the trip, he probably ate like a (medieval) king, for free.

In 1899, $140 was a tidy sum—but it is easy today to look at that sum and forget the overhead. Every animal that got sick, every tent that ripped, every piece of equipment that went bad—it all came out of his profit. Guiding has always been like this, then and now; most guides did not last. Billy had lasted because he diversified so broadly and enthusiastically and made so many valuable contacts.

In Warren Delano, he had just made another one, and, although he could not yet know it, this one would influence his later life greatly. TR would help, too. As Delano noted, Uncle Billy was in his fifties now. He lived in an era when a man's retirement income came out of his mattress or out of a jar buried in the back yard. If he was to survive his golden years—actually he was already living his golden years and had been doing that for decades—he would have to increase his cash flow. His attempts to do so would lead him far afield from Montana.

Hofer later in life, in a photograph possibly taken at his home near Seattle, Washington.

CHAPTER ELEVEN

A Renaissance Man

Billy Hofer had no choice in the matter of leaving guiding. Like so many of us, he had to think about money, as he grew older. It is a pity, because he had so many talents and interests. If only he could have made them pay better. Furthermore, the money Billy earned from guiding Warren Delano and party involved hard, physical labor, and so did every other guiding job. He could not keep on earning his entire income from riding twenty or thirty miles in a snowstorm, just as a routine part of a day's work. He made a number of attempts to find another way, some abortive, some modestly successful, some miserable. He was caught in the Yellowstone trap, one that catches people to this day. He wanted to live outside, riding tall and free through the wilderness, making his own rules as he went along. The economy did not produce many jobs that fit that description.

So he tried to become a businessman, but one whose business still concerned the places he loved. He launched a major effort along these lines in 1907, when the entire park community ran out of patience with boatman E.C. Waters.

Waters was one of the great villains in the history of the park, although throughout his tenure there he managed to survive (because of his political connections) innumerable attempts to expel him. We cannot focus too much attention on him here.[1] He lied, cheated, stole, groveled, insulted, and on and on for years. He was a villain, yes, but do not think of Darth Vader. Think, instead, of Wile E. Coyote of cartoon fame. Waters built the Yellowstone Lake Boat Company and had just launched the largest steamboat ever to operate on Yellowstone Lake—named, grandiloquently, the *E.C. Waters*—when at long last park authorities succeeded in throwing him out. The boat's remains are still visible on the shore of Stevenson Island in Yellowstone Lake, where it was moored and allowed to decompose.

Aubrey Haines summarized the endgame: "E.C. Waters' Yellowstone Lake Boat Company was in financial difficulty after the turn of the century because of his unscrupulous activities. He had alienated the concessioners, the government authorities, and even the employees in the Park, and he had made an unwise investment in a larger boat, the *E.C. Waters*. His boat concession was canceled in 1907 for a multitude of reasons that added up to sufficient cause, and the privilege was given to T. E. Hofer, the old-time guide and friend of the Park. But 'Uncle Billy' Hofer"—note that he was Uncle Billy now—"did not have the necessary capital to launch such an enterprise and had to borrow from Warren Delano to begin operations."[2] In other words, Billy and Delano had stayed in touch, and Delano trusted him to run this substantial business.

President Roosevelt probably also intervened here, to judge from a letter Billy wrote to Delano: "I am after a lease or privilege to put not over 10 Power Launches and 50 row boats on Yellowstone Lake." A passel of former superintendents "and I guess the President will help me to get it. The lease of Waters has run out and he has been so troublesome to the Department he can't get it renewed—I don't want the Steamboats anyway,"[3] wrote Billy, by which he meant the *E.C. Waters* and a second, smaller boat, the *Zillah*. One newspaper, the Salem, Oregon *Daily Capital Journal*, reported that the president had, in fact, intervened: "Bearing a rich concession from the government which was given him by President Roosevelt as a Christmas present, T. E. Hofer...returned yesterday from Washington, D. C.... Hofer brings with him the sole rights and privileges of running a steamboat on the lakes of Yellowstone Park." This was a typical newspaper story of the era (and similar to our own era in that details are often muddled). "Lakes" should have been singular, "steamboat" should have been plural, and here, "steamboat" should actually have been omitted entirely because Billy was interested, at this point, in gasoline-operated powerboats and rowboats only. "The concession promises to be a rich one," said the newspaper, "and Hofer has already made arrangements for five new steamboats which will be built at a cost of about $25,000 and will be in operation next summer." The story then hinted at the sort of cozy scene that requires a $50 million campaign donation today: "Hofer took dinner with President Roosevelt while in Washington and together they reviewed the pleasures of the trip through Yellowstone."[4]

The legal and financial situation was actually rather complex. Waters had been removed from the park—the superintendent actually printed a bulletin-notice barring him from entering—but he fought on. As Bartlett explained, "He might well have been back in business had not a respected scout...started the T.E. Hofer Boat Company with the backing of eastern sportsmen"—by which he meant the Delano family. "On July 1, 1910," continued Bartlett, "Waters sold out to Hofer, and by October of that year the difficult Mr. Waters had removed from the park everything that belonged to him."[5] Thus, for some years, there were two boat companies operating on Yellowstone Lake, Billy's company and the ghost of Waters's company. Billy's eventually extinguished the latter. Substantial sums of money were involved, and a great deal of effort on his part. Billy sent a letter to George Bird Grinnell to apologize for not having written anything lately for *Forest and Stream*: "We are forming a company—$20,000 T.E. Hofer Boat Co—T.E.H. Pres. 110 Shares. $11000." The remaining ninety shares went to three

other shareholders. "We have—2—16 foot 2—18 foot—2— 40
foot & 1—33 foot Cabin Cruisers [coming] besides rowboats." He
was on his way "to St. Joseph Misso to learn the Engines and all
there is to learn in the Shops of the Truscott Boat Mfg Co.,"[6] who
were the people building the boats.

However—to look ahead in time—the T.E. Hofer Boat Company did not survive, for two easy-to-understand reasons that are
actually only visible with inside knowledge. The reason Bartlett
gives us today, in the next sentence, is an explanation that is common in discussions of the matter, but it is incorrect: "Hofer was an
excellent scout and hunter but a poor businessman. In a complicated series of financial deals involving Hofer, his creditors, Waters, Child, and the Northwest Improvement Company, Harry
Child emerged as the man in charge. As of May 27, 1911, the
Yellowstone Park Boat Company was incorporated,"[7] and Billy, to
his great relief, was out of the boat business. The Northwest Improvement Company was a front for the Northern Pacific Railroad
(the secret was not a well-kept one), and Harry Child was a park
businessman who had ambitions about owning every enterprise in
the park. It was inevitable therefore that he would be the one to
take the boat business off Billy's hands.

But Billy was not a poor businessman. A poor businessman
could never have routinely taken parties the size of the deWindt/
Delano excursion (only one of hundreds over the years) all the way
across the park and back without getting anyone killed and without being bankrupted by the overhead. Nor could a poor businessman have trapped animals for zoos back east or run the blue fox
operation in Alaska—we will soon discuss both—businesses that
Billy had started and which he continued to pursue. He had been
born and raised on the water, of course, and could build a boat
from scratch. While it is true that this park operation would be a
world away from sailing a sharpie on Long Island Sound, a mind as
flexible and retentive as his could probably have easily mastered it.

The operation was simple enough, if larger than what he was

used to, and he had the signal advantage of not having to worry too much about liability—a passenger could fall out of one of his boats and drown and he would not necessarily be sued out of existence as a matter of course. Today, only giant corporations run such businesses because only they can afford the liability insurance. The T.E. Hofer Boat Company was partly a ferry service, and the old *Zillah*—whether Billy wanted it or not, his new Boat Company inherited it—was put to work running passengers between West Thumb and the Lake Hotel. Billy's company rented small boats to parties of anglers and operated a fishing tackle store that also sold minor necessities and other items that are no longer on the shelves in Yellowstone tourist stores, such as horse feed.

Billy eventually launched a fleet of larger vessels, the beginnings of which he noted in the letter to Grinnell. The flagship was probably the *Jean D*, a substantial watercraft, with a covered cabin, windows, space for 150 passengers, and, to judge from photographs, lifeboats even more inadequate than those on *Titanic* (the water in Yellowstone Lake may actually be *colder* than the North Atlantic).[8] The *Jean D* was named for Jean Delano, Warren Delano III's daughter. As he began building more boats, however, Billy gave them names so bizarre that they remain a minor mystery in the park to this day, one that each new generation continues to try to solve. It is an exercise that turns out to be both addicting and impossible, like squaring the circle: *Busha, Etcedecasher* (sometimes listed as *Etcedecasha*), *Ocotta, Lockpitsa, Espear, Esportutse, Wood Tuk Colle, Bedupa,* and *Sata*. Amateur cryptanalysts are today invited to have a try at figuring out what the names mean and/or from whence they came. A good guess is that they were the kind of fake Native American names given to tourist traps and children's summer camps, although *Etcedecasher* collided with a Latin dictionary along the way.[9]

Why did Billy Hofer's business fail? What were the two reasons, mentioned above, that today require inside knowledge to understand? First, as we shall see in the rest of this chapter, Billy was still "going a hundred directions at once," as he always had. He actually began to write more often in *Forest and Stream* than he had in years, producing six articles for the journal in 1908 alone. In this limited sense, his business acumen may have failed him, because this boating business required more attention than he was willing to give. That leads us to the second reason, which he stated openly and with some force in a letter to Warren Delano, written just before Harry Child formally took over. It revealed that Child had in fact been running the operation already, for at least a year: "Child *Bossed* and ran the thing last year, I could have made it pay more but he was Chief and I want to get out of it. I'd rather run a little pack train or any thing [else] than to have anything to do for or with the general public."[10]

That last sentence, for anyone who has worked with the traveling public up close in a national park, adds an important detail to the story, namely why he had been avoiding the operation. Billy had been spoiled. He was accustomed to guiding educated and often erudite people: Warren Delano, Theodore Roosevelt, William Pickett, the U.S. Fish Commission, and so on. But as for the general public…well, where should he even begin to discuss it? It was probably all he could do to put up with the screaming babies and dirty diapers, the frustrated, confused, angry adults, the constant complaints about everything, the sweating, sweltering crowds. And how many more of the ridiculous questions from these tourists could he stand? "Do they drain the lake in the winter?" "Why did they build the canyon so deep?" "What time do they turn off Old Faithful?" "Does this boat go to Tom's Thumb?" "Where is the lavatory?" "Where is the lavatory?" "Where is the lavatory?" It all drove him berserk, and thus he let the boating business die because, deep inside, he wanted it dead.

But he had other things to do anyway, some of them of much greater importance. I have scarcely mentioned his work catching animals for zoos back East, but now we will examine it. He did not just catch them for zoos, and in one case at least, this work had extraordinary repercussions that we can look at today. It can be argued that he changed—and not for the first time—the American landscape in a massive way.

He worked first for the Smithsonian's National Zoological Park, the same outfit that everybody today calls the National Zoo. Founded in 1889, it was a primitive affair at first, and so were Billy's earliest efforts at stalking and capturing wild animals. We do not know how he stumbled into the job, although no doubt it happened in the usual way; a nabob from the Boone and Crockett Club was having dinner with a nabob from the Smithsonian Institution, and when the subject of catching animals came up, so did Billy's name. Happily, in 1892, he wrote a five-part series for *Forest and Stream* that described his early work, in this case work dating back to spring, 1891. With straightforwardness unusual for the era, in print at least, he clarified the size of his salary right away: "I will first mention the fact that some time ago I resigned the financial consideration connected with my appointment as Smithsonian Hunter. I was willing to devote all my spare time to the work in hand, but reserved the right to engage at any time in the much better paid occupation of guide and packer."[11]

He was not doing it for a tax write-off (there were no such write-offs in 1891). At least at first, it was a purely charitable effort and not as capital-intensive as some of his work. He simply rode out to Yancey's, where the old man made space for him and his three assistants, including a 13-year-old boy named Dolph who came along "more for the fun he anticipated than the wages I promised to pay him." Also along was a crucial figure in Billy's life whom he had never given much attention in print until now, namely Leo, his dog, who was both a skilled assistant for tasks like this one and a friend. They were deeply attached. Dolph brought his own dog, Bobby, and apart from what help they could scare up at Yancey's, the man, the boy, and the two dogs made up the whole expedition.[12]

During their first day on the job, they caught a black bear cub and an elk calf, in each case just by luckily blundering into them and grabbing them before they could run. They spent some days repairing one of Yancey's old cabins and turning it into a primitive animal shelter (it would serve this purpose for years to come). The elk calf nearly starved until Dolph had the wit to hold his hands over the eyes of one of their mares, so that it would not kick while the elk was suckling. It worked. Dolph, with his country-boy ingenuity, earned whatever money Billy scared up for him. Better prepared now, they went hunting again, this time finding an elk calf and, by a wild piece of luck, a pair of antelope fawns, again by essentially tripping over them.[13]

Two days later, they went out again, heading up the Lamar River valley and climbing Specimen Ridge. Up in the fossil forest, between 1500 and 2000 feet above the river—Billy guessed 2000 feet—Dolph found another elk calf. Before Billy could holler to wait, Dolph grabbed it by one leg, it slipped free, and led Dolph, Billy, Bobby, and Leo on a howling chase. They only found it by accident, 2000 feet below. Climbing back up the ridge, as disgusted as he could be, Billy stumbled into another elk calf, in such dense brush that desperate measures were required to capture it: "I walked zig-zag to within six feet, when I saw it making a motion as if it would run, and I saw that my only chance [to grab it] was to dive head first through the dry brush." He was cut to ribbons, and his shirt was holed as if he had been shotgunned. He at least had caught the day's second elk calf. They hauled the pair back to Yancey's, where Uncle John reported that he had found a fox den (Billy did his collecting in the spring because there were young animals around that would not necessarily kill him if he tried to catch them). They took a shovel, blocked the entrances to the den, and after exhausting labor, exposed the den and caught three young foxes.[14] The cabin at Yancey's was now in constant, open insurrection, the animals howling at all hours and demanding to be fed.

On the next outing, Billy recruited a tourist, his wife, his dog, and a young woman who worked at Yancey's, and left Dolph to guard the petting zoo they were building (Billy had improvised a corral, and it was becoming quite a local attraction). The augmented group now headed up Antelope Creek, near Tower Fall, with Billy's horses and Leo along. They were after the usual, elk calves, when the two women spotted a sow grizzly, "very large," according to Billy. Two cubs trailed behind their massive and extraordinarily dangerous mother. Normally, it would be an occasion for everyone to run for the hills. Instead, Billy and the rest charged the bears.

Defying expected behavior, the bears ran away. "The whole thing had happened in a moment," wrote Billy. "All was noise and confusion, and at one time there were horses, elk, bear, men, women, dogs and cubs, all mixed up…among the fallen timber. We had made all the noise possible in order to bluff the old bear, and had succeeded, yet I was very much surprised. I did not think any bear but a black one could be made to leave her young, and never such a large one as we had just driven away." That encounter ought to have been fatal for one or more of the humans, but, as Billy knew well, you can never tell what you can get away with until you try. The bear had left a single cub high in a tree. Billy lowered it with a rope, and it soon made a star attraction in the petting zoo.[15]

They finished the spring's work soon afterward; the day after their adventure with the grizzly and cubs, Billy rode to Fort Yellowstone and secured Superintendent Anderson's assistance. He sent a wagon and team and a soldier to help. Much of what Billy accomplished in life was directly attributable to his ability to mobilize help without necessarily offering pay. They lost two elk to malnutrition, and the grizzly cub was killed by a fellow grizzly—bears do that—while chained up outside in the middle of the night. In compensation, they found a black bear (a much more tractable species, or at least more easily frightened), collected both of her cubs, and that was that for spring, 1891.[16]

So the effort was, at first, a bit like amateur hour, although as always Billy was learning fast. We have two memoirs that describe how he taught himself to catch one of the more trying animals that the Smithsonian wanted, and which turned out to be his most im-

portant catch of all. In 1930, William Mann, then director of the
National Zoological Park, wrote its history using the memories of
those who had been involved in its earliest years. During that time,
no one there thought to collect any small animals, because such
creatures were then regarded as either pets or pests. At last, during
an era when it looked like the North American beaver was going
to become extinct, the zoo's managers thought they might try to
collect a few, but the only animals they could acquire were dead on
arrival, or nearly so. Mann explained how the organization at last
succeeded in acquiring beavers:

> Finally we turned to the Yellowstone National Park, and
> through the cooperation of Captain George S. Anderson,
> U. S. A., then in charge, made arrangements to procure a
> supply there. The animals were fairly common in localities
> suited to their mode of life, but to get possession of them
> alive and uninjured was not an easy matter. It required
> knowledge of beaver habits and more than the ordinary
> trapper's skill and ingenuity. Fortunately, Captain Anderson
> found ready at his hand the man needed in the person of
> Elwood ("Billy") Hofer, widely known to sportsmen and
> naturalists as a hunter and guide, and he was, with some dif-
> ficulty, persuaded to undertake the capture of the beavers.
>
> By setting nets in their runways and then driving the
> beavers out of their houses, Hofer finally succeeded in col-
> lecting a total of ten American beavers, which were thought
> to be a sufficient number for the purpose. They ranged from
> adult and apparently rather old animals down to young of
> that season.
>
> Shipping crates, carefully designed, were prepared for
> them, each lined with sheet-iron and furnished with a
> tank so that the animals could have their bath. Personally
> conducted by Hofer, they made the long journey from the
> Yellowstone Park to Washington, all arriving safely. Thus
> began the beaver colony at the National Zoological Park.[17]

It was also the beginning of a good deal more. The second memoir was a two-part series written by Billy himself, entitled "Beaver Catching for the Zoo," for *Forest and Stream* in May, 1896.[18] He began by giving us a date: the zoo had sent its request for a ready-made beaver colony in October, 1892. He at first tried using leg traps, choosing the popular Newhouse brand, one of the rare occasions when he had to buy his gear ready-made. He padded the trap jaws with rags, but they still hurt the animals too badly. He tried other methods that failed. At last, after two years of periodic experiments, he formulated the solution that Mann briefly summarized above. He traveled to Yancey's in Pleasant Valley, which, during this era, was full of beavers (it is no longer, for reasons no one has been able to satisfactorily explain). He gave all the details because, he wrote, he had received letters asking for them, and by 1896 he was the world's expert on the capturing of beaver. With the help of two men from Yancey's, he would block all the exits from a beaver house except one, set his net in front of the one open exit, tear a hole in the dam or dams, drain the pond, rip into the house—they have multiple chambers—and chase the beavers toward that one open hole.

One of his helpers usually worked the net, an oversized dip-net hand-made, of course, by Billy. The process was slow, painfully laborious, and regularly failed—but it also regularly succeeded. He worked out complex variants on this basic technique, moving his assistants and the netting around as the local conditions demanded. He had to drain the ponds to get at the houses, which were in deep water otherwise, but discovered that a beaver could build an entire dam in a single night. The three persevered until they at last secured the tenth beaver and thus completed the Smithsonian's request. "We were in a very dilapidated condition," he concluded, and there followed one of the only occasions when Hofer drank sufficiently to feel it: "we had enough for one year. So taking a good dose of Uncle John's 'Kentucky High Step,' we drank success to the beaver."[19]

Why was Billy, as Mann reported, reluctant to take the job, even though Captain Anderson himself, and the Smithsonian Institution itself, were asking? Note what an extraordinary bother it was, taxing Billy's ingenuity to the utmost, during an era when the capture and transportation, alive, of wild animals was vanishingly rare. The only other experts were the people who supplied circuses, and circuses have little use for beavers. He had to make it up as he went along. Furthermore, saving beavers for their own sake may have seemed a bit perverse even to a man like Billy, with so unusual a mind. To say so requires speculation, and we should also note that he was not indifferent to small, obscure animals. In fact, he wrote a long piece about some of them in *Forest and Stream* in 1897, "Visitors at My Camp," that reads as if it were written by John Muir; he had spent forty days with an unidentified client in the backcountry east of the park, and the article was a description—really a celebration—of the birds and rodents that inhabited his camp every day. He and his clients killed only a few rats and mice, and even then tried hazing them first.[20]

At the same time, he called, regularly and for many years, for all the coyotes in Yellowstone National Park to be killed, to protect the elk and bison. "I was very much pleased on my return here not to see one coyote," he reported in May, 1898. "Neither have I heard one. They have been very successful in killing them off," "they" meaning everyone, both local civilians and the Army.[21] He maintained the same opinion about cougars: "One of the good things that has happened here is the killing of seven mountain lions, while down the [Yellowstone] river a few miles and close to the Park boundary three others were killed. These animals are the worst poachers we have in the Park."[22] On this point, he followed the conventional wisdom of his era: predatory mammals were simply evil.

Furthermore—twenty-first century people may find this surprising—beavers were, for Westerners, in the same category as lions, coyotes, and wolves. To this day, country folk dynamite beaver dams and shoot the creatures on sight. To many people, they remain varmints, because of their habit of felling trees and altering watercourses that downstream ranchers do not want altered; Billy had chosen the area around Yancey's because Uncle John Yancey wanted the beavers gone. During their era, they were often seen as merely living pelts; how could an honest mountain man, his contemporaries might wonder, go out of his way to save them? But save them Billy did, in the end reversing the destruction wrought by generations of his fellow woodsmen.

Despite the hardships, he developed a taste for the work. By the time he traveled to the Columbian Exposition in Chicago in 1893, reporters were identifying him as the Smithsonian's animal catcher; the reporter I quoted above identified him exclusively as such (to run the Hunter's Cabin, Billy was "relieved from his task of capturing animals in the Yellowstone, or National Park, for the Smithsonian Institution," the writer here omitting everything else Billy did).[23] Hofer was already a minor celebrity, and the sheer strangeness and routinely comical scenes that resulted from his new "job" often delighted reporters. William E. Curtiss of the *Chicago Record* recorded the following misadventure and, in the custom of that era, other newspapers openly copied it. The piece bounced to the *St. Louis Republic*, bounced finally to Yellowstone National Park Historian Lee Whittlesey, who bounced it to me.[24]

Curtiss actually witnessed the scene, and it is the only record we have of Billy's technique for catching adult bears: "Elwood Hofer, the official hunter and trapper of the United States Government out in the Yellowstone country, not long ago caught a big black bear in one of his patent traps, which also answers as a transportation cage. It is made of iron rods and oak timber—the trap, I mean, not the bear—has a drop at either end, and is baited with honey. When the bear enters and commences to paw the honey the drops fall and lock him in as tight as if he were in an exhibition cage at a menagerie. The cage can then be shipped anywhere the bear is wanted, and Billy Hofer supplies bears and other wild beasts to the Central Park Commissioners of New York and several zoos throughout the country, as well as to the Smithsonian Institution in Washington."[25]

So it seemed that Billy had found if not invented the basic design of the modern bear trap. It is called a "culvert trap" today, because, instead of the wood-and-bars cage that Billy constructed to hold the bear, the modern trap uses the prefabricated steel piping from which road engineers construct culverts (that said, there exist mosaics from the Roman Empire that show men catching bears for gladiatorial shows, and those bear traps look just like Billy's, except that—in the characteristic Roman touch—a slave operated the door). Billy caught his bear, and the comedy ensued:

> Well, Billy hauled the bear down to the railroad terminus at Cinnabar, backed the wagon up against the door of a freight car, ran out a couple of planks for skids, and then hitched a chain to the cage so as to draw it into the car. A pair of mules on the other side of the car were attached to the other end of the chain and the driver was instructed to be very careful in starting with them. He obeyed orders to the best of his ability, and everything went right until the cage was drawn into the car. The bear, being without experience in modern transportation facilities, did not quite comprehend the situation, and expressed his anxiety in a prolonged "Woo-o-o-o-o!" which alarmed the mules and caused them to start across the railroad yards at a 240 gait. They snatched the bear cage through the other door of the car and dragged it over the ground as they ran, first on one side and then on the other. One minute the bear would be standing on his head and the next on his feet. The cage bounded along as if it were light as a chicken coop, and the louder the bear said "Woo-o-o-o-o!" the faster the mules ran, and their fright was not in any measure allayed by having six or seven men yelling after them.

It was an excellent test of the strength of Billy Hofer's cage, for when a field of stumps was reached on the other side of the road, it bounded from one to another until finally it dropped into a place between two stumps that was not wide enough for the cage to pass through. This checked the team with a jerk, and caused them to stop so suddenly that they turned somersaults. But they were on their feet in a moment, and when the bear said "Woo-o-o-oo!" again, they made a desperate jump. The mules being stronger than the chain, they were released, and did not stop running until they were several miles away.

Ever since then, those mules have shied at freight cars. The team of sober-minded horses, which had hauled the cage down from the mountain, was brought up to the stump field and dragged it back to the car. The cage suffered no damage, and the bear got an extra ride for nothing.[26]

Absurd mishaps of this sort were simply a normal part of his new work. It is no wonder that reporters and readers enjoyed them.

The work nevertheless went on. In his regular articles for *Forest and Stream*, Billy began to routinely add a paragraph on what he was shipping to the National Zoological Park. In November 1895, he shipped "Four beaver and quite a number of birds," but unfortunately did not say how he captured the birds.[27] In December 1896, he mailed a menagerie: "I shall send six antelope, one cow elk, four beaver and two black bears. I will leave five elk (bulls). I'm having crates made for them in Gardiner. They are to go by express."[28] Thus a kind of mammalian pipeline evolved between Gardiner and Washington and other points east, with so much traffic on it that jams developed. Almost a year to the day later, he reported that the five bull elk were still waiting to be shipped and were "liable to be turned out, as they are not wanted at the park in Washington."[29] As late as June, 1899, the five elk still languished at Mammoth.[30]

In 1899, Hofer wrote a lengthy article, illustrated with his own photographs, responding to what amounted to a demand from George Bird Grinnell that he tell *Forest and Stream* readers exactly how he went about catching antelope, today called *pronghorn* and then believed among the most easily spooked and speediest animals in North America. He responded by detailing a single long outing he made two years earlier. He rode to Uncle John Yancey's place with Sam Yancey, a relative of the old innkeeper, and with Leo ambling along beside them. He moved into that same unoccupied cabin at Yancey's that he used regularly when catching animals for the Smithsonian; the elder Yancey was nearly always depicted by those who wrote about him as hopelessly disagreeable, but appropriately, the two Uncles were close friends.

Billy then described how he went about his business, having been at it for years now. He and Sam brought Yancey's telescope and Billy's own high-powered field glasses, and they went to a meadow and simply watched: "We commenced operations by riding out every day, sometimes leading a pack animal with sacks, ropes, strings and canvas, and taking a lunch along, for we were often out until dark. We would ride to a prominent point, from which we could see game and command a view of as large an extent of country as possible. Then we would look for antelope." What followed was likely the first thoroughly detailed description of pronghorn antelope behavior in the wild, taking into account the whole environment, the predators, the behavioral defenses of the mother does, their actions in relation to their fawns (or kids), indeed far more than I can summarize here, including an enchanting description of the young, when a female pronghorn at last appeared. Here is a small sample:

> When the antelope thought everything all safe, and no watchful eye of coyote, lynx or other animal was on her, she would circle around a few times more, then stop as though to eat and put her nose to the ground; and then in the field

of the telescope or field glass would appear a small object with its mother. She would let it have a little dinner, then make it stop nursing, and go to her other kid, putting it up the same way—with a poke of her nose—the first kid playing around while its mate had its dinner. The young of the antelope go down on their knees when feeding, like a lamb. After the young have been satisfied the old one moves off slowly with them. They play around, running in circles, stopping suddenly and running the other way, jumping to one side, up in the air, whirling around and going through all kinds of antelope gymnastics, unconsciously practicing every trick that it will resort to to escape from its enemies when it has to shift for itself.[31]

Readers might recall my claim, at the beginning of this book, that Thomas Elwood Hofer should be recognized for what he was: a scientist, really, or at least one of the more accomplished field naturalists of his day. I have tried to mainly let him speak for himself, through the pages of *Forest and Stream*, for which he produced countless descriptions like the one above. What he was doing, although it had another purpose, was otherwise no different from what the young Jane Goodall—the British primatologist— did when she sat down at Gombe with a notebook and just started watching everything the chimpanzees did. Much of Billy's work is out of date scientifically and superseded now, but that does not decrease or nullify his accomplishments.

And the Smithsonian, of course, wanted its captured antelope. Always, with Billy, contemplation had to give way to some task that challenged his hands-on, practical skills to their utmost. In a way, it was like a curse: he always had to put his field glasses down, dream up a creative solution to an impossible problem, then get filthy dirty and exhausted in implementing it. Catching those young antelope, at least, proved surprisingly easy. The watching had been the difficult part; once he knew how to locate them, he simply rode his horse up to walking distance from the spot where they were hiding, strolled up, located them in the grass—the most difficult part—then picked each one up like a housecat. He chose a small window of time in the spring for this task, when the fawns were so young that they offered no resistance. The does, and sometimes the fawns themselves, usually wailed in distress. He was different from a great many scientists in that he felt badly about it.

Catching the animals was of course the easy part. As any warden or zoo manager can tell you, catching wild animals is usually easier (Billy caught a squad of elk calves, too, without having to spend days merely finding the animals). Keeping them alive was the challenge. Billy had already discovered this truth—and again, he had to teach himself all these techniques, learning as he went along, with no guidance on how to proceed: "We had ten to care for, which were almost as bad as ten human young," he stated. He and Sam Yancey had hauled a quantity of baby bottles and similar gear all the way from Gardiner. "We had to gauge the quantity of milk for each one, reduce it with boiled water, and later with rice water, sterilize the milk, wash everything we used about the milk with soda water, wash the babies' faces, jaws and mouth, and dry them carefully to keep them in a healthy condition. Each antelope, as we got it, we marked with a string around its neck."[32]

He admitted to a weakness that wildlife biologists sometimes get into trouble for confessing today, although Dr. Goodall exhibited the same response: "Both Sam and I became very much attached to them. Either of us would wake up in the night if one of them moved about, and often we would get up, light a candle, count them and see that they were all well and comfortable. We used to feed them from six to eight times a day—early in the morning and late at night…. I found I was becoming so attached to them that I would not want to give them up to the Government, so I thought [it] best to give them up at once." He then gave us a glimpse, but only a glimpse, of the next step in the process, as demanding as any that had come before: the trip to Washington. "Teams came from the [Mammoth Hot] Springs and moved all my family to new quarters.... Then I took them [the animals] to Washington, D. C., turning them over to Dr. Frank Baker," who also happened to be the visionary who set up the zoo's first beaver colony. Billy finished: "Any reader or friend of the FOREST AND STREAM will see the little fellows—now more than two years old—by calling at the National Zoological Park. Please don't feed them peanuts or tobacco. I don't wish them to learn bad habits."[33]

And so it went, the animals normally being escorted on their trip to the big city by Billy. More elk and deer made the journey in November 1899.[34] Those five bull elk—they seem never to have made that trip to the capital—formed the nucleus of a small zoo, which was in full swing in 1901. "There is a very interesting collection of animals," wrote Billy, "at the Mammoth Hot Springs—six mule deer, three males and three females. The does have given birth to four beautiful fawns. These little creatures are attracting considerable attention, as are the six little antelope [that] Capt. Pitcher," the new superintendent, "has on hand, to say nothing of the young elk calves. Capt. Pitcher intends to add a few more animals to the collection in the inclosure in front of the hotel, where they will remain until after the close of the season. It is the intention then for them to reach the National Zoological Park,"[35] as needed. Such treatment of wild animals in the park sounds bizarre today, but in fact, it was one of many enclosures and small zoos that existed here and there—both in the park and outside—in the early decades.[36]

Although he might not have known it then, Hofer's greatest success in this context lay not in stocking the National Zoological Park and other collections; it happened instead in distant mountains not too far from his original home. By the turn of the twentieth century, the Adirondacks—the often heavily forested mountains that make up Adirondack Park in upstate New York—were, like so many places, running out of beavers. One careful study tracked the population as it hit its low, down to perhaps five or ten animals in the whole vast massif, rebounding to perhaps fifteen in

1900. At that point, local preservationists took some limited action; one landowner introduced about a dozen into his private forest; another released two onto a private preserve. The State of New York got involved in 1904, purchasing seven beavers, six of which survived the winter to be released the next year. Another private individual released a single animal in 1906.[37]

This unfocused and rather relaxed effort might eventually have succeeded. We cannot know, because in 1906, the New York state legislature got serious, and according to one historian "allocated one thousand dollars to the Forest, Fish and Game Commission to acquire additional beavers. Contracting with the [U.S.] Secretary of the Interior, the Commission purchased twenty-five beavers from Yellowstone National Park." The first shipment, of eight animals, arrived on September 3, 1907. "Four of the eight had died in transit; the survivors were soon released near Old Forge," a town that became a center of the recovery effort, surrounded as it was by hundreds of glacial lakes and ponds. The deaths in transit were part of doing business; again, keeping the animals alive, once caught, was the major challenge. "On October 13th eight healthy beavers arrived from Wyoming," and "two more beavers from Yellowstone entered the Adirondacks' waters" on the eighteenth.[38]

So Yellowstone provided more beavers than had survived in the remnant Adirondack population when it hit its low. Whatever boost the Yellowstone beavers gave to the raw numbers in the Adirondacks, they also helped prevent the kind of genetic bottleneck that results in such situations and which would have meant that the rebounding population carried, undiluted, all the mutations and genetic disorders present in those last five or ten (the "founder effect," geneticists call it). The beavers recolonized their old homes as we might expect them to have done, especially since the State of New York passed multiple laws protecting them. There are today, according to the best guess offered by the New York Department of Environmental Conservation, between 50,000 and 75,000 beavers in the Adirondacks.[39]

You can probably guess who did the heavy lifting involved in getting beavers from Yellowstone to Upstate New York, intact—yes, it was Billy Hofer. The animals already numbered in the thousands in 1921, when *Forest and Stream* ran an article celebrating the success. This essay elicited a letter of mild complaint: "The article on the restocking of the Adirondacks with beaver, printed in your April number, is a gratifying record for all outdoor people." It could, however, have "given a little more detail as to where the Adirondack beaver actually came from. It is my recollection that the authorities of New York State appealed to the Interior Department to furnish them beaver from the Yellowstone Park to be used in restocking the Adirondacks and that the officials of the Yellowstone Park secured the services of T. Elwood Hofer."[40] In fact, an anonymous article, probably written by George Bird Grinnell, had reported in 1910 that the beaver population had then reached "at least forty colonies, and these forty colonies may include one hundred families. They now cover much of the Adirondacks."[41] The article quite explicitly credited Billy as a key player.

Years later, at the request of Syracuse University, Grinnell asked his contacts to dig through the archives in Yellowstone National Park, and they found the original record, written in the telegraphic style common in early park documents: "Eighteen beaver caught at Yanceys August 14 to September 11, 1907, by T. Elwood (Billy) Hofer and shipped by express to J. S. Whipple, Old Forge, N. Y., for New York State, and four died enroute."[42] That makes it sound as if Billy merely mailed the animals, but we know otherwise. According to the Salem, Oregon *Daily Capital Journal*, he accompanied the beaver on their trip, trying without avail to keep all the members of that first group alive. He took eighteen to Washington, DC, presumably left some with the Smithsonian, and took the rest, after dinner with Theodore Roosevelt, directly to Old Forge.[43]

It is remarkable the extent to which what we see today when we go outdoors in North America is the result of actions taken a century and more ago by one Thomas Elwood Hofer. When you catch a nonnative fish in Yellowstone today, it may now occupy those waters because Billy specifically told the U.S. Fish Commission to put it there. Look at the bison in Yellowstone, now so plentiful that their abundance is a problem, and you should remember what Billy—with a great deal of help, of course—did to bring their plight to the nation's attention (he continued to write about them for as long as he worked for *Forest and Stream*). Spot a beaver in the Adirondacks, and you are looking at an animal that, mixed with those original survivors, is a direct descendant of the unhappy few who rode the two thousand miles east on the railroad to New York with Billy at their side.

While he was catching animals and later while he was supposed to be running the T.E. Hofer Boat Company, Billy was also still guiding parties on horseback around the park and beyond its boundaries. From stray references in letters and *Forest and Stream* pieces, we know that he guided people every year, but kept no comprehensive, extant record of them. In passing, in the short autobiography he sent to Horace Albright, he did name one group that should ring a bell for us: "I made one trip without any hunting this time, with Mr. and Mrs. Robt. DeForest and Mr. and Mrs. Lewis Tiffney. The trip was over rather rough country for the ladies of the party."[44] Billy was spelling from memory again (his typewriter did not have a spell checker): Charles Lewis Tiffany was of course the founder of the jewelry empire, the DeForests family friends. The ladies handled it well enough, improvising in the way that Billy would have done. During his own trip with Billy, Warren Delano reported, to his journal, that "I think you will be amused to hear that our tents were once used by Mr. & Mrs Louis Tiffany & Mr. & Mrs. Rob. DeForest. They sewed a lot of hooks about which are still here to which we festoon our small articles."[45] That is just the sort of improvement that Billy himself would have eventually made.

Another influential person who crossed paths with Billy was Anthony W. Dimock, the biggest of big wheels during his era—a financier, steamship owner, commodities speculator, real estate tycoon, and so on. He was not Billy's client, but merely an acquaintance, although their encounters were crucial to Hofer's story in two ways: they helped set Billy up for yet another unusual "job," and Dimock's memories are the only record we have of an exceedingly strange episode involving Hofer that occurred in 1890. In addition to his other projects, Dimock was also, crucially for Billy, an early wildlife photographer, and it turns out that Dimock probably introduced Billy to photography. He met Billy, as he explained in his memoirs, in Yellowstone in the autumn of 1887. "On this Rocky Mountain trip I met Edward Hofer"—and again, the trouble with "Elwood." (No wonder "Billy" caught on). "He showed much interest in my camera work," wrote Dimock, "and spoke of the great opportunities in that direction which came his way." This is the first reference we have to Billy's interest in photography, which may well have been brand new to him at that early date.[46]

We skip ahead here three years for the exceedingly strange episode, which appropriately took place at one corner of what later generations, under the influence of bad science fiction, would call the Bermuda Triangle. Dimock was near Marco Island, Florida, just south of Naples, in the Ten Thousand Islands area of the state, part of which today lies in Everglades National Park. Billy would not, however, recognize present-day Marco Island, in fact would probably be disgusted, as it has been changed for the worse by resort developments. Dimock wrote:

> On the 8th of April, 1890, I was hunting with the camera on the mainland southeast of Marco in Florida. We were near the Royal Palm Hammock, which my companion had never seen, but were separated from it by a stream of water. We discovered a skiff on the bank which had presumably been left there by hunters. We commandeered that skiff and I left a card pinned to a tree stating that I had borrowed the skiff and would return it within an hour. It was several

hours before we got back to find two justly indignant men sitting on the bank waiting for us. The anger of one of them melted away as he reminded me that he was Edward Hofer, erstwhile a Rocky Mountain guide, but now piloting Mr. Andrews through the Ten Thousand Islands of Florida. Again he was interested in my work as I told him of flash-light photographs of alligators which I had taken only the night before, on the 7th of April.[47]

Reading this, one first wonders if that really was some other Hofer and if "Edward" was instead a correct spelling. But Dimock had a third meeting with "Edward," and it sealed the identification of our Billy Hofer. Like so many others in the country, Dimock traveled to the Columbian Exposition. He had claimed, in 1887, to have taken the first proper wildlife photographs in the Rockies—an unlikely claim, but he was surely among the first, given the difficulty of photographing a live animal using the slow shutter speeds of that era (note the ghosts drifting around in the background of Civil War photographs; those were people walking past the camera-lens while the shutter was open). Here is Dimock again: "On September 12th, 1893, I entered the Hunter's Cabin of the Chicago Exposition, where a hunter was exhibiting photographs of wild animals. He was addressing a group of visitors and as I approached him he said: 'I was the first to take photographs of wild animals in their native surroundings,' then pausing a moment and extending his hand toward me he continued, 'excepting that man whom I met years ago in the Rockies and again in Florida engaged in the same work.'"[48]

What was Billy doing "years ago" in Florida? He did briefly mention, in one of his *Forest and Stream* articles, a visit there, although the mention was brief indeed: "I have been from Florida to Alaska,"[49] he wrote, at the beginning of a sentence (and more on Alaska in a moment). So he was there. We know nothing of the Mr. Andrews he was "piloting," but it is highly unlikely that Billy was working as a fishing guide, or was thinking of relocating; the heat and humidity alone would likely have deterred him. He was as cold-adapted as explorers Ernest Shackleton, Robert Peary, Roald Amundsen, or take your pick. More likely, he was just showing this Mr. Andrews how to use a fly rod. That is how an angler catches tarpon, which Billy must have found exciting indeed after spending his adult life dropping little bits of fuzz in front of eight-inch-long trout in the high Rockies. A tarpon can be eight feet long.

So Billy Hofer took an interest in photography at least as early as 1887 and was exhibiting his work by 1893, at the Columbian Exposition. He was something more than just an "amateur" photographer and before long he was publishing his photographs in *Forest and Stream*. His major limitation was technological, and this was the one field he set out to master in which he was substantially dependent on the innovations and manufacturing skills of distant engineers on the East Coast and in Europe. If he had possessed the equipment to, say, grind lenses to maximally fine specifications, he probably would have invented a better camera just working out of what he always called his "cabin" in Gardiner.

Hofer wrote about his photographic challenges in his short autobiography: "I became interested in photographing wild animals. Made winter snow shoe trips before the new camera came out and I got too old for the hard work. My first trip with a camera was with a very heavy Anthony 5 x 8, using glass plates. I got a few buffalo pictures and some elk and antelope. I made several trips with other cameras, but could never get just the camera I wanted until the reflex came out. By this time I had gotten tired of the hard work and exposure, sleeping out all night by open fires and travelling all day hunting for pictures."[50]

Here he identified a single major, technological innovation as crucial to him, the invention of the reflex camera. Inside its chassis, it used a mirror that allowed the photographer to look through the same lens that would take the actual photograph (the mirror provided a "reflection," in time reduced to "reflex"). The user, in other words, did not have to look through a viewfinder, which was offset from the lens and so necessarily provided a different image than that which the actual lens would produce. Today, we associate such cameras with the single-lens reflex camera that dominated the high-end consumer market toward the end of the film era and was so popular that, in today's digital era, when there is no need for mirrors, expensive cameras are still called "SLRs" and imitate the classic design of the film SLR. The technology is surprisingly old—it dates back to the 1860s—but in Hofer's day it would have taken a while for it to filter down to the general public and hence out to Montana.

Not too many Anthony 5x8 cameras have survived, but the manuals do, and they make horrifying reading, in this context. The Anthony was what we might expect from the 1880s, a camera with an adjustable bellows and a wooden tripod that weighed about as much as a set of wooden skis. The "5x8" referred to the size, in inches, of the glass plate that captured the image. The advice that one such manual gives us today on simply taking the photograph remains strongly suggestive of the near-impossibility of using such a camera to photograph wild animals: "After the camera is fixed in position, the focus obtained, the lens covered with the cap, ground glass frame swung back and dry plate holder put in place, withdraw the cardboard slide *nearest the lens*, removing it entirely from the holder; then, without jarring or shaking the camera in the least, remove the cap from the lens and expose for the proper length of time. The time of exposure depends very largely upon the brightness of the day. A view taken on a bright, sunny day requires about one second's exposure. If the day is dark or cloudy, from two to three second's."[51] All that happened after skiing into position, unlimbering the tripod, unhousing the camera, expanding the bellows, and so on and on. The manual, just on exposure, continues in that vein for several hundred words, making it crystal clear why no photograph of an angry moose or charging grizzly exists from the 1880s.

The *Livingston Enterprise* recorded some of Billy's earliest efforts at photographing living wild animals, in the spring of 1888. That anyone would even attempt such a feat was newsworthy. Billy was not exaggerating when he spoke of spending the night by an open fire, waiting for the one chance at a photograph. The newspaper reported that he was tracking "a small band of buffalo that make their headquarters near the Twin Buttes, west of Hell's Half Acre. Mr. Hofer will secure, if possible, a photograph of these last of their tribe for the Forest and Stream. Peter Nelson"—the ubiquitous "Snowshoe Pete"—"saw them once early in the winter and Mr. Hofer will sleep on their trail, if he finds it, until he secures their portraits, if it takes all the winter that remains."[52]

The situation would be familiar to any infantryman or Marine today. Billy was setting up an ambush, and given his technology he had little choice. He would find the bison trail, prepare his camera, aim it in the direction from which the animals would appear, and wait. Almost a month later, on April 28, the *Enterprise* reported that Nelson had spotted another herd, in Hayden Valley, and that Billy was still chasing the animals with his camera, with little success.[53]

Billy kept at it, as he always did, publishing what had to be among the first accounts of anyone's attempts to photograph wildlife in the Rockies, in a long *Forest and Stream* feature from May 1888. Those attempts to photograph bison reported by the *Livingston Enterprise* in fact occurred at the end of at least a full year of experimentation. In the spring of 1887, "I was surprised and delighted to receive as a present from the Forest and Stream Publishing Company a complete photographic outfit." He recorded the challenges involved, and in the process made it clear why early wildlife photographers so routinely used some variant on the verb "hunt" to describe the process. To be successful, the camera-hunter had to be both a talented stalker and cameraman, as Billy made clear with his usual self-deprecating humor:

I first learned that while hunting I must carry the camera

set up, must have my object well lighted and that to obtain good pictures many other favorable conditions must prevail. The thing I found most difficult about it was to get the camera into position while close to game without frightening it before I could focus on the object and then put in plates and fire. Many times after a hard bit of work getting to a favorable position, I would have everything all ready, but the act of drawing the slide or cocking the drop shutter for a shot would alarm the animals, and before I could pull the trigger the game would skip out, leaving me with a camera ready to take a picture of the place where the game had been but a second before; a picture about as satisfactory to a photographer as fine scenery and game sign is filling to a hungry man. Or the game would be standing under the sun with their dark side toward one, the wind blowing from the hunter nearly toward the game, and when everything was about ready the wind would whip around, giving the animals warning of the presence of supposed danger, changing a scene of still life to one of very active life, with buffalo, elk or deer running off in the background, and in the foreground an amateur photographer with an instrument set up ready to make an exposure, a disappointed expression on his face and a few blue streaks in the air.[54]

Billy then gave the details on the hunt for a bison photograph that had made the news in the *Enterprise*. His attempts in the spring of 1888 were among his first extended expeditions with the new *Forest and Stream* equipment, and "expedition" is the right word. He ultimately recruited Snowshoe Pete Nelson and Ed Wilson, the scout who would eventually take his own life. More than any other animal, they wanted photographs of the bison, because plenty of people back East refused to believe that the Yellowstone Park herd even existed. They skied all the way from Fort Yellowstone to Alum Creek in Hayden Valley to get photographic evidence that it did. It is illustrative of the difficulty involved that three of the best scouts and skiers in the Rockies (and probably the world at that time) were only able to produce a few blurry images that *Forest and Stream* found unpublishable.

What Billy and other pioneers in this field (if there *were* any besides Billy) needed was both a handheld camera and a telephoto lens—but that combination required a fatal trade off. A long telephoto lens collected less light, requiring the photographer to leave the shutter open longer...resulting in the usual blurred image when the animal moved. Photographers in Yellowstone had a local advantage: a bright day in winter might, in theory, produce enough light to overcome the problem. It did not work. A correspondent writing *Forest and Stream* reported in 1894 that "Billy Hofer, who used one of these cameras for photographing big game in the Yellowstone Park last winter, found that even over snow and using his largest stop his pictures were under exposed."[55]

Billy himself reported on this trip in a lengthy two-part series in *Forest and Stream* that ran in December, 1893, and included, in the first installment, two of his first publishable photographs.[56] The title of the series was illuminating, however. As with the earlier article, both stories in the series were headlined "Hunting with a Camera." The emphasis was very much on the hunting, not the photography, which did not go so well.

In the end, Billy obtained better equipment, simply because he lived in an era when photography was moving out of the studio and into the hands of ordinary people. By the later 1890s, his longer columns were routinely illustrated with his own photographs; the articles about catching beavers and antelope were graced by his own pictures, and if the animals were difficult to catch, the photographs could not have been easy to take, either. By 1908, he was good enough that Grinnell devoted the entire cover of *Forest and Stream* to one of his photographs. Someone along the way named it "Treed by a Grizzly," and it showed a black bear peeking down, rattled but safe, from the upper limbs of a conifer. Beneath the caption was the line "From a photograph of a Western black bear, by T. E. Hofer."[57]

Hofer was learning all the time, of course, and as always, he had some unusually accomplished tutors. Recall that his first lesson had come from Anthony Dimock, who genuinely knew what he was doing. One of Billy's later tutors was George Shiras III, the congressman from Pennsylvania who is today remembered best as a pioneer of wildlife photography, especially in the use of flash photography at night to catch unsuspecting animals. He also did early work in constructing and perfecting the camera trap, the technique that with modifications is still in use today: a camera was anchored beside a path frequented by the animal that Shiras was after. The shutter was activated when the animal tripped a wire (and, incidentally, set off an exploding pan full of magnesium that must have been quite a surprise). *National Geographic* essentially gave Shiras the July 1906 issue, in which it published 74 of his photographs and in one step went a long way from being the frumpy scholarly journal it had been toward becoming the much-loved dentist's-waiting-room picture book that it is today (indeed, the magazine later called Shiras "Grandfather Flash" and "the father of wildlife photography").[58]

When Shiras arrived in Yellowstone in 1908, he was searching for two animals that he had not had much luck photographing yet: bears and moose. Bears were not much of a challenge to find. His guide ("the redoubtable Billy Hofer," Shiras called him) was still running the T.E. Hofer Boat Company, to his own regret, and was engaged in an everyday chore when Shiras met him at his store: "At the lake we received a hearty greeting from Billy Hofer, who was found in the act of opening a package of Roman candles to be used in firing at the bears, whose ever-increasing depredations made the running of an outfitting store an unprofitable undertaking. That night I slept in one corner of a canvas-covered storehouse and, noticing a large ragged hole in the wall, I told Hofer there seemed to be no trouble about ventilation, when he said: 'I think not, and you may have more before morning, because that hole was made by a black bear night before last, when he butted in and went off with one of my biggest hams.'" When he was finished, Shiras wrote the experience up as a long two-part series in *Forest and Stream*.[59] Whatever else happened to distract Billy, we can be certain he quizzed Shiras at length about both his photographic gear and his photographic techniques.

Shiras returned the following year, after moose this time.[60] Billy was only able to spare one of his more trusted assistants to help, which is unfortunate, because this expedition was to become one of those backcountry journeys that had far reaching ramifications. Shiras had heard that the Yellowstone moose looked different; it was in fact smaller, with a face that appeared unusual to one accustomed to moose elsewhere, and lighter in color. He went out to search for himself. The park moose was in fact a new subspecies, and in spite of the constant creation, destruction, and renaming of subspecies that goes on today in biology, this one has stuck: *Alces americanus shirasi*, which is one of four subspecies of moose in North America.[61]

From all of this, it is easy to conclude that Uncle Billy Hofer would be better known today if—and this was yet another stroke of bad luck—so many of his photographs had not been lost or destroyed. Most went missing when *Field and Stream* swallowed *Forest and Stream*. What we have now are just muddy reproductions of reproductions.

How about this suggestion, as a way of making up for the way history itself has insulted him? Greater Yellowstone is still full of undiscovered creatures. The next time a ranger or biologist discovers a new one, give it the species name *hoferi*, for Thomas Elwood "Billy" Hofer. The honor is long overdue, and it would be truly deserved.

Hofer stands in front of his cottage on Sunlight Beach, Whidby Island, Washington, on May 16, 1931. He was 82. Hofer died in 1933. COURTESY HERITAGE AND RESEARCH CENTER, YELLOWSTONE NATIONAL PARK.

CHAPTER TWELVE

Sunlight Beach

Uncle Billy Hofer completed his journey through life by exchanging one coast and one ocean for another. Born on the Atlantic, he ended up watching the sun set over the Pacific.

Billy is known today almost exclusively to Yellowstone aficionados, and few of them are aware that, while he never quite gave up on the Wonderland that he loved, he began leaving Yellowstone for increasingly lengthy periods starting in 1900, and soon after that moved and regularly spent about half of the year elsewhere. After about 1920, the move became permanent. In his *Forest and Stream* articles, the first suggestion that he was making a major change in his life came in a story published August 11, 1900: "I have been back a few days from Alaska. I have not been in the Park since I took the elk and deer from here for Washington, D. C., last November. In the spring I passed through Livingston on my way to Seattle."[1] His readers must have wondered: what was up? Billy's cryptic references to Alaska and Seattle continued off and on until he dropped this little bombshell into the conclusion of one of his general reports from the park, on December 13, 1902: "The railroad is completed to Gardiner, [and so] by spring I hope to be able to sell out and move my roll of blankets to Seattle and Alaska."[2] He would maintain residences in Yellowstone—the T.E. Hofer Boat Company, among other responsibilities, lay well in the future in 1902—but the place seemed to be losing its charms for him. Note how he structured that sentence, above: we can read in it that the railroad was the reason he had had enough. Yellowstone was simply becoming too civilized for him.

His first exposure to Alaska was on official business. The *Chicago Tribune* reported, on August 5, 1900, that Billy was "just back from the coast of Alaska, where he was sent by the United States government to collect specimens of the great Kodiak bear, alive, for the gardens at Washington. He brought back the bear,"[3] and was passing through Chicago on his way to deliver it, or them—the report is vague on that point. The "gardens" were the National Zoological Park, which must have been heavily geared up to receive such cargo—while a large Yellowstone grizzly may weigh seven or eight hundred pounds, a large Kodiak may weigh twice that. In May 1902, the *Sunday Washington Globe* of Washington, DC described the trap, designed and operated "under the supervision" of Billy Hofer. He had built it on the same pattern as the design that caused such trouble when the mules stampeded at Cinnabar. The Kodiak Island version was, however, sixteen feet long and six high and made entirely of steel.[4]

But at this point, as he shuttled unpredictably between Gardiner, Seattle, and points north, he regularly fell off the map and away from the greater world's attention—as is unsurprising, because that was just where he wanted to be. Our best clues to his years in Alaska lie in the letters he wrote to George Bird Grinnell, about three hundred pages of which have survived from 1905, when his Alaska venture was still getting started, until Billy's death in 1933. Nearly all are handwritten, and when he wrote by hand to Grinnell, he wrote rapidly, not bothering to proofread or make corrections. But the information that we need, at least, is there.[5]

When the Smithsonian sent him to collect those Kodiak bears, Billy looked around maritime Alaska and saw a salty and wet version of the Great Plains he had known in the 1870s. There were few people and no railroads. He liked it. He was four years too late for the Klondike gold rush, and a year too late even for the Nome gold rush that followed it. Besides, he had already been through his share of gold rushes—including Colorado and the Black Hills—and thus knew that they always failed to match their advertising. Instead, he saw another future, in another activity that he knew well: furs. He selected Fox Island as his base of operations,[6] across from the Kenai Peninsula (and not to be confused with the Fox Islands, which make up a significant portion of the inner Aleutians). There is today a tourist lodge on Fox Island, and nothing else. It was far less crowded in 1900. Getting there was difficult on a good day—the key to its appeal for Billy.

He was 51 in 1900, however, time to think about retirement in a society that had no 401Ks, no IRAs, no Social Security, no Medicare, nothing really except individual handouts and charity from religious organizations. And Thomas Elwood Hofer, like the old Patriot Thomas Elwood for whom he was named, was among the least religious men ever produced by what was then an intensely religious society; he probably would have avoided accepting their charity. Billy had to be practical and watch out for his own well-being, as he always did. A retirement home on remote Fox Island would be harsh beyond imagining. He would have to compromise.

He chose Seattle as his logical base of operations. Gardiner would remain his second home, and conveniently for him the Northern Pacific bounced between Seattle and Livingston as straight as a railroad could, when passing through two giant mountain ranges (it did meander through what must have been an annoying jog south toward Walla Walla, before turning north to Spokane). To the extent that he could ever enjoy a place that was all "settled up," as he put it, he liked Seattle. He had a taste for seafood, rarely indulged since he was a teen, as the *Capital Journal* reported: "'Billy' always spends his winters in Seattle [he actually now spent winters in Alaska] near the base of the clam supply and when he pulled into port yesterday his first rush was for the waterfront, where he eagerly began to question J. E. Standley, of Ye Olde Curiosity Shop, as to the clam crop this year. He heard only good news and it put him in the best of humor."[7] This would be an example of what Mark Twain called "good Arkansas journalism"—the editor got a free bucket of clams for that. Seattle was also the throughway to Seward's Folly, the then relatively new "district" of Alaska, so called because it boasted its own district court. It would not even become a territory until 1912. The monstrously large region had been purchased from the Czar in 1867, with Secretary of State William Seward as the motive force. No one knew yet about its gold, and certainly no one knew about the oil.

Billy moved into 414 Union Street, Seattle, almost his last temporary address, and set about seeing what he could make of Fox Island. Without the letters to Grinnell, we would be lost in trying to reconstruct his actions today. He formed the Alaska Blue Fox Propagating Company, which he always abbreviated A.B.F.P.Co., always complete with the periods (the snappy one-word name for a corporation was only just catching on). The goal was stated in the name of the company: it would turn Fox Island into a breeding ground for arctic foxes. It is doubtful Billy knew much about the animal with whom he was throwing in his lot. There was no "blue fox." Arctic foxes (*Vulpes lagopus*) exhibited a blue color phase part of the year, but also produced a variety that, for genetic reasons, was always blue. Billy was also getting in at the start of a small wave of especially persistent ecological destruction. Blue arctic foxes were artificially introduced throughout the Aleutians and other Alaskan islands, especially after fur prices went up during the First World War (the combatants needed warm clothing, in that pre-synthetic age). The foxes, naturally, ate native animals to extinction.

Whatever harm the A.B.F.P.Co. might have done to Fox Island, it was in financial trouble soon after its founding. It produced foxes from the start—that was not the problem. At the surprisingly early date of January, 1903, the New York Zoological Society reported in its bulletin that it received three pairs of blue foxes from Billy.[8] The trouble, happily (happily for us today), shows how the company operated and how it came to grief. The first problem was a simple matter of bad timing. An article in the local column of the *Livingston Enterprise* noted Billy's passage through the town in March, 1904, on his way back from Alaska; counting the 60-day trip to and from, the voyage had consumed six months. "Mr. Hofer and his men secured about 180 pelts.... The value of the pelts is about $4,000 but the Russo-Japanese war has knocked their value about 40 percent, as the principal market for the blue fox is in Russia."[9] Who could have guessed that, just as the island was coming online, Russia would go to war with Japan, of all outlandish enemies, and that the Czar's forces would be eviscerated, leading to a revolution in Russia in 1905, none of which was good for the business of selling furs to Russian aristocrats?

These events were unforeseeable, but the fur industry had structural quirks that would cause just as much trouble. Furthermore, while Billy had avoided the problem associated with every gold rush—that the prospectors who get there first get all the claims worth having—he did not see a similar problem approaching in the fur trade. To quote from a contemporary source, "The great fur events of the year…are the sales held in January, March, June and October of each year in the city of London. The January offerings often consist principally of muskrats, beavers and opossums. It is at the March sales that the choicest collection of the Hudson's Bay Company and the finest consignments shipped to C. M. Lampson and Company and other London brokers are sold at auction to bidders from all parts of the world."[10] The June and October events were for also-rans. This is the world on which Billy staked a considerable sum of money. His livelihood was now tied to the doings of faceless traders in a city on the literal opposite side of the earth, and even at that, it all came down to a single event in March.

In April 1905, he wrote to Grinnell with an update. Again, the sales were taking place in London, and hence in British currency.

During this era, the British pound bought five U.S. dollars. Billy was sending Grinnell news on the "[Fox] Island Lampson & Co March Sales":

> I am sure there is very much to interest you. You will see so many grades and how skins vary. See page 73, Fox, Silver, Lot 1251 160£ 1 skin, then Page 75, Lot 1289 £800 1 skin. I think this is a misprint and should read £80 0 S[hillings] 0 Pen[ce]. Still two years ago 1 skin brought $2500, or rather 500£, and a few years before that one brought 600£, Page 84, Lot 1446. 4 skins brought only 9 shillings each while Lot 1447 brought 220£.... You will see our Blue Fox sales. Only the 18 skins were sold the 75 reached there too late.[11]

Again, it was rather like a gold rush. Just two years earlier, a single skin had brought a small fortune; now four of his skins brought nine shillings—not quite a half-pound.

No wonder he tried to branch out. Keep in mind that this operation was not what we today would regard as politically correct. Billy was selling not just Alaskan animals, but anything he could lay his hands on, as he noted: "See Sea otter, Chinchilla—Real Bastard—Seal, Tiger, Lion, Leopard, Snow Leopard and other skins. These are not all the skins sold. Hudson Bay sales came first and are not on this list."

Lampson was not his only outlet, that is; he also sold to the Hudson Bay Company traders in Canada. Nor was he restricting himself to foxes, as animals to cultivate: "I have been trying to find out something about Chinchilla but it seems almost impossible to get hold of any one who understands the animals in the least. I can gather some things considerable information about what its doing but nothing of much value to any one who would like to try to raise them on some island."[12] Today we know that people have been trying and failing to make chinchillas pay for generations.

The operation was, at this point, still only developing the fatal problems that would kill it. Billy detailed them further later in April. He was faced with the problem that faces seasonal maritime operations along the Alaskan littoral to this day: it is difficult to find, not just quality employees, but employees who are willing to stay at all: "I have cut down running expenses so that its a little more than wages for men. $2000 a year at the most now. Our dry house and outfit at Dog Fish Bay can keep the Island supplied with fish." Dog Fish Bay was on the mainland not far from his island. Unfortunately, he had hit on the solution that employers in the region today return to again and again and that never works: he cut wages and fed the men bad food as a way of trying to keep ahead of the losses that were partly caused by the men always running away. "We have purchased no meal or pork this year and dont think it advisable to do so. We cant get good men to stay on the Island without paying good wages, $900 for one and $600 for the other. These men must furnish all their possession and House hold goods. We furnish buildings and equipment for the Island."

Still, the business was certainly a going-concern at this point, and Billy had learned an important trick: "I have sent a contract for $2500 worth of young foxes to Seattle for signature of party wanting 100 (or 50 pr) foxes, money to be placed in the Bank on signing and due us the day the foxes are put in the shipping boxes on the Island and turned in to purchases against, otherwise no sale. I hope it will go through however because otherwise we get no money until after next March." That bit about the foxes being "put in the shipping boxes" was clever, and it suggests he had been burned in the past. He thus made certain that he got paid no matter what condition the foxes were in when they reached Seattle. He was, however, still dependent on distant transactions that he could neither control nor even see: "I wrote Mr. Fraser"—a ringleader for C.M. Lampson and Co.—"to let the 75 skins go during the June Sales if they would bring the same price as in March."[13] But June was for the second-rate skins, and lower. They could not bring the same price at that date.

Although he was nowhere near giving up on it, the business, like water in a sink, had by 1906 begun to circle the drain—in big, wide, looping circles—and the outcome was in retrospect becoming clear. Billy wrote an unhappy letter to Grinnell from Seattle in March of that year. "I am back here after quite a trip north. Steamers had a rough time this winter along the Alaskan Coast," he began, then unloaded:

> I only got 61 Fox skins this winter not even half what I expected and what we require to make the Island pay. There is no mistake about the Eagles getting foxes and I have been paying a bounty to have the natives kill them. Now I learn after reaching here that Eagles are protected. Of all the d—n notions!.... I'm having the natives I have on the island kill every one they can and pay for any they bring us killed around there for 20 miles. Even the Ravens got some young pups. I have some Eagle feathers with me and some feet to sell but must not let the wardens know it or custom house officers[.] I want to get back for the Company the money I expended for Eagles by selling feathers and feet and will— but whats the matter with the people East, are they daft on protection if so why the—well any thing—dont they protect something worth protecting.... in all due respect to Washington DC, we will kill all the Eagles we possibly can. We who are trying hard to make the Fox business pay (and you are one of the interested parties) are going to protect the Foxes. There is a whole lot of laws and taxes imposed on Alaska that are unjust. Still I guess well put up with it for a while. Its only the same thing repeated from 1776 when England "at long range" made laws for America, and now Washington making laws for Alaska.

The story remains the same today, told generation after generation in the West. A person can approve of the most onerous legislation from Washington protecting some piece of the natural landscape that person wants protected. Once money becomes involved, however, the G-men who had been heroes before become the villains, at least to some people. And Grinnell, among the most prominent conservationists in the nation, was now among "the interested parties," for specific reasons we will soon reach.

Regardless, Billy had set himself up for trouble. He could ski or ride or scramble anywhere he needed to go, in Yellowstone. Now he had to contend with the Gulf of Alaska. Note that he had not made it south in time for the March sale in London: "I tried very hard to get down there with the skins in time for this market [but] our Steamer the 'Dora' was blown to sea.... Reached here the 24th of February. She landed me on Cape Elizabeth on Dec 3rd and went on her way, visiting all the points for which she had mail freight and passengers. The Bertha was up close to the Island about Jan 8th for eight days trying to get into Cook Inlet [but we] could not even make Cape Elizabeth. Blinding snow storms and constant gales. There was no mail or freight coaster in Seldovia from the 3rd December until the Farallon reached there Feb 25th. I missed her [the boat] while on my way up with the natives. Had to stay 24 days at Seldovia until her return."[14] All these places were at the southern end of the Kenai Peninsula. The Cook Inlet is the long, wide embayment that leads to Anchorage, Seldovia being one of the only towns on that far end of the Kenai. The important point for us is that Billy was stuck. Whoever the "natives" were, they managed to get him to Seldovia, to the north of Cape Elizabeth. He could go no farther. He was marooned in Alaska for at least two months just because of the weather, and thus the crucial annual window for shipping fine skins to London passed him by. It must have been intolerably frustrating.

As if Alaska itself were not a stern enough enemy, his next challenge—as he reported to Grinnell at length in July 1907—was a device from a future time, one associated more with the late than with the early twentieth century: the hostile corporate takeover.

Billy had let the capital lie fallow, but the capitalists were active to a great fault. He reported:

> I did not go to Alaska last winter. I thought first that there should be no foxes killed on the Island I wanted to give them a chance to increase. You may remember I had Mr Wrights 60 shares of stock for which I gave a note for $1800, when this became due I was unable to meet the note. In the first place I was supposed to sell his stock so I could pay the note. Not being able to do so I told Wright so, and he would need to take the Stock for the note. [I] Put the note in an innocent parties hands for collection. They commenced suit against me in Seattle. I offered them the 60 shares and 30 I had or rather 28 shares which I had received for work and money. But no they were after money and as I had none…I had to go into Bankruptcy here. The stock was sold and Whites party bought it in for $105—. So I was out of it.[15]

Billy was so angry he could not spell the name of his adversary correctly—the man's name was Wight—and as the letter went on, his handwriting grew ever more violent. He was not, however, "out of it" just yet:

> I had before this, at a meeting of the stock holders, elected Capt. John C. Downing President and Genl Manager and Mrs. Downing treasurer. So I still control the Island. Chas R Olsson whom Whight traded 40 shares has given me his stock to vote and the Trustees voted one 1 share. Now with the votes of the other stock holders I expect to continue running the island and my plan is to vote to buy certain stock with any money we have in the treasury after I sell the skins of the next Killing and turn over to these certain stockholders a percentage of the skins from their stock

on account. I have lost all I ever put in to the company—
about $2,000.00 and don't cry about that but I do want
to protect my friends interest and will! Yourself, Mr. Fred
Delano, Mrs. & Major Pitcher, and two others. I think I
can and will go to Alaska next fall to do so—but more about
that later.[16]

He was writing this letter at the same time he was trying to get
the T.E. Hofer Boat Co. launched, so it would have made sense
for him to turn his back on the financial catastrophe that Fox
Island had become, eat the loss, and look toward the future. He
had done so innumerable times, although involving smaller sums.
Note, however, the names in that second to last sentence. Those
are the investors in the A.B.F.P.Co.: George Bird Grinnell, Frederic Delano, Major John Pitcher—superintendent of Yellowstone
National Park until the previous June—Mrs. Pitcher, "and two
others." These were all people whose good opinion he absolutely
required if he were to stay in any kind of business at all—and more.
These were friends, and the thought of losing their money could
not have been pleasant to Billy.

At least the business with Wight was punctuated, amid the hostile takeover and other modern touches, by a moment of exemplary
Old West business practice. Said Billy: "I am glad I was not in
Seattle on the 4 of July as some one took a shot at him (Mr Wight)
and put a bullet in his hip. Mrs Downing writes [that] it was a
close call for Wight. That the doctors probed 7 inches but could
not find the Bullet. It was a stray bullett so its supposed but—I
know of some people whom he has injured very much and they are
not [located] so very far from where he lives. So Im glad I was not
there but at the Yellowstone with Major Pitcher." Again, he and
the Pitchers were friends—they strolled among the elk at Mammoth regularly after dinner—so he was determined to get their
money back: "I may come on there before very long if not will
write you fully about the affairs of the A.B.F.P.Co. The Co is vir-

tually out of debt and through my efforts and management I had
a native on the Island until this Spring and a white man was there.
He will report to me on the conditions as to numbers of foxes." It
took all his "efforts and management" to get two people to stay,
one of whom decamped.[17]

The fight was still going on the following year, in early May,
1908. Who Charly Olssen was, we cannot even speculate, because
when Billy wrote on business matters, his spelling was almost comically haphazard (when he wrote about elk and flowers, he was fine).
While Olssen was spelled consistently below, as was inevitable with
a name like that, the spelling varied elsewhere. Billy had, however,
adopted another modern touch. As with today's Silicon Valley tech
startup, when cash ran low, he paid employees in stock:

> I got a letter from G.R. Olssen Kodiak Alaska— Charly
> is the man who was five years on the Island and has $4000
> (40 shares) of the Alaska Blue Fox Stock— Wight is trying
> to get hold of this stock, offering to trade west Seattle [real
> estate] lots for it—but Charly wont have anything to do
> with Wight would not give him a proxsey but sent me over
> to vote his share so that with the others I have controll.
> Charly wants to sell and I have offered him $400—for
> it—from letters and other information from the Island I am
> sure we can get back the money and a little more besides
> controlling the whole thing. A man who owns the next
> Island (Pearl) [Perl] would buy Wights stock if he can get
> Olssens, then he would have controll. I would be willing
> for him to have it if I thought he would do the right thing
> by you and the other stock holders, but I'm affraid to trust
> him. They are trying to trade Charly out of it but he won't
> take chances with them. I wrote Charly to make over his
> certificate to Geo Bird Grinnell, New York and send it to
> Capt Downing Pres of the A.B.F.P.Co. and we would either
> send the money direct to here or through Downing, when

the new Certificate was made out to you. If you cant spare the $400 in about a month, I think I can get the money and take it off your hands but I cant do it now[.][18]

A major problem for Billy was that he was trying to contend with this skullduggery while simultaneously running the boat business and his old guiding business. He was actually corresponding with Grinnell from a camp somewhere in the backcountry, as he made clear in a second letter dated May 27:

> Your letter about the stock received some time ago. (I have it at the camp) I will try and make the matter clear about the stock…. As to the matter of my taking it off your hands was, if you did not want it—As these 40 shares give the same controll, in our hands by a big majority, we can do as is best for the investors. Yourself, Mr Delano and the Pitchers. The man I have sent to the Island is all right has been on the Island 26 months, has some $700—invested in stock on Paper, has gone to the Island for the next two years…. I am very busy with the Launches and the work connected with getting fixed for the opening of the season.[19]

The maneuvering continued through the summer. On July 4, Billy wrote to thank Grinnell—he had decided to continue investing—and to report that the foxes were multiplying like the elk in Yellowstone: "I learn from the man I sent to the Island…that there is a lot of foxes. He thinks there are 800 and that every thing was in good shape. He feels as though he could pay a dividend by next March's sales, if skins do not drop, any under…. I am glad you have gotten hold of this stock as we now have control."[20]

There followed a long and ominous silence in the correspondence, ending with this single letter, dated March 27, 1912:

> At last Im getting around to answer your letters as to the

Blue Fox Business. The Lawyer who is closing up the Cos business as per State Law would not allow the bill I had you make out for services. I found you had paid $300 for the stock you got of Chas Olsen, and as there is a certified check for you for $125. at the Lawyers office I make up the Bal out of my own pocket for I remember that you did not want to buy this stock and I said you would not loose the money. I dont know when the Lawyer's going to send the other check but soon I hope. There is some hitch, on acct of the loss of all the books and records in the fire at Capt Downings house in which they lost everything. Capt Downing has been in California for a long time got back a while ago and now on his way to Alaska, he is going to try and visit the Island and ask if by any possibility there is any foxes.[21]

Even at the end of this venture, Billy did not want to give up, dispatching the former "President" of the company on a hunt for the last few foxes. That is the last anyone heard from the A.B.F.P.Co.

So in 1911, the T.E. Hofer Boat Company died, and in 1912, the Alaska Blue Fox Propagating Company followed it to the grave. That would be enough to finish any other entrepreneur. Billy was not finished.

When he moved to Seattle, he recruited, as one of his many partners, Charles Theodore Wernecke, a fur dealer in Livingston for many years, about whom we would know nothing except that his son would go on to become a modestly exalted personage in the mining business in Alaska. Charles Theodore Wernecke, who always went by C.T., was a fellow Montanan—he lived for years in Livingston and even so named his son. Wernecke the younger became the mining potentate in Livingston, and Wernecke the elder was already in the fur business, buying, commissioning, dressing, and selling. The elder Wernecke had moved to Seattle before Billy did, in 1896. The city burned in 1889, and Wernecke caught the rising tide of regrowth, setting up shop at 813 Railroad Avenue, between the docks and the warehouse district. Wernecke, like Mr. Wight and like nearly every-one in town with spare money, dabbled in real estate.[22] That habit proved crucial for Billy in his next venture.

The two went into partnership, in at least two businesses. Billy sometimes used leftover stationery from the fur business to write letters to people like George Bird Grinnell. A note from 1911 in-cluded the letterhead "C. T. WERKECKE / RAW FURS AND SKINS." The next note, from 1912, was headed "WERNECKE & HOFER / FINE ALASKAN FURS."

Billy was not a bad businessman, but he did have some bad luck and more specifically, bad timing. He had just joined forces with a man who spent his life trading furs. In two years, Europe would go to war, and the price of furs would erupt like the guns of August—but Wernecke and Hofer had just lost their breeding island, or at least any infrastructure to make the breeding work. Blue foxes were the height of luxury anyway, and what the world wanted in 1914 was practicality. Recall, however, that in post-fire Seattle, everyone was buying and selling real estate. Billy now benefited from that, and would for the rest of his life.

Facing modern Seattle on the other side of Puget Sound is, among other things, Whidbey Island ("Whidbey" is the spelling today; during Billy's era, people omitted the "e"). It is located to-day directly across the channel from the Boeing Company. Here, Billy began one of his final "jobs," that of real estate mogul. He and Wernecke bought a substantial piece of land here after they formed their partnership, on sheltered water within the Sound. They en-gaged a surveyor and draftsman to plat out a highly professional-looking diagram of what these two visionaries had in mind, but did not have the vocabulary to describe: a planned development, forty years before New Jersey's famous Levittown, although the diagram today shows us precious little planning, just 112 cramped-looking lots served by a central road. Billy and his new partner described the lots as places to build "cottages." The bottom of the diagram read as follows: "SHOWING ALL WATERFRONT LOTS IN

/ SUNLIGHT BEACH ADDITION / WHIDBY ISLAND / INQUIRE OF / WERNECKE & HOFER, Owners."[23] At least a third of the lots were actually tidal-estuary-front, but today that matters little. Billy was way, way out ahead of his time on this one. They were selling lots for $120. Today, a house on Sunlight Beach goes for $2 million.

That was, however, about as far as this particular project ever advanced: both Wernecke and Hofer would not live long enough to see Seattle boom after the Second World War, nor even to see the boom that would make Boeing a household name during the conflict. They did produce a single newspaper advertisement, which, even in the overstuffed manner of that era, still did what a real estate ad would do today:

> The owners claim the following for this Property at Sunlight Beach:
>
> 1. That this property has one of the CLEANEST and WARMEST beaches and is the VERY BEST and SAFEST bathing beach on PUGET SOUND.
>
> 2. That there is an ABUNDANCE of clams, crabs, and fish about this property.
>
> 3. That first class farms adjoin the property which produce all varieties of fruit, vegetables, and farm produce. There is sufficient wood upon each lot to last several summers. Splendid spring water is now, June 1912, being piped thru a four inch wood stave pipe from a clear spring to the property.[24]

And so on, for about a thousand words. Although an identical neighborhood occupies the same piece of land today, the Sunlight Beach Addition as dreamed up on that diagram remained mainly a diagram, with a crucial exception: Billy acquired a lot, an actual piece of land. He was to spend his old age there.

He later recalled that he had to build the "cottage" first, which,

Uncle Billy admitted, was beginning to be a challenge. Still, the tone of his letters to Grinnell, after that last painful bit of duty concerning the dissolution of the Alaska Blue Fox Propagating Company, changed for the better right away. From March 7, 1913—and from now on, any reference to "the Island" is not to Fox Island, but Whidbey Island:

Why is it that for several days Ive been writing to you in my mind and now a letter comes? I said to my self I must write and when I got here, here was your letter of the 31st. I was going to tell you of a little bird that camps under the boat house in the log piles and feeds on water insects picking them from the logs after the tide falls, its not the water wren, but a reddish gray bird, and the other day Sheard [shared] its song, such a range of notes calls and gurgles of sounds very sweet. I watched it for quite a while but when it saw me move it did nothing but cheap. I do not think its a sparrow of any kind but it may be, it had a rather long tail, its smaller. On Feb 22nd I saw the first flock of red winged black birds they were holding a convention on an old barn. Meadow Larks have been singing all winter, have not seen any Night Hawks yet but expect to find them on Sunlight Beach on my return.... I work as much as a 64 year old kind can stand building shacks cottages Gardens and fussing around. Its drawing to the time you will have to take another trip here better settle here and hole up next winter in some secluded mead where you can see the mountains and sea.[25]

As Billy got older, sitting alone with just a pen and paper, his spelling, punctuation, and grammar continued to slide. Throughout his life, as many of you will have noticed, he never learned how to avoid comma splices and run-on sentences. They must have cost him a great many blows with a hickory stick, in those Connecticut schoolhouses, but he carried that bad habit into his old age, and now added a great many more ("Sheard" for "shared" looks deranged, but he did it regularly, apparently without derangement).

There were compensations for him. Having lived most of his life in New England and the high Rockies, he could not get over the bird life around relatively warm Puget Sound. He enjoyed sharing every sighting with Grinnell, an appreciative audience (one of whose lengthiest books is about ducks—about duck shooting, of course, but nevertheless about ducks).[26] In August 1912, after the ugliness over the boat company and the fox company were mostly over, Billy wrote:

> Don't know when you will get this as I expect you are out with some of our people in the west—Im here at the Island for a month or more and was only in town for a few days.
>
> There are very few ducks yet but any quantity of snipe and they are all unknown to me. Several kinds of gulls, one called here sea pigeons, are very plenty.
>
> I put in a small garden to try the ground and every thing I put in it did remarkably well.
>
> There is a herd of deer on the Island but its not an open season yet, doubting I will kill one huh [?] hope I wont be tempted—will be more in danger than the deer as there are so many fool shooters out.
>
> On our land I found three nests ? of the night hawks or Bull Bats—how they are able to fly. Second nest of meadow larks, one albino has been here for 4 years, lots of red winged black birds many ground sparrows…. there were 3 nests of robins but a damn cat got most of the young ones. Ill kill the cat soon as I can get a shot at it—Ive no use for cats. So far we have no English Sparrows out our way. I saw six little garrish yellow birds, five must have been born young though full grown. They hung around their mother

and the food she ate. One was so anxious that it let all its clutch back.[27]

All of this had to have been quite a relief for Billy from the affairs of the fox company.

He continued writing for *Forest and Stream* for some years to come, if at a more relaxed pace, and after 1912, only three of his articles appeared there, the last in August, 1920. The final reference to him in the journal, that call quoted above to recognize his role in restoring the Adirondack beaver, appeared exactly a year later. He did keep guiding. He even fantasized about taking on a new landscape altogether, as he wrote to Grinnell (nearly every letter either began or ended with a plea for Grinnell to leave New York and spend the summer in the West): "You had better try to bring your party over this summer for I'm surely going to pull out of here and go to the Olympic Mountains.... I can do better there and have a pack train for a few years yet. I don't believe they will get wagon roads in there for a while. Ill have boats and salt water fishing as well as trout fishing in fresh water rivers. There is some shooting over there."[28]

Billy would, however, have to stick to what he knew locally—and even then, he was running out of time. His last letter to Grinnell with the return address "Gardiner" was dated November 31, 1910. From then on, he wrote exclusively from Sunlight Beach. He guided at least one more celebrity client that we know about: Ernest Thompson Seton, famous today mainly for helping found the Boy Scouts. Seton had—not an uncommon weakness—a thing for Yellowstone, and Billy had worked with him long before, during a crucial period in Seton's life. In 1897, Seton visited the park, staying at Yancey's. Billy, inevitably as always, took him under his wing, although from Seton's description he did so just to be companionable: they were both at Yancey's, so Billy, who was there regularly, helped him out.

The following year, Seton published *Wild Animals I Have*

Known, which was wildly successful based mainly on its portrait of Lobo, the wolf hunted down by Seton himself.[29] A bestseller, *Wild Animals I Have Known* launched Seton's career as a writer of "realistic" animal books. Unfortunately, he was also at the center of the famous "nature faker" controversy—"unfortunately," because while Seton had his faults, he was an accomplished naturalist. He was also the key figure in an essay that John Burroughs published in 1903, in which Burroughs attacked Seton and others for giving animals human qualities.[30]

But that tendency is as old as humanity (see Aesop's Fables, for instance, and any mythological system you care to name). The timing of Burroughs's charges was especially bad because Seton had just done a service for future generations of Yellowstone fans. His 1897 visit to Yancey's became a long series in *Recreation* magazine, "Elkland." He began his second installment "The other day, when Ellwood Hofer"—"Ellwood," a closer miss at last—"took me to see the big beaver pond, whence he took 3 beaver for the Washington Zoo, I saw at once a chance to publish a careful drawing of a real beaver pond, to replace the fanciful things one sees in books."[31] Seton then provided a careful sketch of the Pleasant Valley beaver colony, a massive affair, and as noted, long vanished for reasons no one can explain. As a result a really important piece of natural history got saved, and the three beavers Billy took from that section did no harm to so prodigious a community.

Seton, trying to recover from Burroughs's attack, produced big books of serious natural history with scary titles like *Life Histories of Northern Animals: An Account of the Mammals of Manitoba*.[32] Billy contributed his story of the cub eaten by an older bear at Yancey's to that volume. When Seton returned in 1912 and again camped at Yancey's, Billy again took him out and showed him around. Seton wrote: "The first day I was in the Yellowstone I was riding along the upland beyond Blacktail Creek with T. E. Hofer. Miles away to the southeast we saw some white specks showing, flashing and disappearing. Then as far to the northeasterly we saw others.

Hofer now remarked, 'Two bunches of Antelope.' Then later there were flashes between and we knew that these two bands had come together. How?"[33] Seton already knew the answer: pronghorn antelope possess one of the flashiest white rump patches in the whole world of grazing animals, serving, of course, mainly as a means of signaling danger, but in this case merely acting as bright white flags of identification.

That (1912) was the end of Uncle Billy Hofer's guiding career. He was 63 years old and had been on the back of a horse or atop a pair of skis since the early 1870s. Undoubtedly he could have kept it up—but probably not to the demanding standards that his own reputation had led every prestigious client to expect. It is at least appropriate that he ended by seeing those antelope. He had developed a deep affection for them, for what they were in themselves, and as a symbol of the vanishing frontier. Recall that he had seen herds of thousands when he was young. He came to hate coyotes and mountain lions mainly because he wanted to protect the antelope, which then appeared to be marching toward extinction. Seton even called them the "doomed Antelope," and wrote that "They do not flourish when confined even in a large area, and we have reason to fear that one of the obscure inexorable laws of nature is working now to shelve the Antelope with the creatures that have passed away."[34] Happily, both he and Billy were wrong.

So Uncle Billy hung up his spurs on Whidbey Island, although he did not quite retire. What few biographical sketches we have from that era depict his final decade as miserable, with one exception, an early edition of Hiram Chittenden's history of Yellowstone National Park, which proclaimed that "He is now out of the Park altogether and is spending the sunset of his life on a beautiful island in Puget Sound."[35]

That was taking a good thing too far. Nevertheless, he was not without support, from friends, of which he had thousands, the major problem being that he kept getting news that another had crossed the Great Divide. But he also had family.

We have not mentioned his family since his cousin decided the boat business on Yellowstone Lake was not to his taste and left Billy at The Outlet in 1880. In fact, the family was not estranged, simply separated, and quite widely. Billy was close to his sister, Catherine A. Kimberly, and to her daughter, Adelade L. Kimberly. The 1910 census showed both still living in Canton, Connecticut, in the county of Hartford.[36] By 1920, they were both living near Billy, on the other side of the continent.[37]

So he was fortunately not alone as the declining years got the better of him. Some of his letters to Grinnell are not written in his hand; one of the women was apparently acting as an amanuensis. By the mid-1920s, Billy Hofer had become significantly dependent on their help, as in this letter to Grinnell: "Sister has gone for the maid—a mile—I am a little lame but not very badly off. Could climb Mt. Washburn yes!—on a horse."[38] The letters he wrote during these years followed a pattern. He would comment on some wildlife management issue in Yellowstone, often in high dudgeon. He would say something about what he was reading. Then he would drift into reminiscences of his earlier life, producing the kind of random memories that the young normally find so annoying in the old—and that historians find delightful.

Quite a few of those memories went into this book already. Others do not fit anywhere else but here, and evoke a vanished world. Here is an example:

> For many years I have amused children with Indian
> singing. Hi yhi, Hi yhi! repeating it many times and some
> times dancing as I used to hear the Indians sing and see
> the bucks dance. If I could get hold of a drum or any thing
> that sounded like an indians drum, so much the better. Id
> always attract their attention and have them smiling, may be
> dancing and singing too. Even babies would and do notice
> the singing? This Ive noticed all over the country. Some
> children would act quite wild. At Georgetown D.C. Billy

Beals children (Billy Beall, Mrs. Jack Pitchers brother) her children would be very wild and noisy when I agreed to have some fun with them. Then close by was a Dr Snyder whos wife Kate Parrish…had three children and were as wild as any. In Alaska 'twas the same and here a child will feel fretfull I will sing? to it and soon have it smiling and keeping time with its body trying to dance. I can sooth as arisen a child with my hi yhi when its mothers sweetest lullaby has no impression….

One instance here a little chap often comes out and we have some Indian music? Last summer his mother took him to the circus. Billy was close to one of the rings. A bunch of Indians came out with their drums and commenced to sing and dance around the ring. The little chap went wild wanted to join them and commenced yelling Uncle Billy! Uncle Billy! He'll never forget it.[39]

Probably almost anyone today can do that. What was different about Billy's performance here was that he had known, and could imitate, the real native songs he heard on the wild plains a half century earlier.

It would be best not to drag this story out, because he lived for a total of eleven years on Whidbey Island, not leaving the place often toward the end. A photograph of his cottage depicts the kind of rot that happens in the Pacific Northwest when buildings are not maintained against the damp. The man who could build or fix anything was at the end of the trail. But there was one last surprise for him, and it issued directly from Yellowstone.

Almost all of Billy's time in Yellowstone, except the very beginning, overlapped with the era when the Army ran the park. At about the time he left, a new division of the Department of the Interior, the National Park Service, took over. It was at that time a small service—small, because there were so few parks—with a family-like feel to it, a feeling heightened by the lingering effect from the Service having been essentially founded by only two men, the industrialist Stephen Mather, who was its first director, and his assistant Horace Albright, who would become superintendent of Yellowstone National Park and eventually director of the NPS. While he was director, he did something that would be rare to the point of eccentricity in the head of a major agency in Washington today: he remembered Uncle Billy Hofer, rusticating on his distant beach, and he determined to save him.

Or at least Albright wanted to save his memories and to do him some honor for the decades of service he had put into Yellowstone. By 1931, things had begun to fall apart for the Hofer family; Billy's sister fell ill with cancer of the liver, and Billy was in no shape to take care of her. Together, they moved in with his niece. Albright would have heard nothing of this had not a writer, Lileota de Staffany, sent a vaguely addressed letter to the "manager" of Yellowstone National Park, explaining that she was working on a piece about early Yellowstone, had found the Hofer family, and found them—crammed together in a single house, struggling against illness and age—to be in pretty bad shape.[40] The letter bounced through the superintendent's office in Mammoth and somehow onto the desk of Horace Albright, then director of the NPS in Washington.

To his eternal credit, Director Albright took action. He wrote Kermit Roosevelt, then Secretary of the Boone and Crockett Club—and of course TR's son—explaining that "I thought perhaps in the Boone and Crockett Club there may be some old timers who knew Hofer well and who would be in position possibly to help him."[41] Albright also contacted George Bird Grinnell directly;[42] Billy had been corresponding with him since the previous century, but he would never have admitted to Grinnell his financial hardship.

Then Albright went a step further: he picked the closest national park, Mount Rainier, and wrote to its superintendent, O.A. Tomlinson, directly: "if possible go over and see Mr. Hofer and ascertain for yourself what his situation is. I am sure that if he is really in such destitute circumstances as Mrs. DeStaffany describes we could stir up rich men in New York to help him."[43] That was not a request that any ranger, park superintendent or not, ignored.

Tomlinson made the trip on May 16 and wrote it up the next day as a single-spaced, narrow-margined report that was military in its thoroughness. Not that he disliked the visit: he had it written up for the Mount Rainier National Park newsletter, and it led to a series of other visits.[44]

Nevertheless, things were not entirely happy on Whidbey Island. Grinnell sent a check, but there was no way to deliver it without hurting Billy's feelings (the plan had been to give it to his sister, who happened on that day not to be home). Affairs otherwise were about as pleasant as one might imagine:

> "Uncle Billy" is pretty feeble. He has palsy in both arms and in his right leg. He seemed to enjoy greatly telling me of his Yellowstone experiences and of his contacts with President Roosevelt, Dr. Grinnell…and many other prominent Yellowstone visitors of the 80's and 90's. He seemed to regret exceedingly his inability to keep up his former correspondence with some of these persons due to his palsy. During our conversation I tried to lead him around to tell me of his conditions but all that I could get out of him was that he is comfortable and has no complaint to make.[45]

Billy's living conditions then, sometimes depicted as catastrophic, were cozy, if cramped.

> "Uncle Billy" and his aged sister live in a very comfortable little cottage at Sunlight Beach on the west coast of Whidby Island. The cottage has a spacious porch glassed in on two sides and stands at the head of a little inlet running in from the main channel of the Puget Sound. From the

cottage wonderful views of Mount Rainier, Mount Baker,
Puget Sound and the Olympic Mountains beyond are had.
Ships to and from the Pacific Ocean pass within sight of
the cottage. During the summer some ten or fifteen families
live in summer cottages near the head of the inlet. During
the remainder of the year "Uncle Billy's" nearest neighbor is
about three fourths mile away. It is a wonderful place for an
old person to spend his declining years.[46]

That was the happy news—although Superintendent Tomlinson
did apparently forget that a view of mountains, for an old mountaineer, can be intolerably tantalizing. Note also the year, 1931.
The Great Depression was in full swing.

> I learned through Mr. Harry G. Woelber, Assistant King
> County Engineer, who maintains a summer cottage at
> Sunlight Beach, that "Uncle Billy" and his sister are almost
> entirely supported by a niece whos[e] husband is a day-
> laborer. The Hofers receive about $75.00 a year from the
> rental of two or three summer cottages. This is their only
> income. Mr. Woelber also told me that because of their
> pride it is very difficult for the summer residents of the little
> colony to help the Hofers. Whenever any of these neighbors
> try to help, "Uncle Billy" or his sister insist on returning the
> favor "with interest."

Mr. Woelber suggested that the best way to assist Uncle Billy
would be to provide $250.00 or $300.00 for installing electric
lights in the cottage and for the purchase of a small radio set. This
amount would be considerably in excess of the actual cost of the
electric wiring and radio set, and the remainder could be used by
the old couple to buy groceries.

> The Hofer cottage is well supplied with books and

"Uncle Billy" told me that he enjoyed reading Vernon Bailey's new book "The Animal Life of Yellowstone National Park". He asked me to pass the following information to Mr. Bailey because he is unable to write. "Elk and all other members of the deer family grow a fine, silky hair between the coarser or heavier hair which he calls 'quills.' This fine hair keeps the animals warm and it is the hair they shed in the spring. Birds use this shedded silky hair for lining their nests."[47]

Hofer spent a lifetime accumulating such data, and in the end, it was hard to know what to do with it, except to try to share it. Tomlinson promised to notify the author. That note set the tone for the rest of the visit, spent reminiscing about Yellowstone, with Tomlinson trying to figure out how to deliver the financial aid without it being noticed.

Albright was delighted with the report, if not with the news in general, and forwarded it in various directions, including to Grinnell and Kermit Roosevelt—and through them, to all of the Boone and Crockett Club.[48] Tomlinson visited again, as he reported to Albright, and arrived at a subterfuge that allowed him to deliver Grinnell's gift, which was in fact only a check for $25:

I made a second trip to Whidby Island on May 29 and gave Dr. Grinnell's $25.00 to "Uncle Billy" Hofer. When I handed the money to the old fellow I told him Dr. Grinnell wanted to make him a present in appreciation of his many kindnesses during their contacts in the Yellowstone, but as the Doctor didn't know the brand of cigars "Uncle Billy" smokes or his situation, he thought it best to send him the money and let him choose his own present. The old fellow was most grateful and remarked that the amount was pretty large for cigars.

Mrs. Tomlinson accompanied me and in conversation with "Uncle Billy's" sister learned that the old couple have gradually sold their small buildings piece by piece until they have only a few lots left. She also learned that the old lady's daughter and her husband are employed at a resort on the Olympic Peninsula. The daughter plays a piano in an orchestra and her husband takes care of a cabin camp. The daughter and son-in-law visit the old couple frequently and look after their needs as well as they can.[49]

So things could have been a good deal worse for Billy Hofer and his sister—their daily life must have actually been pretty good at times—but of course they could not last. Liver cancer was not normally survivable, in the early 1930s. Tomlinson made another trip to Whidbey Island to try to get Billy to accept another donation—more money had arrived from the East Coast—and wrote the following to Grinnell: "I went over to Whidby Island yesterday and gave the $75.00…to Mrs. Peterson, T. E. Hofer's niece. I found that Hofer's sister is in a pretty bad way. She has cancer of the liver and must make periodical trips to the doctor's office at Everett to be drained." The fluid weeping out of her diseased liver, that is, filled her abdominal cavity, and the pressure had to be relieved with a large syringe. "Mrs. Peterson and her husband are taking care of the expenses in connection with the medical attention."[50]

Billy's sister Catherine hung on for a long time—they were a tough bunch—but she died the 12th of January 1932. Billy wrote to Grinnell in the frame of mind we might expect of him:

I received your last letter some time ago Hard work for me to write…. I lost my sister the 12th of January she died of cancer of stomach [sic] I miss her very much I have my niece with me or rather I'm with her. I had expected to go first but Sister got the best of me. I did not know what was the matter with her untill after she was dead and of the 75 dollars... sent by Mr Tomlinson Supt Mt Rainier Park. Then my niece told me. She had to use most of it for expenses conected with her illnes and burial. Fortunately all bills are paid I hope I'll go soon but just now cannot afford to die. Itd cost $125—to plant me—but I'm thinking I can get the best of them by being dumped over board in Puget Sound. Don't like to be planted in the ground.[51]

Nevertheless, he would be so planted, and the national park system would have some say in just how. When the inevitable happened, Adelade wrote directly to George Bird Grinnell: "Wish to let you know that 'Billy' Hofer passed away on Sun. Apr. 23rd at 10:10 p.m. He went peacefully, for which I am thankful. He had been growing more shaky and weaker, but aside from that he had been about his little duties each day. The Sun. he went, he had been to the Barber's, and had a hair cut, and shampoo, and had nice visits with the people here at the beach, for over the week-end. We buried him Wed. 16th next to my mother, in the little cemetery at Bayview. Mr. Tomlinson was there, and later visited a while with us. He told us of calling you last summer. Uncle was fond of you, and appreciated all you did for him in these latter years."[52]

He is still at Bayview Cemetery on Whidbey Island, next to his sister. A standard obituary appeared in the Yellowstone National Park's *Superintendent's Monthly Report*,[53] and in regional newspapers.[54] But Tomlinson did more. In a letter to Albright, he explained what he had done: "I am sorry that I have to report the death on April 23, 1933 of T. E. 'Uncle Billy' Hofer, one of the pioneer guides of Yellowstone National Park.... I attended the funeral and burial services and placed a National Park Service wreath on the grave."[55] Then Horace Albright wrote to Adelade:

My dear Mrs. Peterson:
The Superintendent of Mount Rainier National Park, Mr. Tomlinson, has told me of the death of your uncle, Mr.

Hofer. This was shocking news to me because I had felt that he was strong enough to live several years more and had been looking forward to a chance to see him when I come West this summer.

He was one of the finest of the early Yellowstone guides and his passing takes away from us one of the last of the pioneers of Yellowstone Park. His name is a permanent thing in the literature of the park and stories of his work there will go down through the ages. I know how much you and your husband did for Mr. Hofer during the past few years. It was a labor of love, of course, but the work was appreciated too by Mr. Hofer's old friends who thought so much of him and whose lives were enriched by their contact with him even though it was a good many years ago that they were under his influence. For myself, I want to express my gratitude to you for your part in caring for our old pioneer friend.[56]

That was well put, Mr. Director. Uncle Billy was never quite forgotten, never completely "lost," despite my title for this book. He did, however, recede into the background. Let us return to the analogy with which this book began, and compare Billy Hofer to John Muir. The two were near contemporaries and led remarkably similar lives, appropriately in the two mountain parks that start with "Y" and that tourists today always confuse. Muir ended up so famous that he is on the California quarter. Billy is known almost exclusively to the—admittedly large—fellowship of people who get hung up on, and become lifetime aficionados of, Yellowstone National Park.

Billy's obscurity happened because Thomas Elwood Hofer simply could not abide civilization, at least not for long periods of time. He could visit Washington to drop off some beavers and have dinner with Theodore Roosevelt, but he always retreated to the back of beyond. This was a man who considered Whidbey Island to be "civilization." He could never have tolerated, say, a year-long speaking tour of the Northeast.

Billy put it best in his own words, which are also the best way to end this story:

> After years devoted to my particular line of work, and so many new roads being built, a desire of people to travel my way was growing less, and I getting older and the country filling up. I started the T. E. Hofer Boat Co., ran it two years, and then sold out. That last two years put me in contact with the general public, and that was not pleasant. I much preferred a small party and away in the wilds of the mountains where we would not meet a living soul from the time we started until our return. I made hundreds of friends whom I will not name, but no one can appreciate more than I how much we became attached to and like one whom we have traveled with in a wild and rough country, where there are "times that try men's souls" and you learn what they are as in no other possible way—no one who has proved himself "all right" in mountains is ever forgotten by his friends. I've trav[e]led there with Lords, Barons, Presidents, Generals and men from many countrie[s]. Some I have forgotten, but most of them I remember as most true men and good Americans. Most of them were glad to be away [from the] "madding crowd" and live once more in the glorious mountains.[57]

Such a person as T. Elwood "Billy" Hofer is not likely to become a major celebrity. He can, however, become a legend.

Citations

ACKNOWLEDGMENTS

1. *Yellowstone's Ski Pioneers: Peril and Heroism on the Winter Trail* (Worland: High Plains Publishing, 1995), p. 49.
2. Broadbent's findings are online at https://creator.zoho.com/ notes/yellowstone-np-in-forest-and-stream/#Page:Home, under the title "Yellowstone NP in *Forest and Stream.*" This work partly resulted in her MA thesis, *Sportsmen and the Evolution of the Conservation Idea in Yellowstone: 1882-1894* (Bozeman: Montana State University, 1997).

INTRODUCTION

1. According to the *Oxford English Dictionary*, the word "ski" ultimately comes from Old Norse—the Norwegians have been skiing a long time. Excluding isolated occurrences in 1755, 1885, and 1893, the word was not in use in English until the twentieth century—except in the pages of *Forest and Stream.*
2. The term "lurk," in this sense, is so obscure today that definitions appear only in specialty skiing publications: "The Telemark Lurk," [Internet], *Telemark Skier*, accessed June 16, 2016, available at: http://www.telemarkskier.com/the-telemark-lurk/.
3. *Yellowstone's Ski Pioneers: Peril and Heroism on the Winter Trail* (Worland: High Plains Publishing, 1995), p. 33.
4. "An Act to Establish a National Park Service, and for Other Purposes," in Larry M. Dilsaver, ed., *America's National Park System: The Critical Documents* (Lanham: Rowman and Littlefield, 1994), p. 46.
5. Paul Schullery and Lee Whittlesey, "The Documentary Record of Wolves and Related Wildlife Species in the Yellowstone National Park Area Prior to 1882," in John D. Varley and Wayne G. Brewster, eds., *Wolves for Yellowstone? A Report to the United States Congress.* Volume IV: Research and Analysis (Mammoth Hot Springs: National Park Service, 1992).

6. Paul Schullery, *Searching for Yellowstone: Ecology and Wonder in the Last Wilderness* (Helena: Montana Historical Society, 2004), p. 42.

7. Paul Schullery, *Yellowstone's Ski Pioneers*, pp. 50-51.

8. David Quammen, *The Song of the Dodo: Island Biogeography in an Age of Extinctions* (New York: Scribner, 1996), pp. 40-41.

9. Quammen, pp. 40-41.

10. Thomas E. Hofer, "Winter in Wonderland," Part 2, *Forest and Stream*, April 14, 1887, p. 247.

11. Hofer, "Winter in Wonderland," Part 2, p. 247.

12. John Muir, *The Yosemite* (San Francisco: Sierra Club, 1988), p. 49.

13. Hunter S. Thompson, *Fear and Loathing on the Campaign Trail '72* (New York: Fawcett, 1973), p. 253.

CHAPTER 1

1. The term "whip-saw" has become relatively rare. The *Oxford English Dictionary* defines it as "A frame-saw with a narrow blade, used esp. for curved work." For Billy and his cousin, portability was obviously a major consideration.

2. William D. Pickett, "Sailing on the Yellowstone Lake," *Forest and Stream*, March 7, 1908, p. 369.

3. Lee H. Whittlesey, *Yellowstone Place Names* (Second ed., Gardiner, Montana: Wonderland Publishing, 2006), pp. 250-251.

4. Aubrey L. Haines, *The Yellowstone Story: A History of Our First National Park* (Vol. 2, Rev. ed., Boulder: University Press of Colorado, 1996), p. 478.

5. Lee H. Whittlesey, *Death in Yellowstone: Accidents and Foolhardiness in the First National Park* (Second ed., Lanham: Roberts Rinehart, 2014), p. 170.

6. George Herendeen was an experienced frontiersman and one of Pickett's favorite packers. "George Herendeen was a first-class man," Pickett later recalled, "and he was not at all afraid of a bear" (Pickett in George Bird Grinnell, ed., "Memories of a Bear Hunter," *Hunting at High Altitudes: The Book of the Boone and Crockett Club*, New York: Harper), p. 176. As we will see, that was the highest praise Pickett could give. Herendeen was unavailable for Pickett's annual hunt the next year, 1881, and Billy took his place.

7. Pickett, "Sailing on the Yellowstone Lake," p. 370.

8. The whole story is told in Robert Alexander Gunn's *Forty Days Without Food!: A Biography of Henry S. Tanner, M.D.* (New York: Metz, 1880).

9. Pickett, "Sailing on the Yellowstone Lake," p. 370.

10. Hiram Martin Chittenden, *The Yellowstone National Park: Historical and Descriptive* (St. Paul: J. E. Haynes, 1927), p. 345.

11. Thomas E. Hofer to Horace Albright, 27 April 1926, Merrill Burlingame Special Collections, Renne Library, Montana State University Bozeman, Jack E. Haynes Papers and Haynes Inc. Records, 1915-1965, Collection 1504, Box 121, File 21.

12. Chittenden, *The Yellowstone National Park: Historical and Descriptive*, 1927, p. 344.

13. Lincoln, Charles H., *A Calendar of John Paul Jones Manuscripts in the Library of Congress* (Washington: GPO, 1903), p. 134.

14. Gutis, Mark, "USF Alliance (1778)," [Internet], "3decks: Naval Sailing Warfare History," accessed June 16, 2016, available at: http://3decks.pbworks.com/w/page/916084/USF%20Alliance%20 (1778).

15. Society of the Sons of the Revolution in the State of New York, *Yearbook of the Society of Sons of the Revolution in the State of New York* (New York: Exchange Printing, 1893), p. 289, gives Thomas Elwood's whole operational career, and also reveals that the Hofers had family in New York, although they associated little with them. The yearbook states that the Society of the Sons of the Revolution for New York accepted as members, in 1889, both George Grannis Stow and William Lewis Stow, because both were great-grandsons of "Lieutenant Thomas Elwood, Private, Captain David Dimon's Company, Fairfield Connecticut Militia, 'Lexington Alarm;' Private, Captain David Dimon's Company, 5th Regiment Connecticut Line, Colonel David Waterbury, May 10-December 14, 1775; Lieutenant of Marines on frigate *Alliance,* Captain Peter Landais, afterwards Captain Barry, August 24, 1778; retired from service, May 1, 1783." Jones had captained the ship after Landais.

16. Chittenden, *The Yellowstone National Park: Historical and Descriptive*, 1927, pp. 344-345.

17. Emerson Hough, "'*Forest and Stream*'s' Yellowstone Park Game Exploration," *Forest and Stream*, June 23, 1894, p. 531. The novel Hough here refers to is surely *Evelina or the History of a Young Lady's Entrance into the World*, the 1778 sentimental favorite by Fanny Burney.

18. Hough, "'*Forest and Stream*'s' Yellowstone Park Game Exploration," *Forest and Stream*, June 23, 1894, p. 531.

19. Edmund S. Morgan, *The Puritan Dilemma: The Story of John Winthrop* (Boston: Little, Brown, 1958), p. 81.

20. Benjamin Trumbell, *A Complete History of Connecticut, Civil and Ecclesiastical: From the Emigration of Its First Planters, from England, in the Year 1630, to the Year 1764, and to the Close of the Indian Wars* (Vol. 1, New Haven, 1818), p. 72.

21. This claim is widely associated with Max Weber's 1905 *The Protestant Ethic and the Spirit of Capitalism* (Rev. ed., New York: Oxford University Press, 2010).

22. A Connecticut historian, Walter W. Woodford, looked at the history of the motto in "The Unsteady Meaning of 'The Land of Steady Habits,'" [Internet], Connecticut Humanities, accessed June 16, 2016, available at: http://connecticuthistory.org/the-unsteadymeaning-of-the-land-of-steady-habits/.

23. Morgan, *The Puritan Dilemma*, pp. 7-8.

24. "Census of Population and Housing," [Internet], United States Census Bureau, accessed June 16, 2016, available at: http:// www.census.gov/prod/www/decennial.html.

25. The list of inventions that have issued from New Haven is impressive. See Economic Development Corporation of New Haven, "Greater New Haven Firsts: Region of Inventions, Sports Firsts, Medical Milestones and Notable Residents," [Internet], accessed July 17, 2016, available at: http://www.rexdevelopment.com/about-us/ gnh-firsts.

26. Letter from Thomas E. Hofer to George Bird Grinnell, April 25, 1905, Yale Beinecke Library, George Bird Grinnell Papers, MS 1388, Series 2, Box 27 (reel 37), page 746.

27. Shannon Smith Calitri, "'Give Me Eighty Men:' Shattering the Myth of the Fetterman Massacre," *Montana: the Magazine of Western History*, 54, Autumn, 2004, 44-59.

28. To a remarkable degree, we still rely, for our knowledge of the decline of the American bison, on research done in the nineteenth century by the influential zoologist and conservationist William Temple Hornaday, for whom a peak in Yellowstone National Park is named (Whittlesey, *Yellowstone Place Names*, Second ed., 2006, p. 179). Unsurprisingly, Billy would come to know Hornaday well.

29. "Census of Population and Housing," [Internet], United States Census Bureau, accessed June 16, 2016, available at: http:// www.census.gov/prod/www/decennial.html.

30. John Muir, "The Wild Parks and Forest Reservations of the West," William Cronon, ed., *John Muir: Nature Writings* (New York: Library of America, 1997), p. 721.

31. Edward Abbey, "Freedom and Wilderness, Wilderness and Freedom," *The Journey Home: Some Words in Defense of the American West* (New York: Penguin, 1991), p. 229.

32. The 1910 Census, for instance, showed a Catherine A. Kimberly, Hofer's sister, living in Canton. United States Census, County: Hartford, State: Connecticut, Roll T624_131, Page 1A, ED 138, image 2.

33. Chittenden, *The Yellowstone National Park: Historical and Descriptive*, 1927, p. 345.

34. Emerson Hough, "Chicago and the West," *Field and Stream*, January 1904, p. 854. Hough had for years written a column called "Chicago and the West" for *Forest and Stream*, then transferred both the column and its name to the new magazine *Field and Stream* not long before he published this installment.

35. Sir Edward Coke's *Institutes of the Lawes of England* was published in sections over a period of 16 years, and exists in innumerable editions. The laws concerning "infants" are at 171b.

36. Letter from Thomas E. Hofer to George Bird Grinnell, August 15, 1921, Yale Beinecke Library, George Bird Grinnell Papers, MS 1388, Series 2, Box 27 (reel 37), page 926.

37. George Bird Grinnell, *Bent's Old Fort and Its Builders* (Topeka: Kansas State Historical Society, 1923).

38. Letter from Thomas E. Hofer to George Bird Grinnell, January 9, 1923, Yale Beinecke Library, George Bird Grinnell Papers, MS 1388, Series 2, Box 27 (reel 37), pages 939-940.

39. John Wesley Powell, *Canyons of the Colorado* (Meadville: Flood and Vincent, 1895), p. 120.

40. Thomas E. Hofer, "Beaver Catching for the Zoo," Part I, *Forest and Stream*, May 16, 1896, p. 412.

41. Thomas E. Hofer, "Yellowstone Park Game," *Forest and Stream*, February 7, 1903, p. 104.

42. Letter from Thomas E. Hofer to George Bird Grinnell, May 6, 1925, Yale Beinecke Library, George Bird Grinnell Papers, MS 1388, Series 2, Box 27 (reel 37), pages 953-54.

43. Hofer's language and content in this letter suggest a familiarity with Charles A. Siringo's classic memoir *A Texas Cow Boy or, Fifteen Years on the Hurricane Deck of a*

Spanish Pony (Chicago: M. Umbdenstock, 1885). That he knew the book must today remain speculation—but given his omnivorous reading habits, it is not farfetched speculation.

44. Letter from Thomas E. Hofer to George Bird Grinnell, May 9, 1923, Yale Beinecke Library, George Bird Grinnell Papers, MS 1388, Series 2, Box 27 (reel 37), pages 942-43.

45. "The Pistol in Bozeman: William Roberts and Elias J .Keeney Both Killed," *Deer Lodge* (MT) *The New North-West*, November 7, 1879, p. 1. See also Lee H. Whittlesey, *Gateway to Yellowstone: The Raucous Town of Cinnabar on the Montana Frontier* (Lanham: Rowman and Littlefield, 2015), especially pp. 78-82, which mentions the gunfight and gives a brief biography of Joe Keeney, brother to the victim and long a presence in the early years of Yellowstone National Park and environs. Both the reporter for *The New North-West* and Hofer appear to have confused the brothers, an understandable mistake given the similarity in their names. Eli Keeney died in the gunfight, while his brother Elias J. Keeney, who went by his middle name, Joe, and who was also present, survived to live a long, roguish life.

46. Robert V. Goss, "Yellowstone Biographies: 'H,'" [Internet], Geyser Bob's Yellowstone Park History Service, accessed June 16, 2016, available at: http://geyserbob.org/bio-h.html.

47. Letter from Thomas E. Hofer to George Bird Grinnell, December 31, 1925, Yale Beinecke Library, George Bird Grinnell Papers, MS 1388, Series 2, Box 27 (reel 37), page 960.

48. "Gov. Roosevelt Has a Defender," *Chicago Tribune*, August 5, 1900, p. 3.

49. George Bird Grinnell, "The Mountain Sheep and Its Range," *American Big Game in Its Haunts: The Book of the Boone and Crockett Club.* (New York: *Forest and Stream* Publishing, 1904), pp. 294-95.

50. See, for instance, Robert V. Goss, "Yellowstone Biographies: 'H,'" [Internet], Geyser Bob's Yellowstone Park History Service, accessed June 16, 2016, available at: http://geyserbob.org/bioh.html.

51. Nathaniel P. Langford, "The Wonders of the Yellowstone," [Internet], *Scribner's Monthly* May 1871: 1-17; June 1871: 113-28, Cornell University Library Making of America, accessed July 17, 2016, available at: http://cdl.library.cornell.edu/ moa/ browse.jour-nals/scmo.1871.html.

52. "Brief Bits from Bozeman," *The Anaconda* (MT) *Standard*, April 18, 1894, page 8.

CHAPTER 2

1. The *Oxford English Dictionary* gives this definition for tillicum.

2. Thomas E. Hofer to Horace Albright, 27 April 1926, Merrill G. Burlingame Special Collections, Renne Library, Montana State University Bozeman, Jack E. Haynes Papers and Haynes Inc. Records, 1915-1965, Collection 1504, Box 121, File 21.

3. Thomas E. Hofer to Horace Albright, 27 April 1926, Merrill G. Burlingame Special Collections, Renne Library, Montana State University Bozeman, Jack E. Haynes Papers and Haynes Inc. Records, 1915-1965, Collection 1504, Box 121, File 21.

4. Libraries of books have been produced about these events, much of them worthless or out of date, or meant for specialists, but some good titles have appeared in recent years, intended for a general readership. Among them are Robert M. Utley, *The Lance and the Shield: The Life and Times of Sitting Bull* (New York: Ballantine, 1993); Nathaniel Philbrick, *The Last Stand: Custer, Sitting Bull, and the Battle of the Little Bighorn* (New York: Viking, 2010); James Donovan, *A Terrible Glory: Custer and the Little Bighorn: The Last Great Battle of the American West* (New York: Little Brown 2008); and Larry Sklenar, *To Hell with Honor: Custer and the Little Bighorn* (Norman: University of Oklahoma Press, 2000).

5. Google Earth and Google Maps, for instance, contain nearly all the place names Hofer mentions.

6. Specifically Major General Jesse L. Reno, killed at the Battle of South Mountain in 1862, during the run-up to the Battle of Antietam.

7. Evan S. Connell, *Son of the Morning Star: Custer and the Little Bighorn* (New York: Harper Collins, 1984), pp. 343-44.

8. William A. Allen, *Adventures with Indians and Game, or Twenty Years in the Rocky Mountains* (Chicago: Bowen, 1903), p. 62.

9. Allen, *Adventures with Indians and Game*, p. 67.

10. Allen, *Adventures with Indians and Game*, p. 68.

11. Allen, *Adventures with Indians and Game*, pp. 71, 73.

12. Thomas E. Hofer to Horace Albright, 27 April 1926, Merrill G. Burlingame Special Collections, Renne Library, Montana State University Bozeman, Jack E. Haynes Papers and Haynes Inc. Records, 1915-1965, Collection 1504, Box 121, File 21.

13. "Joseph M. V. Cochran—First Homesteader & 'Josephine' River Boat," [Internet], Yellowstone Genealogy Forum, accessed June 16, 2016, available at: http://www. rootsweb.ancestry. com/~mtygf/cochran.html.

14. Independent scholars Dave Eckroth and Harold Hagen remain the premier authorities on the battle. See Lorna Thackeray, "Baker Battlefield Still Revealing Its Secrets," [Internet], *Billings* (MT) *Gazette*, February 21, 2004, accessed July 17, 2016, available at: http://billingsgazette.com/news/local/baker-battlefield-still-revealing-its-secrets/article_0177b609-c88a-5423-b80f-c0b502e7f823. html. A second article on the battle from the same issue and author, "1872 Fight Near Billings Captivates Local Historians," is at http://billingsgazette.com/news/local/fight-near-billings-captivates-localhistorians/article_06675343-1ec4-5d53-943d-c3505c9bd821.html.

15. The *Helena* (MT) *Independent Record* reported on October 29, 1922 that Baker was "attacked by Sitting Bull at Baker's battle ground, now occupied by the town of Huntley," p. 17.

16. Thomas E. Hofer to Horace Albright, 27 April 1926, Merrill G. Burlingame Special Collections, Renne Library, Montana State University Bozeman, Jack E. Haynes Papers and Haynes Inc. Records, 1915-1965, Collection 1504, Box 121, File 21.

17. The library on the Nez Perce war of 1877 is nearly as large as that on the Little Bighorn. One classic study is Alvin M. Josephy, Jr.'s *The Nez Perce Indians and the Opening of the Northwest* (Boston: Houghton Mifflin, 1997). A more recent volume is Jerome A. Greene's *Nez Perce Summer 1877: The U.S. Army and the Nee-Me-Poo Crisis* (Helena: Montana Historical Society, 2000).

18. Today, the spelling, at least on maps, omits the apostrophe in "Henrys." Possessive apostrophes in place-names can be a source of confusion. The US Geological Survey—and, within that agency, the US Board on Geographic Names—routinely drop apostrophes in place-names on maps, but not in textual documents. Other agencies and groups follow their lead.

19. Greene, *Nez Perce Summer 1877*, p. 145.

20. In many places, the route that the Nez Perce followed remains today a matter of debate. Some authorities believe they entered the national park north of the future West Yellowstone, on Duck Creek. The tribe also, of course, was not a homogenous unit: it routinely broke up and reformed, sending out scouting parties, foraging parties, raiding parties, etc.

21. Writing much later, Billy noted them, too: "The weed-grown remains of the old Henderson cabin, burnt by the Nez Perces just outside the Park in 1877, can be seen by the tourist along the Cinnabar road; but not one in a thousand knows of it" ("In the Yellowstone Park," *Forest and Stream*, June 29, 1901, p. 502). The easily-visible remains are gone today, having been likely removed by the NPS when the area of the old Henderson ranch was added to the park in 1932 (Whittlesey, *Gateway to Yellowstone*, pp. 2-3, 183).

22. Greene, *Nez Perce Summer 1877*, p. 191-93.

23. Billy here used an eccentric spelling for the borderlands between Montana and the Dakotas and the Canadian West, usually called the "Whoop-Up Country" after Fort Whoop-Up, the whiskey trading post at Lethbridge, Alberta. The name spread because of the drunken anarchy that characterized this section of the West as much as any other. See Paul F. Sharp, *Whoop-Up Country: The Canadian American West 1865-1885* (Minneapolis: University of Minnesota Press, 1955).

24. Thomas E. Hofer to Horace Albright, 27 April 1926, Merrill G. Burlingame Special Collections, Renne Library, Montana State University Bozeman, Jack E. Haynes Papers and Haynes Inc. Records, 1915-1965, Collection 1504, Box 121, File 21.

25. The tour guides were following both tradition and a pamphlet, *Yellowstone's Bannock Indian Trails* (Yellowstone Interpretive Series Number 6, Mammoth Hot Springs: Yellowstone National Park, 1956), in which one of the Park Service's more accomplished naturalists, Wayne F. Repogle, carefully reconstructed the trail—and by chance, traced an ancient wagon road instead. In an unpublished memo-to-file in the Yellowstone National Park Heritage and Research Center ("Report: Clark's Fork Miner's Road/Bannock Indian Trail: July 2006," YNP Archives), former ranger Robert Flather at last identified the error.

26. Greene, *Nez Perce Summer 1877*, pp. 144-45, discusses Tendoy and the Lemhi Shoshone in the context of the Nez Perce.

27. We do not know much about Billy's cousin, who accompanied him regularly—although not constantly—during his adventures in the later 1870s and early 1880s, and during his first park trips. We do know that this cousin went by "C. E. Hofer," from a note in the *Bozeman* (MT) *Avant Courier*, August 26, 1880, p. 3, "Boat on Yellowstone Lake," that records the construction of their sharpie.

28. Thomas E. Hofer to Horace Albright, 27 April 1926, Merrill G. Burlingame Special Collections, Renne Library, Montana State University Bozeman, Jack E. Haynes Papers and Haynes Inc. Records, 1915-1965, Collection 1504, Box 121, File 21.

29. Whittlesey, *Yellowstone Place Names*, Second ed., 2006, p. 268.

30. It is well beyond the scope of this book to trace the intricate record of Yellowstone's early exploration. The classic history of the establishment of the park through 1872 remains Aubrey Haines's *Yellowstone National Park: Its Exploration and Establishment* (Washington: GPO, 1974) and his two-volume history of the place after 1872 is also a classic: *The Yellowstone Story: A History of Our First National Park* (Rev. ed., Boulder: University Press of Colorado, 1996).

31. Joseph L. Sax, *Mountains without Handrails: Reflections on the National Parks* (Ann Arbor: University of Michigan Press, 1980), p. 5.

32. J. Horace McFarland, quoted in Horace M. Albright, *The Birth of the National Park Service: The Founding Years, 1913-33* (Salt Lake City: Howe Brothers, 1985), p. 8.

33. Alfred Runte, *National Parks: The American Experience* (Rev. ed. Lincoln: University of Nebraska Press, 1987), pp. 11-12.

34. Billy's narrative of his 1879 tour of the park is the one part of the autobiography he sent Albright that is haphazard enough as to be difficult to read. As an eyewitness tour of the park at a very early date, however, it deserves to be rescued from obscurity, and so is reproduced here:

a. "Soon after crossing Tower Creek we met Col. W. D. Pickett and two men. He wanted us to go back to Camp on Tower Creek and give him [Pickett] the news. He had been out several weeks without any news. We camped the next day at the Grand Canyon of the Yellowstone. Here was camped Gen. Whipple, Gen. Sackett, and an escort of the 2nd Cavalry under a second leut. Gen. Whipple had two sons with him, and there were two citizens, Mr. [Charles W.] Hoffman of Bozeman, and a New York banker. Jack Bean was in charge of the pack train. We traveled with this party to the Mud Geyser, camped there and rode up to the Yellowstone Lake, then by the old Howard road to Nez Perce Creek, lower basin. Here we traveled a road, the first ever built in the park, to the upper basin. This road was built by Virginia City people, up the Madison. After spending several days Gen. Whipple's party had left for Fort Ellis—we moved on to the lower basin, down the Virginia City road to where we struck a new cut road branching off up the Gibbon, built by Col. Norris.

b. "This was a very rough trail for a wagon, slashed through the timber. At the Gibbon meadows we found the road camp with Col. Norris. Here I first saw Lut[h]er B. Kelley, Yellowstone Kelly, but not to get acquainted with him. There was another scout and guide but I can't remember his name. They were telling of Two Ocean Pass. This interested me and I treasured the same in my memory, intending some day to see it. Jack Burnett [Baronett] was there, and another old guide. We had fallen in at Upper Geyser Basin with a trapper known as Wolf, or Coyote because he could imitate the barks and howls of those animals to perfection. His right name was Henry Fancher. We traveled with him all the way to Bozeman. We visited Norris Basin and saw everything there of interest. Traveled over the very rough country to Mammoth Hot Springs, where we found James McCartney. He was not there on our way out. McCartney was a proprietor of the Pioneer Hotel, now used by the chinese as a laundry. Three were several buildings, a little log store and bath houses, a stable and attempts at a "raw hide" saw mill. Down on Gardiner River, just above Boiling River was another log building, which was started years ago with the intention of making it a hotel, by a man by the name of McGuirk. There were a number of active hot springs there that have since dried up, and all traces of them have disappeared—on the flat where now stands the town of Gardiner, just within the line, were a few buildings belonging to McCartney. We did not know then exactly where the boundaries were. The 45 parallel I think was run later that year."

c. We will meet most of the people above in this book. Some are more obscure, but are interesting in their own right. Mathew McGuirk, for instance, was among the park's very first businessmen, having moved into the Mammoth area in 1871 as a squatter. He planned to profit from the "healing" powers of the hot springs, but failed to register a proper claim, and Superintendent Langford evicted him. Lee H. Whittlesey, *This Modern Saratoga of the Wilderness!: A History of Mammoth Hot Springs and the Village of Mammoth in Yellowstone National Park* (Mammoth Hot Springs: Yellowstone National Park, unpublished manuscript under review).

d. Henry Fancher appeared regularly in the regional newspapers for years, his name attached to one bit of misbehavior or another. In 1886, he was tried in Livingston for having stolen a revolver. Fancher argued that, since the complainant had drawn the revolver and intended to shoot him with it, he was within his rights to take the weapon away and hang onto it for a while. The judge agreed: case dismissed ("Local Layout," *Livingston Enterprise*, May 29, 1886, p. 3). In 1892, he was in trouble with the law again, although the charge is not known to us. In the State of Montana v. Fancher, he failed to appear and forfeited his recognizance. If he ever reappeared, that fact, too, is not known to us ("District Court," *Livingston Enterprise*, November 19, 1892, p. 1).

35. Probably the best-known book concerning this shift in attitude toward wildland fire is Stephen J. Pyne's *Fire in America: A Cultural History of Wildland and Rural Fire* (Princeton: Princeton University Press, 1982). About half of Yellowstone National Park itself burned during the unusually hot and dry summer of 1988. The park is today a prodigious open-air exhibition showing how all sorts of natural environments recover from fire—and incidentally showing how rapidly that can happen. Two studies of the 1988 fires and their aftermath are Mary Ann Franke's *Yellowstone in the Afterglow: Lessons from the Fires* (Mammoth Hot Springs: National Park Service, 2000) and George Wuerthner's *Yellowstone and the Fires of Change* (Salt Lake City: Dream Garden Press, 1988).

CHAPTER 3

1. The term "global warming" inevitably brings to mind warming caused by human production of carbon, but another likely cause of colder weather in the past in Greater Yellowstone was the Little Ice Age. During this time, starting in the later medieval period and continuing through the twentieth century, temperatures plunged worldwide, with significant local variations in the intensity of the cold. Nothing like a scientific consensus exists about the duration of the Little Ice Age or its causes. Nor can any scientist presently disentangle its effects from the posited temperature increases caused by burning fossil fuel.

2. Thomas E. Hofer to Horace Albright, 27 April 1926, Merrill G. Burlingame Special Collections, Renne Library, Montana State University Bozeman, Jack E. Haynes Papers and Haynes Inc. Records, 1915-1965, Collection 1504, Box 121, File 21.

3. Allen K. Andersen, *Geochemistry of Inkpot Spring, Sulphur Creek-Sevenmile Hole Area, Yellowstone Caldera, Wyoming* (MS Thesis. Pullman: Washington State University, 2010), p. 74.

4. Billy was spelling from memory again, and only came close with the names. They were spelled Gilmer and Salisbury. See Lee H. Whittlesey, *Storytelling in Yellowstone: Horse and Buggy Tour Guides* (Albuquerque: University of New Mexico Press, 2007), p. 203.

5. Thomas E. Hofer to Horace Albright, 27 April 1926, Merrill G. Burlingame Special Collections, Renne Library, Montana State University Bozeman, Jack E. Haynes Papers and Haynes Inc. Records, 1915-1965, Collection 1504, Box 121, File 21.

6. Theodore Roosevelt, "In Cowboy-Land," *Century Illustrated Magazine*, June 1893. Roosevelt re-tells Woody's story of the Sioux war party on pp. 282-283.

7. Emerson Hough, "'*Forest and Stream*'s' Yellowstone Park Game Exploration," *Forest and Stream*, June 16, 1894, p. 508.

8. For data on climate, I am thankful to Dr. Mike Tercek, a theoretical ecologist and climate scientist who has done a great deal of work in Yellowstone National Park. Climate data in the older parks was of course taken by hand, and Tercek has developed computer software to collect the older data and flag erroneous entries. His data is available on his climate website, http://www.climateanalyzer.org/. When compared to average climate for 1971-2000, the snowfall for March 1894 at Mammoth—when Billy took Hough on his ski trip from Mammoth to the Boiling River—was over 200% of average, with comparable figures for January and February 1894.

Corroborating testimony of this sort is one reason I have called Billy a reliable observer, and I believe he was indeed highly reliable. From our vantage point today, whenever he makes a seemingly outlandish claim, the corroboration turns up eventually. When writing for publication, he would occasionally leave out information embarrassing to his clients or other VIPs—understandable, given the business he was in. When he did not know or remember a piece of information, he freely admitted it. He was essentially in the entertainment business, yet avoided the classic Western tall tale, perhaps realizing that the truth, when speaking about Yellowstone, always outperformed fiction.

9. In his Grinnell/Albright biographical notes, Billy at this point gives a quick summary of the whole history of boating on the lake as he knew it up to the date he arrived, and again, as a very early eyewitness account, it deserves to be rescued from obscurity. This section begins with his arrival at the lake shore:

"Here we camped in a cabin put up by [E. S.] Topping[g] and another man [FranWilliams] years before, where they built a sailboat. I do not remember the date, but think it was '74 or '75 [1874-1876]. Nothing was left of it then but a beam and a rudder. It had been used in '79 by a party to cross some of their baggage, but was leaky and that year went over the falls. There had been one other boat upon the Lake, a canvas boat with a wooden frame ["The Annie"], made by members of the Hayden expedition, for sounding the Yellowstone Lake. Five years after I built my boat I found the framework of this canvas boat on Steamboat point and cached it in some fir trees, but it was burned when the fire swept the point. We whip-sawed all our lumber and built our sharpie about one-third of a mile from where now stands the Lake Hotel, using the same saw pit Topping[g] did for his lumber. A few years after this boat went over the falls, having been used by some camping party in our absence and left neglected on the shore."

10. In *Yellowstone Place Names*, Second ed., 2006, Whittlesey gave a brief history of Topping and Topping Point, pp. 250-251.

11. No one is certain where the word came from; the *Oxford English Dictionary* said that it "apparently" came from the word sharp, but did not elaborate.

12. A thorough but highly readable description of the New Haven sharpie can be found in Howard I. Chapelle's *The Migrations of an American Boat Type* (Contributions from the Museum of History and Technology: Paper 25. Washington: Smithsonian, 2009). Chapelle covers the New Haven design on pp. 136-147.

13. Pickett, "Sailing on the Yellowstone Lake," *Forest and Stream*, p. 369.

14. Philetus W. Norris, *Annual Report of the Superintendent of the Yellowstone National Park to the Secretary of the Interior for the Year 1880* (Washington: GPO, 1881), p. 11.

15. Norris, *Annual Report,* 1880, p. 5.

16. Whittlesey, *Yellowstone Place Names,* Second ed., 2006, p. 101.

17. Norris, *Annual Report,* 1880, p. 37.

18. Both "Hofer" and "Topping" were routinely misspelled in early documents; Billy himself misspelled "Topping" habitually, and he lived for a while on Topping Point. Billy's cousin, C. E. Hofer, was misidentified as his brother in other early sources. For instance, Newell F. Joyner, in his chronology of Yellowstone history, had the "Hofer Brothers" building the *Explorer* in 1880 ("Yellowstone History, Pictures–Charts–Diagrams, with sources," mimeograph, Yellowstone National Park, National Park Service, July 8, 1929, Yellowstone National Park Research Library, heading 18). Billy always spoke only of working with a cousin. After the Yellowstone Lake boating venture, the two do not seem to have worked together again, in Yellowstone at least.

19. "New Haven Sharpie: Oyster Tonger," [Internet], *Mystic Seaport: The Museum of America and the Sea*, accessed June 16, 2016, available at: http://www.mysticseaport. org/locations/sharpie/.

20. Norris, *Annual Report,* 1880, p. 5.

21. According to the *Oxford English Dictionary*, navigator often meant "sailor" in the 19th century, and calls the usage "Obsolete" today. The word does not here carry our sense of "navigator," as a sailor with specialized knowledge about maps and direction-finding. There was never any need for a navigator on Yellowstone Lake, even in 1880. When the weather cooperated, then as now, the views were so open and unobstructed that it would have been nearly impossible to get lost.

22. Christine Bold, *The Frontier Club: Popular Westerns and Cultural Power,* 1880-1924 (New York: Oxford University Press, 2013), p. 199.

23. In George Bird Grinnell's *Jack, the Young Explorer: A Boy's Experiences in the Unknown Northwest* (New York: F. A. Stokes, 1908), pp. 273-274, Hugh Johnson, the old guide, said "Now, there's a place down south of here on Boulder Creek up near its head, where two men, both of whom I know well, Colonel Pickett and Billy Hofer, found eighteen or twenty skulls of sheep all by one rock.... The two men who found these skulls were both good mountain men and they both believe that this was a place where a lion lay and killed his food as the sheep passed along the trail under the rock." This experience matched exactly one narrated by Billy himself in another of Grinnell's books—see below.

24. Billy appeared briefly in Grinnell's *American Big Game Hunting: The Book of the Boone and Crockett Club* (New York: Forest and Stream Publishing, 1901), p. 336. He appeared regularly in Grinnell's *Hunting at High Altitudes: The Book of the Boone and Crockett Club* (New York: Harper and Brothers, 1913) and Grinnell's *American Big Game in its Haunts: The Book of the Boone and Crockett Club* (New York: Forest and Stream Publishing, 1904), where the incident with Pickett and the sheep skulls appeared, on p. 292.

25. "Boat on Yellowstone Lake," *Bozeman* (MT) *Avant Courier*, August 26, 1880, p. 3. The story gives the cousins' names as C. E. and E. Hofer.

26. Letter from Thomas E. Hofer to George Bird Grinnell, no date, probably March 10, 1918, Yale Beinecke Library, George Bird Grinnell Papers, MS 1388, Series 2, Box 27 (reel 37), page 1026.

27. Chittenden, *The Yellowstone National Park*, 1927, p. 345.

28. Thomas E. Hofer to Horace Albright, 27 April 1926, Merrill G. Burlingame Special Collections, Renne Library, Montana State University Bozeman, Jack E. Haynes Papers and Haynes Inc. Records, 1915-1965, Collection 1504, Box 121, File 21.

29. For background on Pickett, see George Bird Grinnell's *Hunting at High Altitudes*, much of which was devoted to Pickett's memoir of his bear hunting days—one reason Billy appeared so regularly therein. It included a full description of the 1881 hunt (pp. 186-206). Paul Schullery also devoted a full chapter of *The Bear Hunter's Century* to Pickett (Harrisburg: Stackpole, 1988).

CHAPTER 4

1. Thomas E. Hofer to Horace Albright, 27 April 1926, Merrill G. Burlingame Special Collections, Renne Library, Montana State University Bozeman, Jack E. Haynes Papers and Haynes Inc. Records, 1915-1965, Collection 1504, Box 121, File 21.

2. Thomas E. Hofer to Horace Albright, 27 April 1926, Merrill G. Burlingame Special Collections, Renne Library, Montana State University Bozeman, Jack E. Haynes Papers and Haynes Inc. Records, 1915-1965, Collection 1504, Box 121, File 21.

3. Grinnell, *Hunting at High Altitudes*, p. 186.

4. Grinnell, *Hunting at High Altitudes*, pp. 187-188.

5. For more on the technicalities of the express bullet design, and every other ballistic issue of interest to Pickett, see Thomas F. Freemantle's *The Book of the Rifle* (London: Longmans, Green, 1901), especially the fifth chapter.

6. "History of Park County," [Internet], Park County Montana, accessed July 17, 2016, available at: http://www.parkcounty.org/ History/.

7. Two species of bear are native to the contiguous United States, the black bear (*Ursus americanus*) and the grizzly (*Ursus arctos horribilis*). Websites and the like intended for tourists will always claim that the two are easy to confuse, but in fact they are quite distinct. The crucial differences are in size, power, aggressiveness, a hump on the grizzly's back, and its flat face, as opposed to the black bear's protruding face. A large Yellowstone black bear might weigh 250 pounds, and will rarely do serious harm to people. A large Yellowstone grizzly might weigh 800 pounds. They kill and eat people

with some regularity. The standard text on human-bear misadventures—and on telling the two species apart in a hurry—is Stephen Herrero's *Bear Attacks: Their Causes and Avoidance* (Rev. ed., Guilford: Lyons Press, 2002).

8. Haines, in *The Yellowstone Story* and in his *Exploration and Establishment*, includes multiple maps of the park as it changed through time. The National Park Service also has a webpage with a useful graphic that transposes the original park over the modern boundaries, which were reset in 1929 and 1932 to more closely follow the natural contours of the land and include features missed by the original, simple outholding. "Birth of a National Park," [Internet], National Park Service, Yellowstone National Park, accessed 17 July 2016, available at: https://www.nps.gov/yell/learn/historyculture/yellowstoneestablishment.htm.

9. Grinnell, *Hunting at High Altitudes*, pp. 188-189.

10. Grinnell, *Hunting at High Altitudes*, pp. 189-191.

11. Grinnell, *Hunting at High Altitudes*, p. 191.

12. Grinnell, *Hunting at High Altitudes*, p. 316. Near the creek, Grinnell wrote, "Captain Andrew S. Bennett was killed" fighting the Bannock, "and the little stream carries his name to-day." *Hunting at High Altitudes*, p. 285.

13. Grinnell, *Hunting at High Altitudes*, p. 191.

14. Grinnell, *Hunting at High Altitudes*, pp. 208-209.

15. Grinnell, *Hunting at High Altitudes*, pp. 193-194.

16. Tercek, Rodman, and Thoma gave a brief overview of the annual precipitation cycle in Greater Yellowstone (Mike Tercek, Ann Rodman, and David Thoma, "Trends in Yellowstone's Snowpack," *Yellowstone Science*, Spring 2015, p. 20).

17. Grinnell, *Hunting at High Altitudes*, p. 194. This entire scene, as Pickett narrated it, is confusing in the present day because of the locations Pickett gave. He, Billy, and Corey were trying to cross Bennett Creek from north to south. Through this stretch, today, Bennett Creek actually runs parallel to the Clark's Fork of the Yellowstone. Pickett, however, described the Crow fording "at the mouth of Pat O'Hara Creek" (p. 193), which never reaches Bennett Creek today; flowing almost due north, it debouches into the Clark's Fork in the stretch of the river that runs close to Bennett Creek. In other words, it appears that Pickett misremembered the Clark's Fork as Bennett Creek, and both groups were actually crossing the former, which would account for the violence of the watercourse: then and now, the Clark's Fork is the largest by far of any of these streams.

   However, both Pickett and Grinnell were absolutely clear about the identity of Bennett Creek. That Pickett called it by its former name—its correct former name—only confirms its identity. Further, Pickett wrote that they built their raft "a few miles" (p. 191) from the Clark's Fork. Pickett, the arch-engineer, would not have built so awkward a thing as that raft miles from its destination. One possible explanation is that a creek cannot be expected, in the twenty-first century, to stick to the same course it followed in the nineteenth. Satellite photographs of the area show multiple, fossil streambeds.

   There is also a Clark Fork River in northwest Montana. It is easily and inevitably confused with the Clark's Fork of the Yellowstone, far to the southeast.

18. There is of course another Sheep Mountain in Wyoming, near the ski resort town of

Jackson, and two more along the north boundary of Yellowstone National Park. It is a relatively common place-name in the northern Rockies.

19. Grinnell, *Hunting at High Altitudes*, p. 195.

20. Grinnell, *Hunting at High Altitudes*, pp. 201-202.

21. Grinnell, *Hunting at High Altitudes*, p. 202.

22. Emilene Ostlind summarized the key events in the arrival of cattle in the Bighorn Basin: "The late 1870s and the 1880s brought cattle and sheep operations to the Bighorn Basin, starting with John Chapman's Two Dot Ranch on a tributary of the Clark's Fork River and Judge William Alexander Carter's ranch on the Stinking Water River, later renamed the Shoshone River. Carter Creek and Carter Mountain are named for this rancher....The German aristocrat Otto Franc von Lichtenstein, who in Wyoming shortened his name to Otto Franc, was one of a number of Europeans among the Bighorn Basin's early ranchers. Franc established the famous Pitchfork Ranch along the Greybull River in 1879.... With the coming of the ranchers, bison were extirpated from most of their original range in the basin by the mid-1880s." Emilene Ostlind, "The Bighorn Basin: Wyoming's Bony Back Pocket," [Internet], Wyoming State Historical Society, accessed 17 July 2016, available at: http://www.wyohistory.org/encyclopedia/bighorn-basin-wyoming. See also Laurence M. Woods, *Wyoming's Bighorn Basin to 1901: A Late Frontier* (Spokane: Arthur H. Clark Company, 1997).

23. Grinnell, *Hunting at High Altitudes*, pp. 228-229.

24. Grinnell, *Hunting at High Altitudes*, p. 178.

25. Thomas E. Hofer, "The National Park," *Forest and Stream*, June 16, 1887, p. 452.

26. Grinnell, *Hunting at High Altitudes*, p. 204.

27. Grinnell, *Hunting at High Altitudes*, p. 206.

28. Donovan, *A Terrible Glory*, pp. 10-11.

29. The "man named Nelson" may have been Pete Nelson, long a fixture of the park community, but Nelson was and is such a common name in the region that we cannot know the man's identity for certain. We will meet "Snowshoe Pete" Nelson again in this book, and repeatedly.

30. Thomas E. Hofer to Horace Albright, 27 April 1926, Merrill G. Burlingame Special Collections, Renne Library, Montana State University Bozeman, Jack E. Haynes Papers and Haynes Inc. Records, 1915-1965, Collection 1504, Box 121, File 21.

31. "History of Cooke City," [Internet], Colter Pass, Cooke City, and Silver Gate Chamber of Commerce, accessed 16 June 2016, available at: http://www.cookecitychamber.org/#!history/czhj.

32. The remnants of the wagon road are visible in places across the northern range today, including a crystal clear segment up a draw near Blacktail Plateau Drive. Ironically, it was this trail that generations of park residents mistook for the Bannock Trail, the hunting trail that was a worry during the Bannock uprising in 1878.

33. Thomas E. Hofer to Horace Albright, 27 April 1926, Merrill G. Burlingame Special Collections, Renne Library, Montana State University Bozeman, Jack E. Haynes Papers and Haynes Inc. Records, 1915-1965, Collection 1504, Box 121, File 21.

34. Haines, *The Yellowstone Story*, Vol. 1, p. 260.

35. "Northern Pacific Branches," p. 3.

36. Hals Lake and Arvid Lake—see below.

37. George Wood Wingate, *Through the Yellowstone Park on Horseback* (New York: O. Judd, 1886). The Northern Pacific survey team did leave some traces of themselves on the landscape. Arvid Lake and Hals Lake were named for the two topographers who produced the map in Wingate's book, and Grant's Pass was named for M. G. Grant, the chief engineer. The survey team was at work in the park from July 1 to September 28, 1882. Whittlesey, *Yellowstone Place Names*, Second ed., 2006, pp. 40, 121, 126.

38. Lee Whittlesey covers the arrival of the Northern Pacific at Cinnabar—and further explains the delay in reaching Gardiner— especially on pp. 10-14 and 268-270, note 2, of *Gateway to Yellowstone: The Raucous Town of Cinnabar on the Montana Frontier* (Lanham: Rowman and Littlefield, 2015).

39. Paul Schullery, *Searching for Yellowstone: Ecology and Wonder in the Last Wilderness* (Helena: Montana Historical Society, 2004), p. 93.

40. Schullery, *Searching for Yellowstone*, p. 95.

41. "Sportsmen & Tourists," Advertisement, *Forest and Stream*, April 5, 1883, p. 199.

42. "Publisher's Department," *Forest and Stream*, April 5, 1883, p. 193.

CHAPTER 5

1. "Last week Field swallowed Forest: venerable *Forest and Stream* went out of existence, absorbed by its chief competitor," *Time* reported on 16 June 1930. "The Press: Forest, Field, and Stream," [Internet], *Time Magazine*, accessed 17 July 2016, available at: http:// content.time.com/time/magazine/article/0,9171,739586,00.html.

2. George B. Grinnell, "Letter of Transmittal," in William Ludlow, *Report of a Reconnaissance from Carroll, Montana Territory, on the Upper Missouri, to the Yellowstone National Park, and Return, Made in the Summer of 1875* (Washington: GPO, 1876), p. 61. The complete story of the massive, commercial slaughter of mammals in the Greater Yellowstone Ecosystem, southern Montana, and northern Wyoming, as well as the mammals' general histories from 1796 through 1881 is in Lee H. Whittlesey, Paul D. Schullery, and Sarah E. Bone, "The History of Mammals in the Greater Yellowstone Ecosystem, 1796-1881: A Cross-disciplinary Analysis of Thousands of Historical Observations," manuscript in review, two volumes (1,705 pages), National Park Service, Yellowstone National Park, Mammoth, Wyoming. Grinnell is, of course, quoted and utilized throughout.

3. John F. Reiger, *American Sportsmen and the Origins of Conservation* (Third ed., Corvallis: Oregon State UP, 2001).

4. Reiger, p. x.

5. Reiger, p. xi.

6. A highly readable biography of Grinnell is Michael Punke's *Last Stand: George Bird Grinnell, the Battle to Save the Buffalo, and the Birth of the New West* (New York: HarperCollins, 2007). Punke detailed Grinnell's early association with *Forest and Stream* on pp. 115-23.

7. Thomas E. Hofer to Horace Albright, 27 April 1926, Merrill G. Burlingame Special

Collections, Renne Library, Montana State University Bozeman, Jack E. Haynes Papers and Haynes Inc. Records, 1915-1965, Collection 1504, Box 121, File 21.

8. Patrick H. Conger, "Visitors to the Park." *Report of the Superintendent of the Yellowstone National Park for the Year 1882* (Washington: GPO, 1882), p. 9.

9. John H. Eicher, and David J. Eicher, *Civil War High Commands* (Stanford: Stanford University Press, 2002).

10. Schullery, *Yellowstone's Ski Pioneers*, p. 49.

11. Schullery, *Searching for Yellowstone*, p. 179.

12. "Winter in Wonderland," *Forest and Stream*, April 7, 1887, p. 221.

13. "Winter in Wonderland," *New York Herald*, April 15, 1887, p. 7.

14. A fine source on Frederick Schwatka's 1887 attempt on wintertime Yellowstone is Schullery, *Yellowstone's Ski Pioneers*. It in turn owes much to a seminal article by William L. Lang, "'At the Greatest Personal Peril to the Photographer': the Schwatka-Haynes Winter Expedition in Yellowstone, 1887," *Montana: the Magazine of Western History*, Winter 1983, pp. 14-29.

15. Jeffrey T. Meyer, *Alpine Experiments: The National Parks and the Development of Skiing in the American West* (MA Thesis, Missoula: University of Montana, 2015), pp. 32-33.

16. "On Snowshoes through the Park," *Forest and Stream*, March 31, 1887, p. 197. As a physical expression of the compositor's art, during the mid-1880s, *Forest and Stream* would never have won any awards: every page was a sea of black ink dense with information. The first page normally carried unsigned editorials that either set forth the journal's opinion on pressing conservation issues, or else called attention to a major feature in this week's number. Given journalistic custom, these pieces would normally be Grinnell's responsibility, and from the opinions expressed—the style, the wit, and other routine internal evidence—most reveal themselves self-evidently to be Grinnell's work. Someone as busy as he was, however, would likely have farmed work out to editorial assistants. We can be certain, at least, that on such occasions, he approved of what the assistants were saying. For the sake of convenience, this book will refer to these editorials as Grinnell's work, but the reader should recall that a few may be the work of secretaries, and at this early date in the history of the publication, we can only rarely say for sure that an unsigned editorial was not written by Grinnell.

17. "Winter in Wonderland," *Forest and Stream*, April 7, 1887, p. 221.

18. "Winter in Wonderland," *Forest and Stream*, April 7, 1887, p. 222.

19. "Yellowstone Park Notes," *Livingston* (MT) *Enterprise*, January 1, 1887, p. 3.

20. "Winter in Wonderland," *Forest and Stream*, April 7, 1887, p. 222.

21. The illustrations appeared in the first and last installment of the series, on April 7, p. 222, and April 28, p. 294.

22. An obscure item, today, a miner's candle was one attached to a spike, in various designs, that could be stuck into a beam. It could also be stuck in a hat, and so served as a nineteenth-century version of a modern skier's or caver's headlamp. For explanations and a range of images, see "Lighting Used in the Wisconsin Lead and Zinc Mines," [Internet], The Mining and Rollo Jamison Museums, accessed July 17, 2016, available at: http://mining.jamison.museum/ lighting-used-in-the-wisconsin-lead-and-zinc-mines.

23. "Winter in Wonderland," *Forest and Stream*, April 7, 1887, p. 222.

CHAPTER 6

1. The town of Gardiner is spelled with an "i." Though named for the same person, the river is not so spelled.

2. Scott R. Herring, *Lines on the Land: Writers, Art, and the National Parks* (Charlottesville: University of Virginia Press, 2004), pp. 44-48.

3. The Cornell Lab of Ornithology has a page on the American dipper: https://www.allaboutbirds.org/guide/American_Dipper/id.

4. Schullery, *Yellowstone's Ski Pioneers*, p. 54.

5. The identity of "Snowshoe Pete" was long a mystery until, in 2013, the Yellowstone National Park Historian, Lee Whittlesey, found some hard information. The *Livingston* (MT) *Herald* reported his departure in March, 1896 ("Exit Telephone Pete," March 26, 1896, p. 3). He was leaving Yellowstone at last, departing for Sweden with his savings, $1,400. Whittlesey has also found references to him in the park archives dating from not long after the Yellowstone Park Association set up the telephone network, in 1886 (Whittlesey, Personal Communications, March 1, 2013, March 15, 2013), so he was already both winter postman and winter lineman by the time Billy and Tansey started their ski. The most intriguing account appeared in the *Livingston Enterprise* on February 19, 1887, during Billy's trip ("Park Letter: Thrilling Adventure of Telephone Superintendent Nelson at Gibbon River," p. 3). According to the *Enterprise* correspondent, G. L. Henderson, a massive avalanche had blocked Nelson's path near Norris Geyser Basin, and the only way through that he could find was the cavern the Gibbon River had carved. He followed the cavern until it gave way and buried him. The story may have been an extraordinarily mangled account of the accident Billy narrated. More likely, Nelson was simply buried by an avalanche in a separate incident, after nearly dying of hypothermia earlier in the month, because that was the business he was in.

6. "Winter in the Yellowstone," *Forest and Stream*, April 14, 1887, p. 245.

7. At least 1,336 newspaper and 209 magazine articles appeared just in the period 1872-1883, and these numbers exclude all other kinds of literature, like book chapters, books, and so on. See Lee H. Whittlesey, "Yellowstone: From Last Place Discovered to International Fame," *Site/Lines: A Journal of Place*, Fall 2009, p. 9.

8. Thomas E. Hofer, "Winter in Wonderland: Through the Yellowstone Park on Snowshoes," Part II, *Forest and Stream*, April 14, 1887, p. 246.

9. "Winter in Wonderland," Part II, p. 246-47.

10. Kerry Murphy, Tiffany Potter, James Halfpenny, Kerry Gunther, Tildon Jones, and Peter Lundberg, "The Elusive Canada Lynx: Surveying for Yellowstone's Most Secretive Threatened Carnivore," *Yellowstone Science*, Spring 2005, pp. 7-15.

11. James Halfpenny, Personal Communication, June 21, 2011.

12. In their massive analysis of animal sightings in the early history of Greater Yellowstone, Whittlesey, Schullery, and Bone agree that the lynx was present in significantly greater numbers during this era. Their conclusions: "Consolo-Murphy and Meagher (1995) looked at YNP sighting records (post-1920) and concluded that there was little evidence to support historic or present populations of lynx, and they tentatively attributed it to either 'their occurring only rarely or a result of the lack of effort exerted to document the existence' of this carnivore within the ecosystem. Our historical data have now convinced us that it was the latter reason, not only because of the present

historical study but also because of naturalist Ernest Thompson Seton's 1897 observations. Seton stated that lynx in YNP were 'somewhat common in the woods,' and he also stated that acting superintendent George S. Anderson told him that lynx in YNP generally were 'quite common.'...

a. "Park sighting records (archival card files) after our study period (1887-2003) contain at least 73 records of observations or tracks of lynx made by employees or visitors. Additionally, there are 34 references to lynx in U.S. Army or NPS ranger logbooks (1895-1926), including at least six individuals trapped or shot in YNP. Taken all together, these references suggest an historical park-wide distribution of lynx as well as larger numbers in YNP then than today (Murphy et al. 2005, p. 7).

b. "Because the lynx has been rare in YNP, one of the surprises of the present study was to find more historical references to lynx than we expected, leading us in our initial (1992) study to wonder whether the lynx population before 1882 was somewhat greater than today, and now to affirm that the animal was indeed present in greater numbers in YNP during the nineteenth century. Within the historical accounts from our study-period, the database recorded 5 'total sightings' of lynx, which included one general observation, one killed animal, and 3 'observed animals.'"

c. Lee H. Whittlesey, Paul D. Schullery, and Sarah E. Bone, "The History of Mammals in the Greater Yellowstone Ecosystem, 1796-1881: A Cross-disciplinary Analysis of Thousands of Historical Observations," manuscript in review, two volumes (1,705 pages), National Park Service, Yellowstone National Park, Mammoth, Wyoming.

13. "Local Layout," *Livingston Enterprise*, March 5, 1887, p. 3.

14. Excelsior and especially Great Fountain geysers were the major stars during this era. The most reliable source on matters concerning Yellowstone geysers is T. Scott Bryan's classic guidebook *The Geysers of Yellowstone* (4th ed., Boulder: University Press of Colorado, 2008).

15. "Winter in Wonderland: Through the Yellowstone Park on Snowshoes," Part III, *Forest and Stream*, April 21, 1887, p. 270.

16. "Winter in Wonderland," Part III, p. 271.

17. "Winter in Wonderland: Through the Yellowstone Park on Snowshoes," Part IV, *Forest and Stream*, April 28, 1887, p. 294.

18. Shown this passage, a longtime Yellowstone resident and experienced skier made the following comment to me: "This was incredibly brave of them. Most experienced winter travelers today would shy away from such deep-snow country and at such high elevations, especially when there was a blizzard going on. The danger borders on craziness in my estimation, so my hat is off to Billy here."

19. This was probably Carrington Island.

20. "Winter in Wonderland," Part IV, p. 294.

21. The official height is 308 feet. "Canyon Village: Frequently Asked Questions," [Internet], National Park Service, Yellowstone National Park, accessed June 16, 2016, available at: https://www.nps.gov/yell/planyourvisit/canyonfaq.htm.

22. "Winter in Wonderland: Through the Yellowstone Park on Snowshoes," Part V, *Forest and Stream*, May 5, 1887, p. 318.

23. Theodore Roosevelt, "Wilderness Reserves: The Yellowstone Park," in *Theodore Roosevelt: Wilderness Writings* (Ed. Paul Schullery. Salt Lake City: Peregrine Smith, 1986), pp. 152-153.

24. "Winter in Wonderland," Part V, p. 318.

25. For an early use of the term ski-run, see Lewis R. Freeman, "Ski Runners of the Yellowstone," *National Magazine*, February, 1904, pp. 611-614.

26. "Winter in Wonderland," Part V, p. 319.

27. "Running season" is a not-uncommon variant from this era for "rutting season," the time during the autumn when the elk bulls fight to see which will reproduce this year.

CHAPTER 7

1. "Game in the Park," *Forest and Stream*, April 21, 1887, p. 275.

2. "The National Park," *Forest and Stream*, May 5, 1887, p. 321.

3. The "news" articles Billy wrote from the park were often signed "H." or "E. H.," but also often "E. Hofer," and it was always clear from these signatures when it was Billy's work. In addition to the two above that ran before "Winter in Wonderland" ended, the following list includes all the short news articles he wrote, omitting only lengthy feature stories that this book will examine later: "The National Park," April 16, 1887, p. 452; "Bison in the Park," June 23, 1887, pp. 474-475; "Game in the Park," August 25, 1887, p. 88; "Notes from the Park," September 8, 1887, p. 126; "Yellowstone Park Notes," September 29, 1887, p. 162; "Notes from the Park," November 3, 1887, p. 285; "Park Notes," November 10, 1887, p. 305; "Winter in the Park," January 26, 1888, p. 8; "Game in the Yellowstone Park," March 15, 1888, p. 147; "The National Park," July 12, 1888, p. 494; "The Yellowstone National Park," January 3, 1889, p. 478; "Notes on the Yellowstone Park," April 25, 1889, p. 275; "The National Park," July 25, 1889, p. 3; "Lots of Big Game," February 20, 1890, p. 84; "Game in the National Park," June 25, 1890, p. 453; "Stocking the Yellowstone," July 31, 1890, p. 34; "Winter in the National Park," February 19, 1891, p. 83; "Game in the National Park," March 19, 1891, p. 170; "News from the Yellowstone Park," July 2, 1891, pp. 476-477; "Game in the Yellowstone," December 17, 1891, p. 427; "Game in the National Park," February 4, 1892, p. 102; "Spring in the National Park," June 9, 1892, p. 539; "Yellowstone Park Notes," July 28, 1892, p. 72; "National Park Game," February 16, 1893, p. 137; "News from Yellowstone Park," October 19, 1895, p. 338; "Yellowstone Park Game," November 16, 1895, p. 425; "Yellowstone Park Game," December 12, 1896, pp. 465-466; "Among Protected Game," December 11, 1897, p. 462; "Visitors at My Camp," December 11, 1897, p. 463; "Yellowstone Park Notes," January 8, 1898, p. 23; "National Park News," May 7, 1898, p. 368; "The Yellowstone Park Bears," September 10, 1898, p. 204; "The Yellowstone Park Game," March 25, 1899, p. 224; "In the Yellowstone Park," June 10, 1899, p. 443; "The Yellowstone Park," June 17, 1899, p. 466; "The National Park," July 1, 1899, p. 8; "Notes from the Yellowstone Park," August 11, 1900, p. 106; "In the Yellowstone Park," June 29, 1901, p. 502; "Fires in the Yellowstone," August 10, 1901, p. 102; "Park Animals for Washington," November 23, 1901, p. 404; "In the Yellowstone Park," December 13, 1902, p. 467; "Game in the National Park," January 10, 1903, p. 25; "Yellowstone Park Game," February 7, 1903, p. 104; "In the Yellowstone Park," March 21, 1903, p. 222; "The President's Park Trip," June 13, 1903, p. 464; "Spring in the National Park," April 30, 1904, p. 355; "National

Park Game," May 13, 1905, p. 373; "Yellowstone National Park," June 17, 1905, p. 478; "Animal Life in the Yellowstone," September 23, 1905, p. 248; "National Park Game," November 4, 1905, p. 366; "Yellowstone Park Notes," March 28, 1908, p. 491; "Yellowstone Park News," May 16, 1908, p. 772; "In Yellowstone Park," July 4, 1908, p. 12; "From the Yellowstone Lake Shore," August 8, 1908, p. 212; "Treed by a Grizzly," September 5, 1908, p. 361; "Yellowstone Park Notes," November 14, 1908, pp. 772-773; "Spring in the Yellowstone Park," July 3, 1909, p. 15; "Timber Dying in Yellowstone Park," July 31, 1909, p. 175; "Domesticate the Elk," March 26, 1910, p. 492; "The Use of Game," May 20, 1911, pp. 775-776; "Yellowstone Park Notes," July 22, 1911, p. 137; "Yellowstone Park Game," January 13, 1912, p. 49; "Where the Credit Belongs," April 13, 1912, p. 463; "Overstocked Winter Ranges of Elk," June 1915, pp. 362-363; "The Yellowstone Park Bill," August 1920, p. 446.

4. "The National Park," *Forest and Stream*, May 5, 1887, p. 321.

5. The *New York Herald* reported Billy's journey in three major feature stories: "Through the Yellowstone," April 8, 1887, p. 5; "Among the Frozen Geysers," April 22, 1887, p. 7; and "The Elk's Mountain Home," May 6, 1887, p. 5.

6. For an in-depth explanation of the geology of Greater Yellowstone, see Robert B. Smith and Lee J. Siegel, *Windows into the Earth: The Geologic Story of Yellowstone and Grand Teton National Parks* (New York: Oxford University Press, 2000).

7. Haines, *The Yellowstone Story*, Vol. 2, pp. 88-89. Haines also includes a version of Jordan's 1889 map of the fishless waters in the park, on p. 90.

8. "Large Trout from the Yellowstone," *Forest and Stream*, March 11, 1886, p. 130.

9. Thomas E. Hofer to Horace Albright, 27 April 1926, Merrill G. Burlingame Special Collections, Renne Library, Montana State University Bozeman, Jack E. Haynes Papers and Haynes Inc. Records, 1915-1965, Collection 1504, Box 121, File 21.

10. Thomas E. Hofer to Horace Albright, 27 April 1926, Merrill G. Burlingame Special Collections, Renne Library, Montana State University Bozeman, Jack E. Haynes Papers and Haynes Inc. Records, 1915-1965, Collection 1504, Box 121, File 21.

11. Haines, *The Yellowstone Story*, Vol. 2, pp. 478-480.

12. "Winter in Wonderland," Part IV, April 28, 1887, p. 294.

13. [George Bird Grinnell], "Though Two-Ocean Pass," *Forest and Stream*, 15 parts, January 29-April 30, 1885.

14. Whittlesey, *Yellowstone Place Names*, Second ed., 2006, p. 257.

15. [Grinnell], "Through Two-Ocean Pass," Part XV, April 30, 1885, p. 266.

16. "In the Sporting World," *Spokane (WA) Spokesman-Review*, March 17, 1901, p. 10.

17. Richard A. Bartlett, *Yellowstone: A Wilderness Besieged* (Tucson: University of Arizona Press, 1989), p. 143.

18. Bartlett, *Yellowstone: A Wilderness Besieged*, p. 250.

19. Bartlett, *Yellowstone: A Wilderness Besieged*, p. 143.

20. W. H. Phillips, *Letter from the Acting Secretary of the Interior, Transmitting, in Response to Senate Resolution January 12, 1886, Report of W. H. Phillips on the Yellowstone Park* (Washington: GPO, 1886).

21. Phillips, *Letter from the Acting Secretary*, p. 15.

22. "Park Matters," *Livingston Enterprise*, March 28, 1885, p. 3.

23. "The Park Railroad Bill," *Forest and Stream*, July 1, 1886, pp. 447-449.

24. "The Park Railroad Bill," p. 448.

25. Thomas E. Hofer to Horace Albright, 27 April 1926, Merrill G. Burlingame Special Collections, Renne Library, Montana State University Bozeman, Jack E. Haynes Papers and Haynes Inc. Records, 1915-1965, Collection 1504, Box 121, File 21.

26. Bartlett, *Yellowstone: A Wilderness Besieged*, p. 58.

27. Henry Adams, *The Education of Henry Adams: An Autobiography* (Boston: Houghton Mifflin, 1918), p. 350.

28. Bartlett, *Yellowstone: A Wilderness Besieged*, p. 58.

29. Whittlesey, *Yellowstone Place Names*, Second ed., 2006, p. 144.

30. Thomas E. Hofer to Horace Albright, 27 April 1926, Merrill G. Burlingame Special Collections, Renne Library, Montana State University Bozeman, Jack E. Haynes Papers and Haynes Inc. Records, 1915-1965, Collection 1504, Box 121, File 21.

31. Thomas E. Hofer to Horace Albright, 27 April 1926, Merrill G. Burlingame Special Collections, Renne Library, Montana State University Bozeman, Jack E. Haynes Papers and Haynes Inc. Records, 1915-1965, Collection 1504, Box 121, File 21.

32. Thomas E. Hofer to Horace Albright, 27 April 1926, Merrill G. Burlingame Special Collections, Renne Library, Montana State University Bozeman, Jack E. Haynes Papers and Haynes Inc. Records, 1915-1965, Collection 1504, Box 121, File 21.

33. Lee H. Whittlesey, *Death in Yellowstone: Accidents and Foolhardiness in the First National Park* (Second ed., Lanham: Roberts Rinehart, 2014), pp. 102-103.

34. Thomas E. Hofer to Horace Albright, 27 April 1926, Merrill G. Burlingame Special Collections, Renne Library, Montana State University Bozeman, Jack E. Haynes Papers and Haynes Inc. Records, 1915-1965, Collection 1504, Box 121, File 21.

35. Schullery, *Searching for Yellowstone*, pp. 86-87.

36. "History of Fisheries Management in Yellowstone," [Internet], Yellowstone National Park, National Park Service, accessed July 17, 2016, available at: https://www.nps.gov/yell/learn/nature/ fish_management_history.htm.

37. Thomas E. Hofer, "Game in the Park," *Forest and Stream*, August 25, 1887, p. 88.

38. Barton W. Evermann, "A Reconnaissance of the Streams and Lakes of Western Montana and Northwestern Wyoming," *Bulletin of the United States Fish Commission for 1891* (Washington: GPO, 1893), pp. 3-60. Evermann Creek near Two Ocean Pass in the Bridger-Teton National Forest was subsequently named for this early researcher.

CHAPTER EIGHT

1. Haines, *The Yellowstone Story*, Vol. 2, p. 3.

2. Thomas E. Hofer, "The National Park," *Forest and Stream*, May 5, 1887, p. 321.

3. Thomas E. Hofer, "The National Park," *Forest and Stream*, May 5, 1887, p. 321.

4. Thomas E. Hofer, "Bison in the Park," *Forest and Stream*, June 23, 1887, p. 475.

5. Dan R. Sholly, and Steven M. Newman. *Guardians of Yellowstone* (New York: Morrow, 1991), pp. 136-141.

6. Thomas E. Hofer, "Notes from the Park," *Forest and Stream*, November 3, 1887, p. 283.

7. Thomas E. Hofer, "Park Notes," *Forest and Stream*, November 10, 1887, p. 305.

8. Thomas E. Hofer, "Lots of Big Game," *Forest and Stream*, February 20, 1890, p. 84.

9. The original has this as the "Lamon" River, clearly a typographical error; there was no such river, and the Lamar was formerly called the East Fork of the Yellowstone (Whittlesey, *Yellowstone Place Names*, Second ed., 2006, pp. 146-147). To judge from the characteristic errors—sideways letters, p's and q's not minded, etc.—*Forest and Stream* was still typeset by hand at this date, a process guaranteeing such errors. The compositors' work was hit-and-miss. Some issues were nearly free of errors. Others, especially if they had a great many obscure Western place names in them, were a mess.

10. Thomas E. Hofer, "Game in the National Park," *Forest and Stream*, June 25, 1890, p. 453.

11. Thomas E. Hofer, "Game in the National Park," *Forest and Stream*, March 19, 1891, p. 170.

12. James A. Pritchard, *Preserving Yellowstone's Natural Conditions: Science and the Perception of Nature* (Lincoln: University of Nebraska Press, 1999).

13. I make this statement even though the scientific literature for the Greater Yellowstone Ecosystem is now vast. A recent example— note its lengthy bibliographies—is P. J. White, Robert A. Garrott, and Glenn E. Plumb, eds., *Yellowstone's Wildlife in Transition* (Cambridge and London: Harvard University Press, 2013).

14. Thomas E. Hofer, "Timber Dying in Yellowstone Park," *Forest and Stream*, July 31, 1909, p. 175.

15. Thomas E. Hofer, "Overstocked Winter Ranges of Elk," *Forest and Stream*, August, 1915, p. 362.

16. Thomas E. Hofer, "Animal Life in the Yellowstone," *Forest and Stream*, September 23, 1905, p. 248.

17. Thomas E. Hofer, "Game in the National Park." *Forest and Stream*, June 25, 1890, p. 453.

18. Thomas E. Hofer, "Lots of Big Game," *Forest and Stream*, February 20, 1890, p. 84.

19. Mary Meagher, Th*e Bison of Yellowstone National Park* (National Park Service Scientific Monograph Series Number One, Mammoth Hot Springs: Yellowstone National Park, 1973), pp. 17. Mary Ann Franke's *To Save the Wild Bison: Life on the Edge in Yellowstone* (Norman: University of Oklahoma Press, 2005) is an updating of Meagher's earlier work.

20. "Immense Collection of Hides," *Bozeman Avant Courier*, June 2, 1881, p. 3.

21. Thomas E. Hofer, "Game in the National Park," *Forest and Stream*, March 19, 1891, p. 170.

22. Whittlesey, *Death in Yellowstone*, Second ed., pp. 250-52.

23. Haines, *The Yellowstone Story*, Vol. 2, p. 445.

24. Anderson had a long and interesting career in the Army, retiring a Brigadier General. He died in 1915. Haines included a biography of him in *The Yellowstone Story*, Vol. 2, pp. 454-455, but the best short biography is probably his obituary in *Forest and Stream* ("Death of General Anderson: His Work Largely Responsible for the Yellow-

stone Park of To-day," April 1915, pp. 234-235). Written and signed by Grinnell, it ends on a note of sincere mourning: "His death leaves a vacancy that cannot be filled."

25. Thomas E. Hofer, "Game in the Yellowstone," *Forest and Stream*, December 17, 1891, p. 427.

26. "Game in the Yellowstone," *Forest and Stream*, December 17, 1891, p. 427.

27. Thomas E. Hofer, "Spring in the National Park," *Forest and Stream*, June 9, 1892, p. 539.

28. Thomas E. Hofer, "Yellowstone Park Notes," *Forest and Stream*, July 28, 1892, p. 72.

29. Thomas E. Hofer, "News from the Yellowstone Park," *Forest and Stream*, July 2, 1891, p. 476.

30. Now spelled Polecat Creek, this stream is a small tributary of the Snake River that flows past Flagg Ranch, just outside the south boundary of Yellowstone National Park.

31. Thomas E. Hofer, "National Park Game," *Forest and Stream*, February 16, 1893, p. 137.

Chapter Nine

1. Emerson Hough, "'*Forest and Stream*'s' Yellowstone Park Game Exploration," *Forest and Stream*, May 5, 1894, pp. 377-78. In this first installment of the long series of articles that told the story of his journey, Hough reported the Howell arrest at length, having interviewed nearly all of the participants.

2. Hough wrote a regular column for *Forest and Stream*, called "Chicago and the West." Hough's complete, fourteen-part series, "'*Forest and Stream*'s' Yellowstone Park Game Exploration," has been recently collected into a single volume, with explanatory notes, in *Rough Trip through Yellowstone: The Epic Winter Expedition of Emerson Hough, F. Jay Haynes, and Billy Hofer* (Scott Herring, ed., Helena: Riverbend, 2013).

3. See note eight for chapter three—again, I am grateful to Dr. Mike Tercek for such figures, which are available on his website, http://www.climateanalyzer.org/.

4. It is permanently confusing, but we are stuck with it. Again, the town of Gardiner and the Gardner River, though both named for the mountain man Johnson Gardner, are spelled differently. That history is astonishingly complex. Whittlesey, *Yellowstone Place Names*, Second ed., 2006, p. 112.

5. Hough, "Yellowstone Park Game Exploration," June 9, 1894, pp. 486-487.

6. Hough, "Yellowstone Park Game Exploration," June 9, 1894, p. 487.

7. Hough, "Yellowstone Park Game Exploration," June 16, 1894, p. 508.

8. Hough followed the normal practice of this era, capitalizing his own publication and leaving the competition in lower case.

9. Letter from Thomas E. Hofer to George Bird Grinnell, no date, probably March 10, 1918, Yale Beinecke Library, George Bird Grinnell Papers MS 1388, Series 2, Box 27 (reel 37), page 1024. A microfilm copy is owned by the University of California. I am grateful indeed to Yellowstone National Park Historian Lee Whittlesey, who transcribed the letter. Having decades of experience reading the handwriting of fron-

tiersmen, Whittlesey told me he found the letter "very legible." The paper is, however, damaged, the ink faded, the microfilm blurry, and I thought it looked like Mayan hieroglyphs.

Two other letters from Hofer to Grinnell support this point. Billy wrote the first in 1922: "Hough was more interested in getting a picture of Howell than in getting an account of his capture.... I told Hough to rush through the message, night letter, to the F. & S [*Forest and Stream*].... I saw a chance for the story to stir up the country about the park." Thomas E. Hofer to George Bird Grinnell, April 20, 1922, Yale Beinecke Library, George Bird Grinnell Papers, MS 1388, Series 2, Box 27 (reel 37), pages 933-34. The second letter came a year later: "Yes he was a hard man to get along with on that snowshoe trip. I had to urge and had to make him send that dispatch about Ed Howell killing the Buffalo. That gave us Law in the Park." The tone of both letters make it sound as if Billy disliked Hough, but there is little other evidence he did. The second letter was written a few weeks after Hough died, and appears to reflect merely a lingering frustration with Hough for not recognizing that history was being made in front of his eyes, and in failing to comprehend the larger ramifications of the story, that night at Captain Anderson's house. Thomas E. Hofer to George Bird Grinnell, May 13,1923, Yale Beinecke Library, George Bird Grinnell Papers, MS 1388, Series 2, Box 27 (reel 37), page 945.

10. Emerson Hough, "The Survivors," *Saturday Evening Post*, December 11, 1920, p. 104.

11. Hough, "Yellowstone Park Game Exploration," June 16, 1894, p. 509.

12. Hough, "Yellowstone Park Game Exploration," June 23, 1894, p. 531.

13. Hough, "Yellowstone Park Game Exploration," June 23, 1894, p. 531.

14. Hough, "Yellowstone Park Game Exploration," June 30, 1894, p. 554.

15. Hough, "Yellowstone Park Game Exploration," July 7, 1894, p. 2.

16. Hough, "Yellowstone Park Game Exploration," July 7, 1894, p. 3.

17. Hough, "Yellowstone Park Game Exploration," July 7, 1894, p. 3.

18. Hough, "Yellowstone Park Game Exploration," July 7, 1894. The description of the night and morning are on pp. 3-4.

19. Hough, "Yellowstone Park Game Exploration," July 14, 1894, p. 24.

20. Hough, "Yellowstone Park Game Exploration," July 14, 1894, p. 25.

21. Mathews had left the Riverside soldier station alone, in defiance of Captain Anderson's strict order against traveling without a companion, and simply disappeared. His remains finally turned up on June 9, 1895. Whittlesey, *Death in Yellowstone*, Second ed., pp. 111-12, 300; Hough, "Yellowstone Park Game Exploration," July 21, 1894, p. 47.

22. In twenty-first century Nordic skiing slang, the pair grew "stilts." Their skis made them six or more inches taller than their actual height, because of the mass of snow adhering to the bottoms.

23. Hough, "Yellowstone Park Game Exploration," August 4, 1894, p. 92.

24. Hough, *Saturday Evening Post*, December 11, 1920, p. 107.

25. Hough, "Yellowstone Park Game Exploration," August 11, 1894, p. 115.

26. Hough, "Yellowstone Park Game Exploration," August 11, 1894, p. 115. Nearly ev-

eryone who met Woody had trouble with his first name. Billy misspelled it in letters; Hough here spelled it "Taswill." Tazewell Woody was, as Hough noted, friendly with Theodore Roosevelt, who described him in an article in *Century Illustrated Magazine*, June 1893, pp. 282-283. Had Woody not been so deathly silent, he would have been as famous as any frontier celebrity you care to name.

27. Hough, "Yellowstone Park Game Exploration," August 18, 1894, p. 135.

28. Hough, "Yellowstone Park Game Exploration," August 18, 1894, p. 136.

CHAPTER TEN

1. Bartlett, *Yellowstone: A Wilderness Besieged*, p. 321.

2. Haines, *The Yellowstone Story*, Vol. 2, pp. 68-69.

3. John Lounsbury, personal communication, January 3, 2017; Lee H. Whittlesey, personal communications, November 3, 2016 and January 12, 2017.

4. Serious attempts to construct railroads through Yellowstone National Park have had a tangled and lengthy history. Bartlett, in *Yellowstone: A Wilderness Besieged*, pp. 309-316, followed them through their multiple deaths and resurrections.

5. Haines, *The Yellowstone Story*, Vol. 2, p. 67.

6. For an explanation of how this informal filibuster actually worked, see Punke, *Last Stand*, pp. 153-58.

7. Theodore Roosevelt, *The Wilderness Hunter: Sketches of Sport on the Northern Cattle Plains*, two volumes in one (New York: G. P. Putnam's Sons, 1893), vol. 1, pp. 209-210.

8. Roosevelt, *The Wilderness Hunter*, Vol. 1, p. 211.

9. Roosevelt, *The Wilderness Hunter*, Vol. 1, p. 213.

10. Roosevelt, *The Wilderness Hunter*, Vol. 1, pp. 213-214.

11. Whittlesey, *Yellowstone Place Names*, Second ed., 2006, pp. 198, 213.

12. Roosevelt, *The Wilderness Hunter*, Vol. 1, pp. 235-237.

13. Thomas E. Hofer to Horace Albright, 27 April 1926, Merrill G. Burlingame Special Collections, Renne Library, Montana State University Bozeman, Jack E. Haynes Papers and Haynes Inc. Records, 1915-1965, Collection 1504, Box 121, File 21.

14. Roosevelt, *The Wilderness Hunter*, Vol. 2, p. 61.

15. Hubert Howe Bancroft, *The Book of the Fair* (Chicago: The Bancroft Company, 1893), pp. 449-450.

16. Michael Steiner, "Parables of Stone and Steel: Architectural Images of Progress and Nostalgia at the Columbian Exposition and Disneyland," *American Studies*, Spring 2001, pp. 54-55.

17. Steiner, "Parables of Stone and Steel," p. 54.

18. Theodore Roosevelt, and George Bird Grinnell, eds., *American Big-Game Hunting: The Book of the Boone and Crockett Club* (New York: *Forest and Stream* Publishing, 1901), pp. 334-336.

19. Bold, *The Frontier Club*, p. 17.

20. "Kelpie," "*Forest and Stream* at the Fair," *Forest and Stream*, January 6, 1894, p. 3.

21. Emerson Hough, "Chicago and the West," *Field and Stream*, February 1904, p. 854. Hough by this time had transferred his "Chicago and the West" column to *Field and Stream*, although he also still wrote for *Forest and Stream*.

22. Jerry Keenan, *The Life of Yellowstone Kelly* (Albuquerque: University of New Mexico Press, 2006), p. 164.

23. "Gov. Roosevelt Has a Defender," *Chicago Tribune*, August 5, 1900, p. 3.

24. Woody told Hough that Roosevelt was "the best big-game shot he ever knew": "Yellowstone Park Game Exploration," August 11, 1894, p. 115. Roosevelt himself reported that Woody would only become talkative when he was pleased with TR because his shooting was exceptionally good: "In Cowboy-Land," *Century Illustrated Magazine*, June 1893, p. 282. Indeed, it may be that Roosevelt's shooting was the only force in the world that could render Woody voluble, and the long narratives Woody delivered when thus pleased are indirect testimony to the accuracy of the rifle-fire.

25. "Gov. Roosevelt Has a Defender," *Chicago Tribune*, August 5, 1900, p. 3.

26. "Gov. Roosevelt Has a Defender," *Chicago Tribune*, August 5, 1900, p. 3

27. "Told About Roosevelt," *Indianapolis* (IN) *Journal*, August 20, 1900, p. 3.

28. Emerson Hough, "Chicago and the West," *Forest and Stream*, March 28, 1903, p. 246.

29. A good and brief summary of Roosevelt's trip around the West is Rebecca Hein's "President Theodore Roosevelt's 1903 Visit to Wyoming," [Internet], Wyoming State Historical Society, accessed July 17, 2016, available at: http://www.wyohistory.org/encyclopedia/president-theodore-roosevelts-1903-visit-wyoming.

30. See generally, John Burroughs, *Camping with President Roosevelt* (New York: Houghton Mifflin, 1906). Because the party was relatively small and the press incarcerated in Gardiner, we have only a couple of eyewitness accounts of their time in Yellowstone. A recent article in *Yellowstone Science* by Jeremy Johnston ("Trailing Theodore Roosevelt through Yellowstone: The Written and Visual Records of Roosevelt's 1903 Visit," Spring 2007, pp. 23-26) collects a number of extraordinarily rare photographs from the trip, including at least two, and probably more, of Billy (the photographers, long dead, did not always identify their subjects).

31. Burroughs, *Camping with President Roosevelt*, p. 19.

32. Theodore Roosevelt in George Bird Grinnell, ed., "Wilderness Reserves," *American Big Game in Its Haunts: The Book of the Boone and Crockett Club* (New York: *Forest and Stream* Publishing, 1904), pp. 33-34.

33. Burroughs, *Camping with President Roosevelt*, pp. 24-25.

34. Burroughs, *Camping with President Roosevelt*, pp. 30-31.

35. Thomas E. Hofer, "The President's Park Trip," *Forest and Stream*, June 13, 1903, p. 464.

36. Whittlesey, *Death in Yellowstone*, Second ed., pp. 150-51.

37. H. A. deWindt always went by "H. A." According to the *Harvard Crimson*, his first name was Heyliger. He was in the class of 1881; Warren Delano III, a little older, was in the class of 1874 (Billy's clients skewed toward the Ivy League). "Harvard Men

at the West," [Internet], *Harvard Crimson*, April 26, 1892, accessed June 16, 2016, available at: http://www.thecrimson.com/ article/1892/4/26/harvard-men-at-the-west-harvard/?print=1

38. As with all aristocratic families, the relationships are elaborate and the names are confusing; the Delanos, for instance, produced an uncountable number of boys named Warren. A brief and reliable summary of the Delano family history is at the website for the Franklin Delano Roosevelt Presidential Library and Museum, under "Delano Family Papers, 1568-1919: Collection Historical Note." Available at: http://www.fdrlibrary.marist.edu/archives/collections/ franklin/index.php?p=collections/findingaid&id=27

39. The journal is in the Franklin Delano Roosevelt Presidential Library and Museum, Delano Family Papers, 1568-1919, Box 54, "Diary of Warren Delano III, Trip to Wyoming and Yellowstone Park, August 16, 1899-September 18, 1899." I am grateful to Ruth and Leslie Quinn, who visited the museum in Hyde Park, New York, and transcribed the diary.

40. "Diary of Warren Delano III," p. 8.

41. "Diary of Warren Delano III," pp. 12-13.

42. "Diary of Warren Delano III," pp. 13-14.

43. "Diary of Warren Delano III," pp. 88-90, 92. Their "Beaman Anisden" was most likely Beam Amsden, who married early Gardiner settler Louise Spiker, after she and her husband John Spiker split up. Both Beam and Louise are interred today in the Gardiner cemetery. Aubrey L. Haines, oral-history interview with (daughter) Edith Spiker Ritchie, November 7, 1961, audiotape 61-3, YNP Archives.

44. "Diary of Warren Delano III," p. 18.

45. "Diary of Warren Delano III," pp. 19-22.

46. "Diary of Warren Delano III," pp. 90-91.

CHAPTER ELEVEN

1. A recent treatment of the whole lurid tale is *Wrecked in Yellowstone: Greed, Obsession, and the Untold Story of Yellowstone's Most Infamous Shipwreck*, by former Billings Gazette reporter Mike Stark (Helena: Riverbend, 2016). At the same time, Leslie Quinn, among the most informed voices on this issue, has an interesting and compelling revisionist take. In his view, Waters was merely doing what was necessary to survive as a park concessionaire. Any business conducted in an isolated national park in the mountains is almost impossibly challenging. Given the difficulties involved in transportation, supply, infrastructure, staffing, etc., only a ruthless businessman could last. When I was a Yellowstone concession manager, park visitors accused me literally thousands of times of engaging in "highway robbery." Quinn's argument clearly has some merit.

2. Haines, *The Yellowstone Story*, Vol. 2, p. 50.

3. Thomas E. Hofer to Warren Delano III, July 18, 1907, Franklin Delano Roosevelt Presidential Library and Museum, Delano Family Papers, 1568-1919, Papers of Warren Delano III, General Correspondence 1891-1919, Container 50.

4. "Billy Hofer to Run Line of Steamboats," *Salem* (OR) *Daily Capital Journal*, January 10, 1908, p. 3.

5. Bartlett, *Yellowstone: A Wilderness Besieged*, p. 193.

6. Letter from Thomas E. Hofer to George Bird Grinnell, March 9, 1908, Yale Beinecke Library, George Bird Grinnell Papers, MS 1388, Series 2, Box 27 (reel 37), page 775.

7. Bartlett, *Yellowstone: A Wilderness Besieged*, p. 193.

8. Annalies Corbin and Matthew A. Russell, eds., *Historical Archeology of Tourism in Yellowstone National Park* (New York: Springer, 2010), includes descriptions and photographs of both *Jean D* and *Zillah*, pp. 87-95.

9. Ruth and Leslie Quinn, definitely the reigning experts on the history of Yellowstone Lake watercraft, provided this information about the names Billy gave his vessels. They are, at present, still working on the mystery.

10. Thomas E. Hofer to Warren Delano III, May 25, 1911, Franklin Delano Roosevelt Presidential Library and Museum, Delano Family Papers, 1568-1919, Papers of Warren Delano III, General Correspondence 1891-1919, Container 50.

11. Thomas E. Hofer, "Catching Wild Animals," Part I, *Forest and Stream*, February 25, 1892, p. 173.

12. Hofer, "Catching Wild Animals," Part I, p. 173.

13. Thomas E. Hofer, "Catching Wild Animals," Part II, *Forest and Stream*, March 3, 1892, p. 195.

14. Thomas E. Hofer, "Catching Wild Animals," Part III, *Forest and Stream*, March 10, 1892, p. 224.

15. Thomas E. Hofer, "Catching Wild Animals," Part IV, *Forest and Stream*, March 17, 1892, p. 247.

16. Thomas E. Hofer, "Catching Wild Animals," Part V, *Forest and Stream*, March 24, 1892, p. 271.

17. William M. Mann, *Wild Animals In and Out of the Zoo* (New York: Smithsonian, 1930), pp. 116-117.

18. The two articles were both called "Beaver Catching for the Zoo." Part I ran in *Forest and Stream* on May 16, 1896, pp. 391-392, and Part II on May 23, pp. 411-412.

19. Hofer, "Beaver Catching for the Zoo," Part II, p. 412.

20. Thomas E. Hofer, "Visitors at My Camp," *Forest and Stream*, December 11, 1897, p. 463.

21. Thomas E. Hofer, "National Park News," *Forest and Stream*, May 7, 1898, p. 368.

22. Thomas E. Hofer, "The Yellowstone Park Game," *Forest and Stream*, March 25, 1899, p. 224.

23. Bancroft, *The Book of the Fair*, p. 50.

24. Whittlesey used the article in his 2015 book *Gateway to Yellowstone*, pp. 103-104.

25. William E. Curtis, "The Bear, the Cage, and the Mules," *St. Louis Republic*, September 16, 1900, p. 6, quoted fully in Whittlesey, *Gateway to Yellowstone*, pp. 103-104.

26. Curtis, "The Bear, the Cage, and the Mules," p. 6.

27. Thomas E. Hofer, "Yellowstone Park Game," *Forest and Stream*, November 16, 1895, p. 425.

28. Thomas E. Hofer, "Yellowstone Park Game," *Forest and Stream*, December 12, 1896, p. 465.

29. Thomas E. Hofer, "Among Protected Game," *Forest and Stream*, December 11, 1897, p. 462.

30. Thomas E. Hofer, "The Yellowstone Park," *Forest and Stream*, June 17, 1899, p. 466. The five bulls also received a mention in "The Yellowstone Park Bears," September 10, 1898, p. 204.

31. Thomas E. Hofer, "Antelope Catching for the Zoo," *Forest and Stream*, August 19, 1899, p. 143.

32. Hofer, "Antelope Catching for the Zoo," p. 144.

33. Hofer, "Antelope Catching for the Zoo," p. 144.

34. Thomas E. Hofer, "Notes from the Yellowstone Park," *Forest and Stream*, August 11, 1900, p. 106.

35. Thomas E. Hofer, "In the Yellowstone Park," *Forest and Stream*, June 29, 1901, p. 502.

36. Whittlesey discusses the private zoos that sprung up just outside the park in *Gateway to Yellowstone*, pp. 100-103. For a discussion of zoos inside the park during its early years, see Alice W. Biel, *Do (Not) Feed the Bears: The Fitful History of Wildlife and Tourists in Yellowstone* (Lawrence: University Press of Kansas, 2006), pp. 7-17. Biel includes a discussion of an infamously ill-run zoo operated by E. C. Waters, the man Billy Hofer replaced as the Yellowstone Lake boat concessionaire.

37. Peter Aagaard, *The Rewilding of New York's North Country: Beavers, Moose, Canines and the Adirondacks* (MA Thesis, Missoula: University of Montana, 2008), pp. 46-50.

38. Aagaard, *The Rewilding of New York's North Country*, p. 50.

39. "Beaver," [Internet], Adirondack Ecological Center, State University of New York College of Environmental Science and Forestry, Newcomb Campus, accessed July 17, 2016, available at: http://www.esf.edu/aec/adks/mammals/beaver.htm.

40. "Yo," "Beaver for Adirondacks," *Forest and Stream*, August, 1921, p. 358.

41. "Beaver Increasing," *Forest and Stream*, November 5, 1910, p. 732.

42. YNP archival document quoted in Charles Eugene Johnson, "An Investigation of the Beaver in Herkimer and Hamilton Counties of the Adirondacks," *Roosevelt Wild Life Bulletin*, August 1922, p. 163. Grinnell noted that his information was "taken from Mr. Chester Lindsley's record of animals shipped from the Park."

43. "Billy Hofer to Run Line of Steamboats," *Salem (OR) Daily Capital Journal*, January 10, 1908, p. 3.

44. Thomas E. Hofer to Horace Albright, 27 April 1926, Merrill G. Burlingame Special Collections, Renne Library, Montana State University Bozeman, Jack E. Haynes Papers and Haynes Inc. Records, 1915-1965, Collection 1504, Box 121, File 21.

45. "Diary of Warren Delano III," p. 20.

46. Anthony W. Dimock, *Wall Street and the Wilds* (New York: Outing Publishing, 1915), pp. 447-448.

47. Dimock, *Wall Street and the Wilds*, pp. 448-449.

48. Dimock, *Wall Street and the Wilds*, p. 449.

49. Thomas E. Hofer, "Yellowstone Park Game," *Forest and Stream*, February 7, 1903, p. 104.

50. Thomas E. Hofer to Horace Albright, 27 April 1926, Merrill G. Burlingame Special Collections, Renne Library, Montana State University Bozeman, Jack E. Haynes Papers and Haynes Inc. Records, 1915-1965, Collection 1504, Box 121, File 21.

51. *How to Make Photographs with the Anthony Camera* (Boston: Perry Mason, 1890), p. 5.

52. G. L. Henderson, "Park Paragraphs," *Livingston Enterprise*, March 31, 1888, p. 1.

53. G. L. Henderson, "Park Paragraphs," *Livingston Enterprise*, April 28, 1888, p. 1.

54. Thomas E. Hofer, "Hunting with a Camera," *Forest and Stream*, May 31, 1888, p. 370.

55. J.B. Burnham, "Cameras for Stalking Game," *Forest and Stream*, December 22, 1894, p. 554.

56. Thomas E. Hofer, "Hunting with a Camera," *Forest and Stream*, 2 parts, December 23, 1893, pp. 538-539; December 30, 1893, pp. 563-564.

57. Thomas E. Hofer, "Treed by a Grizzly," *Forest and Stream*, September 5, 1908, cover image.

58. Jessie Wender, "Meet Grandfather Flash, the Pioneer of Wildlife Photography," [Internet], *National Geographic*, accessed July 17, 2016, available at: http://proof. nationalgeographic.com/2015/11/20/ meet-grandfather-flash-the-pioneer-of-wildlife-photography/.

59. George Shiras III, "Silver-Tip Surprises During a Hunting Trip for Big Game with the Camera on the Upper Yellowstone River," *Forest and Stream*, Part I, July 10, 1909, p. 48. Part II ran under the same title in the July 17, 1909 issue, pp. 88-91.

60. George Shiras III, "Moose of the Upper Yellowstone Valley," *Forest and Stream*, 2 parts, July 23, 1910, pp. 130-131; July 30, 1910, pp. 171-172.

61. The designation is sometimes *Alces alces shirasi*, but Congressman Shiras is still there in the taxonomic designation. "Geographic Variation," [Internet], University of Connecticut, accessed July 17, 2016, available at: http://hydrodictyon.eeb.uconn.edu/ eebedia/images/6/6c/Subspecies_2013.pdf.

CHAPTER 12

1. Thomas E. Hofer, "Notes from the Yellowstone Park," *Forest and Stream*, August 11, 1900, p. 106.

2. Thomas E. Hofer, "In the Yellowstone Park," December 13, 1902, p. 467.

3. "Gov. Roosevelt Has a Defender," *Chicago Tribune*, August 5, 1900, p. 3.

4. "The Kadiak [sic] Bear: Attempts to Catch the Largest Carnivore in Existence," *Sunday Washington Globe*, May 11, 1902, p. 2.

5. The letters are in the Yale Beinecke Library, George Bird Grinnell Papers, MS 1388, Series 2, Box 27 (reel 37).

6. "Billy Hofer to Run Line of Steamboats," *Salem* (OR) *Daily Capital Journal*, January 10, 1908, p. 3.

7. "Billy Hofer to Run Line of Steamboats," p. 3.

8. *Zoological Society Bulletin*, January, 1903, p. 63.

9. *Livingston Enterprise*, March 26, 1904, p. 3.

10. Marcus Peterson, *Fur Traders and Fur Bearing Animals* (Buffalo: Hammond, 1914), p. 46.

11. Letter from Thomas E. Hofer to George Bird Grinnell, April 25, 1905, Yale Beinecke Library, George Bird Grinnell Papers, MS 1388, Series 2, Box 27 (reel 37), pages 744-46.

12. Letter from Thomas E. Hofer to George Bird Grinnell, April 25, 1905, Yale Beinecke Library, George Bird Grinnell Papers, MS 1388, Series 2, Box 27 (reel 37), pages 744-46.

13. Letter from Thomas E. Hofer to George Bird Grinnell, April 28, 1905, Yale Beinecke Library, George Bird Grinnell Papers, MS 1388, Series 2, Box 27 (reel 37), pages 747-48.

14. Letter from Thomas E. Hofer to George Bird Grinnell, March 22, 1906, Yale Beinecke Library, George Bird Grinnell Papers, MS 1388, Series 2, Box 27 (reel 37), pages 749-54.

15. Letter from Thomas E. Hofer to George Bird Grinnell, July 22, 1907, Yale Beinecke Library, George Bird Grinnell Papers, MS 1388, Series 2, Box 27 (reel 37), pages 764-69. The *Livingston Enterprise* reported on January 26, 1907 ("Local Layout," p. 5) that "Thomas E. Hofer, better known as 'Billy' Hofer, of Gardiner, has been declared a bankrupt in the United States court." A second sentence stated that the meeting of the creditors would be held in Billings on February 4.

16. Letter from Thomas E. Hofer to George Bird Grinnell, July 22, 1907, Yale Beinecke Library, George Bird Grinnell Papers, MS 1388, Series 2, Box 27 (reel 37), pages 764-69.

17. Letter from Thomas E. Hofer to George Bird Grinnell, July 22, 1907, Yale Beinecke Library, George Bird Grinnell Papers, MS 1388, Series 2, Box 27 (reel 37), pages 764-69.

18. Letter from Thomas E. Hofer to George Bird Grinnell, May 6, 1908, Yale Beinecke Library, George Bird Grinnell Papers, MS 1388, Series 2, Box 27 (reel 37), pages 779-80.

19. Letter from Thomas E. Hofer to George Bird Grinnell, May 27, 1908, Yale Beinecke Library, George Bird Grinnell Papers MS 1388, Series 2, Box 27 (reel 37), pages 781-82.

20. Letter from Thomas E. Hofer to George Bird Grinnell, July 4, 1908, Yale Beinecke Library, George Bird Grinnell Papers MS 1388, Series 2, Box 27 (reel 37), pages 783-87.

21. Letter from Thomas E. Hofer to George Bird Grinnell, March 27, 1912, Yale Beinecke Library, George Bird Grinnell Papers MS 1388, Series 2, Box 27 (reel 37), pages 801-802.

22. Jane Gaffin, *Livingston Wernecke: An Idol in Yukon Mining Annals and the House of the Guggenheims* (Whitehorse: Jane Gaffin, 2006).

23. "Sunlight Beach Addition," Yale Beinecke Library, George Bird Grinnell Papers, MS 1388, Series 2, Box 27 (reel 37), page 1017.

24. Yale Beinecke Library, George Bird Grinnell Papers MS 1388, Series 2, Box 27 (reel 37), pages 1053-55.

25. Letter from Thomas E. Hofer to George Bird Grinnell, March 7, 1913, Yale Beinecke Library, George Bird Grinnell Papers MS 1388, Series 2, Box 27 (reel 37), page 812.

26. George Bird Grinnell, *American Duck Shooting* (New York: *Forest and Stream* Publishing, 1901).

27. Letter from Thomas E. Hofer to George Bird Grinnell, August 16, 1912, Yale Beinecke Library, George Bird Grinnell Papers MS 1388, Series 2, Box 27 (reel 37), pages 803-804.

28. Letter from Thomas E. Hofer to George Bird Grinnell, June 29, 1906, Yale Beinecke Library, George Bird Grinnell Papers MS 1388, Series 2, Box 27 (reel 37), pages 761-63.

29. Ernest Thompson Seton, *Wild Animals I Have Known* (New York: Charles Scriber's Sons, 1898). See also H. Allen Anderson, ed., "Ernest Thompson Seton in Yellowstone," *Montana: the Magazine of Western History*, 34(2), Spring, 1984, pp. 46-59.

30. John Burroughs, "Real and Sham Natural History," *Atlantic Monthly*, March 1903, pp. 298-309.

31. Ernest Thompson Seton, "Elkland II: The Beaver Pond," *Recreation* 1897, p. 202.

32. Ernest Thompson Seton, *Life-Histories of Northern Animals: An Account of the Mammals of Manitoba* (New York: Charles Scribner's Sons, 1909), p. 725.

33. Ernest Thompson Seton, *Wild Animals at Home* (Garden City: Doubleday, Page, 1922), p. 84.

34. Thompson, *Wild Animals at Home*, pp. 83, 85.

35. Hiram Martin Chittenden, *The Yellowstone National Park: Historical and Descriptive* (Cincinnati: Stewart and Kidd, 1915), p. 341.

36. The 1910 census shows a Catherine A. Kimberly, 57, and Adelade L. Kimberly, 32, Town: Canton, County: Hartford, State: Connecticut, Roll T624_131, Page 1A, ED 138, image 2.

37. The 1920 census shows a Hofer, Thomas E., 70, and a Kimberly, Catherine, 67, Town: Useless Bay, County: Island, State: Washington, Roll T625_1923, ED20, p. 1A, image 994. My mention here of Billy's sister Catherine A. (nee Hofer) Kimberly is also a logical place to mention what remains probably the single most controversial, and little-known, issue with regard to Billy Hofer. Because of their mutual childhood spent together, Catherine may well have been the only person besides Billy's parents who was privy to this information, and if so, she probably took the secret to her grave. If true, the secret may well have been the reason that Billy never married, and it may have even figured, if only partly, into why he preferred life in remote areas away from civilization. The secret, if true, is not well documented (we know of only one mention, and it is from the oral-history account of one of Billy's contemporaries), and thus it may not have even been true, but accurately reporting the historical record requires me to at least mention it, so that future researchers can possibly either confirm it or send it into disrepute.

Historian Lee Whittlesey learned long ago from the J. E. Haynes papers (specifically, the information came from OTO Ranch owner James N. "Dick" Randall, as interviewed in 1952 by Jack Ellis Haynes), that Thomas Elwood "Billy" Hofer may have been born hermaphroditic, but in what physical form—there are at least five— is unknown. That source—Randall—refers specifically to T. Elwood Hofer as "Morphodite Bill." Here is the actual quotation, as recorded by park photographer Jack E. Haynes, who kept meticulous records in alphabetical form for his annual updating of the *Haynes Guide to Yellowstone National Park:* "Hofer, Billie (T. E.), sometimes known as 'Morphodite Bill' off the record is [the same as] the Hofer variously known. He had no brother. There was only one Hofer in the park at that time." From this, it appears that Dick Randall was speaking "off the record" to Jack Haynes and did not wish his own name to be used by Jack as a source for this information, but it also appears that in speaking of "only one Hofer," Randall wanted to make clear that he was indeed talking about T. Elwood "Billy" Hofer. "Morphodite" is merely another word for "hermaphrodite." See Jack Ellis Haynes, notes for his interview with J. N. "Pretty Dick" Randall, interviewed by J. E. Haynes, June 10, 1952, in Haynes Collection, box 112, file 20, Montana State University, Bozeman, Montana, copy sent by Whittlesey to Paul Schullery. The book about Dick Randall's life, which does not mention this allegation, is Roberta Cheney and Clyde Erskine, *Music, Saddles, and Flapjacks: Dudes at the OTO Ranch* (Missoula: Mountain Press Publishing Company, revised 2000).

Inherently, this is the kind of allegation that is, and will likely continue to be, difficult to prove, and so far the only evidence we have that backs it up is Warren Delano's mention that Hofer had a "high-pitched voice." Accordingly, I will say no more about it here, other than that I must present the possibility in order to complete what is currently extant in the historical record.

38. Letter from Thomas E. Hofer to George Bird Grinnell, May 6, 1925, Yale Beinecke Library, George Bird Grinnell Papers MS 1388, Series 2, Box 27 (reel 37), pages 953-57.

39. Letter from Thomas E. Hofer to George Bird Grinnell, no date, Yale Beinecke Library, George Bird Grinnell Papers MS 1388, Series 2, Box 27 (reel 37), pages 1018-20.

40. Letter from Lileota De Staffany to "Manager, Yellowstone National Park," April 17, 1931, Thomas E. Hofer ("Uncle Billy") Correspondence, Accession #91-188, YNP Archives.

41. Letter from Horace Albright to Kermit Roosevelt, April 30, 1931, Thomas E. Hofer ("Uncle Billy") Correspondence, Accession #91-188, YNP Archives.

42. Letter from Horace Albright to George Bird Grinnell, April 30, 1931, Thomas E. Hofer ("Uncle Billy") Correspondence, Accession #91-188, YNP Archives.

43. Letter from Horace Albright to O. A. Tomlinson, April 30, 1931, Thomas E. Hofer ("Uncle Billy") Correspondence, Accession #91-188, YNP Archives.

44. "Echoes from the Past," *Mt. Rainier Nature Notes,* June, 1931, p. 1.

45. Letter from O. A. Tomlinson to Horace Albright, May 17, 1931, Thomas E. Hofer ("Uncle Billy") Correspondence, Accession #91-188, YNP Archives.

46. Letter from O. A. Tomlinson to Horace Albright, May 17, 1931, Thomas E. Hofer ("Uncle Billy") Correspondence, Accession #91-188, YNP Archives.

47. Letter from O. A. Tomlinson to Horace Albright, May 17, 1931, Thomas E. Hofer ("Uncle Billy") Correspondence, Accession #91-188, YNP Archives.

48. Letter from Horace Albright to O. A. Tomlinson, May 25, 1931, Thomas E. Hofer ("Uncle Billy") Correspondence, Accession #91-188, YNP Archives.

49. Letter from O. A. Tomlinson to Horace Albright, June 1, 1931, Thomas E. Hofer ("Uncle Billy") Correspondence, Accession #91-188, YNP Archives.

50. Letter from O. A. Tomlinson to George Bird Grinnell, September 4, 1931, Thomas E. Hofer ("Uncle Billy") Correspondence, Accession #91-188, YNP Archives.

51. Letter from Thomas E. Hofer to George Bird Grinnell, March 10, 1932, Yale Beinecke Library, George Bird Grinnell Papers MS 1388, Series 2, Box 27 (reel 37), page 997.

52. Letter from Adelade Peterson to George Bird Grinnell, May 3, 1933, Yale Beinecke Library, George Bird Grinnell Papers MS 1388, Series 2, Box 27 (reel 37), pages 1007-1008.

53. Roger W. Toll, *Superintendent's Monthly Report*, Yellowstone National Park, May 5, 1933, p. 17.

54. "'Uncle Billy' Hofer Passes Away Sunday," *Walla Walla* (WA) *Farm Bureau News*, April 27, 1933; Coupeville (WA) Island County Times, April 28, 1933.

55. Letter from O. A. Tomlinson to Horace Albright, April 27, 1933, Thomas E. Hofer ("Uncle Billy") Correspondence, Accession #91-188, YNP Archives.

56. Letter from Horace Albright to Adelade Peterson, May 8, 1933, Thomas E. Hofer ("Uncle Billy") Correspondence, Accession #91-188, YNP Archives.

57. Thomas E. Hofer to Horace Albright, 27 April 1926, Merrill G. Burlingame Special Collections, Renne Library, Montana State University Bozeman, Jack E. Haynes Papers and Haynes Inc. Records, 1915-1965, Collection 1504, Box 121, File 21.

Index

About the Author

Scott Herring is a writer and historian who teaches advanced writing to science students at the University of California, Davis. He received his Ph.D. there after a long sojourn working in Yellowstone National Park.

Also by Scott Herring

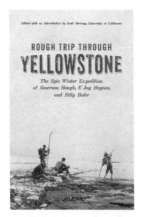

Rough Trip Through Yellowstone:
The Epic Winter Expedition of Emerson
Hough, F. Jay Haynes, and Billy Hofer

Edited and Annotated by Scott Herring
Format: Trade Paperback
ISBN: 978-1-60639-066-5
Author: Emerson Hough
List Price: $14.95

Includes nine Yellowstone National Park
photos by F. Jay Haynes

In the winter of 1894, the magazine *Forest and Stream* sent one of its most talented writers, Emerson Hough, to Yellowstone National Park to document the decline in bison. Under the tutelage of legendary guide Billy Hofer, Hough learned to ski on 12-foot-long wooden slats. He witnessed the arrest of notorious poacher Ed Howell—caught red-handed skinning a bison—and met pioneering photographer F. Jay Haynes.

Undertaking a tough, 200-mile trip on skis, Hough, Haines and Hofer came up with the best census of the park's bison and elk that anyone had yet achieved. Hough wrote up the expedition in a series of 14 articles. His reporting motivated the United States Congress to pass the anti-poaching Lacey Act and helped turn public opinion against a proposed railroad through the park.

Moreover, Hough's articles are immensely entertaining. He remains one of the wittiest writers ever to describe the park, and his series, edited and annotated by University of California writing professor Scott Herring, is as fun to read as it is historically significant.

More Fine Books About Yellowstone

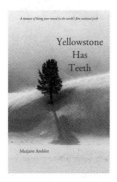

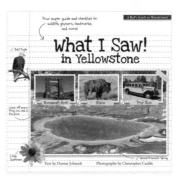

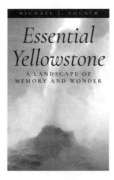

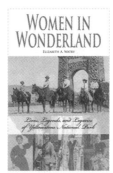